FIFTY
FAVORITE
FLY-FISHING
TALES

FIFTY FAVORITE
FLY-FISHING
TALES

Expert Fly Anglers Share Stories from the Sea and Stream

Chris Santella

Foreword by Brian O'Keefe

STEWART, TABORI & CHANG ~ NEW YORK

This book is dedicated to everyone who has ever told or enjoyed a good fishing tale.
After all, when the fish aren't cooperating, a good story may be all we have left!

––––––––––

Library of Congress Cataloging-in-Publication Data

Fifty favorite fly-fishing tales : expert fly anglers share stories from
the sea and stream / [compiled by] Chris Santella.
p. cm.
ISBN-13: 978-1-58479-444-8
ISBN-10: 1-58479-444-5
1. Fly fishing—Anecdotes. I. Santella, Chris.

SH456.F49 2006
799.12'4—dc22

2006012833

Photograph credits: Pages 2, 10, 16, 21, 30, 34, 44, 72, 74, 82, 90, 92, 104, 122, 126, 146,
166, 180, 186, 198, 214, and 220: photographs © Brian O'Keefe; pages 14, 24, 40, 42, 60,
138, 152, 192, 202, and 204: photographs © Tom Montgomery; page 47: photograph
© Mike Copithorne; pages 50 and 53: photographs © Jeff Currier; pages 56, 57, and 58:
photographs © Ralph Cutter; page 67: photograph © John Ecklund; pages 76 and 78:
photographs © Frontiers staff; page 110: photograph © Julie Lowing; pages 160 and 176:
photographs © TerryGunn.com; page 206: photograph © Jim Teeny.

Published in 2006 by Stewart, Tabori & Chang
An imprint of Harry N. Abrams, Inc.

Printed and bound in Thailand
10 9 8 7 6 5 4 3 2 1

HNA ▮▮▮▮▮
harry n. abrams, inc.
a subsidiary of La Martinière Groupe

115 West 18th Street
New York, NY 10011
www.hnabooks.com

CONTENTS

ACKNOWLEDGMENTS

This book would not have been possible without the generous assistance of the expert anglers who were kind enough to share their stories—tales that had previously been reserved for the campfire or the pub—with me and readers like you. To these men and women, I offer the most heartfelt thanks. I would especially like to thank Brian O'Keefe for his wonderful photos and K.C. Walsh, Jean Williams, and Paul Bruun, who offered encouragement and made many introductions on my behalf. I also wish to acknowledge the unwavering support of my agent, Stephanie Kip Rostan, and the fine efforts of my editor, Jennifer Levesque, designer Helene Silverman, and copy editor Don Kennison, who helped bring the book into being. Since I began fly fishing in 1979, I've shared many stories—and lived a few more—with a wide range of fishing buddies. This cast includes Howard Kyser, Peter Marra, Ken Matsumoto, Jeff Sang, Joe Runyon, Mark Harrison, Peter Gyerko, Tim Purvis, Geoff Roach, Bryce Tedford, Darrell Hanks, Sloan Morris, Hamp Byerly, John Dethman, and Mike Ishida. I look forward to living more stories on the river and flats with these friends and friends to come. I would be remiss not to thank my parents, Andrew and Tina Santella, who fostered an early love of reading that led to an appreciation of stories and storytelling—and who always encouraged me to experience new things. Last but certainly not least, I want to extend a special thanks to my wife Deidre and my daughters Cassidy Rose and Annabel Blossom, who've humored difficult deadlines and many weekends when daddy's "gone fishing" with patience and grace. It won't be long before we'll all be able to get out on the river together!

FOREWORD

Storytelling is an art, and the fly-fishing world is full of great artists. Our stage is the world's oceans, rivers, and lakes; our main players are leaky rowboats, dilapidated fishing vehicles, game wardens, mean dogs, rattlesnakes, dysfunctional relatives, screaming guides, and other assorted mischief makers.

On the road to and from our beloved waters, a good portion of a fly angler's conversation concerns the reliving of the mind-boggling or sentimental experiences that make a good fishing story. With *Fifty Favorite Fly-Fishing Tales*, Chris Santella has rounded up a collection of one-of-a-kind tales from some of fly fishing's most colorful personalities. (Reading through the epic adventure I shared with Chris, I still cringe and chuckle at the exploits of my youth!) I think anyone who has fished with a grandfather, or from a canoe, or anywhere in Montana, or with anyone who brings more beers than flies has an outrageous story that's just waiting to be told. This book will make some people laugh and others cry, perhaps at the same time . . . because we've all been there.

—BRIAN O'KEEFE

INTRODUCTION

Most of us around the angling brother- and sisterhood have at one time or another enjoyed regaling—or being regaled—with a good fishing story. Sometimes the fish grow a bit over the years in the telling. And sometimes events that *really transpired* seem far too outlandish to be true. Whatever the case, many a slow day of fishing—and many winter evenings when the season's first cast seems eons away—have been saved by a good fishing tale . . . whopper or not!

It is my own love of a good fly-fishing yarn that inspired me to compile *Fifty Favorite Fly-Fishing Tales*. To create the book, I invited fifty noteworthy fly fishers—including some living legends of the sport—to share some of their favorite fly-fishing stories culled from their vast experiences. These stories take us from the caves of Gunung Buda in Borneo where Ralph Cutter casts in darkness for blind catfish to the wilds of the Alaska peninsula where J. W. Smith boxes with grizzly bears to protect his tent camp. Tales range from the comical (Jack Gartside poaching trout from a moat to support himself in London) to the poignant (Jean Williams helping a type-A father connect with his son by connecting them with a wary rainbow trout in the Colorado Rockies) to the absurd (George Anderson fly fishing for saltwater crocodiles in Cuba). Some tales tell of large fish landed, others of large fish lost, and others of near-death experiences and similar striking events that occurred on the way to and from the river. Combined, it's my hope that the tales herein reflect the rich experience of fly fishing and how its metaphors extend beyond the river and the salt to touch our lives.

Most of the individuals I interviewed by phone or in person; a few shared written versions of the tale in question, which were amended to suit the "as told to" format the book uses. To give a sense of the breadth of their fly-fishing backgrounds, a bio of each individual is included after each tale. I've also added a brief footnote that speaks to either the fishery or curious minutiae featured in the tale.

Every fly fisher I've ever known has a few good stories to share, and I'm sorry that I was unable to find room for everyone's tale. However, I think you'll find the stories that are included far-reaching, amusing, and perhaps even inspirational.

THE STORIES

GEORGE ANDERSON

THE BITE IS ON

The popularity of programs like *Corwin's Quest* and *The Crocodile Hunter* speaks to the public's fascination with predatory creatures. Is it the raw power and amoral killing potential of the beasts profiled on such programs that pulls viewers in? Or is it the chance—ever so slight—that the featured beast might snack on the program's host?

Producers of fly-fishing programs who hope to boost ratings might take a cue from Animal Planet's sundry offerings—specifically, to incorporate more aggressive encounters between man and man-eating predators. Should they be at a loss for a host, they would do well to consider George Anderson, who already has most of the footage for Episode One in the can.

"I first got the idea that we could catch crocodiles on a fly rod when I was in Belize some years ago," George began. "We'd see the crocs by the docks at night. We could spot them a half mile away with a Q-Beam spotlight we brought down, and you'd see four or five sets of ruby-red eyes bobbing above the water. I had some big sailfish flies, poppers with foam heads, that were just about right for the task, and I teamed them up with eighty-pound-test coated-wire leaders. Hooking a croc on a fly rod is easier than you'd think. If you can show the crocs a surface fly that makes a lot of commotion, they're gonna eat it. Saltwater crocs don't have tons of stamina, but they're certainly strong. On a few occasions when I was using tippet heavier than eighty pounds, they broke my fly line. I had friends videotape the croc-fishing escapades a few times and shared the video with the Ketchum Release people. They responded by making me a special saltwater catch-and-release tool with a three-foot handle.

"A few years back I was fishing down in Jardines de la Reina, an archipelago south of Cuba, with a group of friends. We were staying on one of the houseboats that cater to anglers, the *Tortuga*. There are a lot of saltwater crocs in the region, and in the course of a few days I had hooked a few in fun. A buddy named Tom who was fishing with me must have gotten tired of these antics, because he made me a challenge: 'Bet you five hundred dollars you can't catch a croc with your bare hands.' I knew a little bit about croc behavior—sometimes, when they feel threatened, they just lie still on the bottom—so I figured I could collect on this wager. After dinner that night I dragged my buddy out with me, armed with the Q-Beam

OPPOSITE: Stalking the flats around Jardines de la Reina, where tarpon, bonefish, permit —and crocodiles—make for excellent sport.

and little else. I was darting the light around in the shallows, and pretty soon I came upon a small croc, resting on the bottom. We got closer and, as I figured, it just lay there, perhaps thinking that we wouldn't notice it if it didn't move. I reached down and scooped him up with my hands—he was about four or five feet long. 'I'd like my five hundred dollars now,' I said. Tom said, 'I wanted you to get me an eight-foot croc.' At this, the croc wriggled out of my hands and into the water. I reached down and grabbed it by the hips. Before I knew what happened, it twisted around, grabbed my left hand in its mouth, and chomped down. *OW!* Even the small crocs have needle-sharp teeth, and he ripped most of the meat off my little finger.

A crocodile has a glance about.

"At this point, we had the bright idea of taking the croc back to the *Tortuga*, where our friends had been drinking and whooping it up. We figured that we could tape the croc's mouth shut, visit some sleeping berths with the croc and the video camera, and have a little fun. Things went pretty much as planned, at least for a while. Our buddies were half asleep

GEORGE ANDERSON

TALE 1
2
3
4
5
6
7
8
9
10
11
12
13
14
15
16
17
18
19
20
21
22
23
24
25
26
27
28
29
30
31
32
33
34
35
36
37
38
39
40
41
42
43
44
45
46
47
48
49
50

in their bunks, we'd sneak in, flip the lights and introduce a little scaly companion into their bed, and then they'd freak out and we'd capture their reaction on film. After a few such visits, we opened the door to Room #4. I thought it was one of our guys in the top bunk, and slipped the crocodile under the sheets. It turned out that I'd had the accommodations slightly confused, and instead of being one of our guys in the bunk, it was a British couple. They didn't find our little prank very amusing; in fact, the next day they informed the captain of the *Tortuga* that they could not be expected to spend the rest of the week on the boat with 'those rowdy Americans,' and were spirited off to another craft.

"This past year I was down in Jardines de la Reina again, fishing with a guide named Coqui, one of the very best guides I've ever had. I had a few different rods with me, a seven-weight for bonefish and a ten-weight for permit. We were fishing one morning when Coqui pointed out a large cayman in the distance. I asked him to go closer. As we poled the boat over, the croc submerged. It was in only two feet of water. You don't often see the saltwater crocs out in the sunlight, and I figured that the odds of getting him to take a fly on top—or sub-surface, for that matter—were low. Blame it on the bet from the year before or just another lapse of judgment, I decided I wanted to catch this croc. To do so, I'd have to snag him with a big fly. I found the heaviest fly in my box, a Del Brown Merkin tied on a ½, and dropped it down. It took a few tries but eventually I got him in the back. It didn't take long for me to get him up to the boat, and I wanted to get a picture of me holding the animal. I asked Coqui to give me the bow rope so I could tie it around the croc's head and pull him into the boat. I had the rope and grabbed hold of the croc around the front foot. He lashed around quickly and almost got my hand. That should've told me to let him go, but it didn't. I put the rope over his head and, in the meantime, a surgeon friend who was present—and capturing all of this on tape—was clearing the rods and everything else out of the cockpit so they wouldn't get broken when we got the croc into the boat. When the cockpit was clear, I skidded the croc up over the bow. He then made one of the fastest hundred-and-eighty-degree spin moves I've ever seen—Kobe Bryant would've been proud—and buried his jaws into my ankle. I looked down and said, 'We've got a problem.' Fortunately, his lower jaw had sunk into the heel cup of my Sperry's—otherwise, it would've been in my Achilles tendon. I grabbed his jaws and pulled as hard as I could for about fifteen seconds. Had the croc started thrashing around he would have torn me up, but he stayed still. I got his jaws open and removed my leg. I then slammed my hand down on his mouth, closed it good, picked him up, and got my video shots. My surgeon friend was laughing his head off as blood came gushing out of my leg. I said, 'Are we ready for the release?' Then I hurled the croc off the boat.

"The croc's teeth had sunk right to the bone. At first my surgeon friend wanted us to go back to the *Tortuga*, but I said, 'We've got all sorts of bonefish around us. We've got salt water, bandages. We're gonna fish.' He patched me up as best as he could and we fished. When we got back to the boat, everyone asked us how we did. I said, 'Well, we got some bonefish, and got one about a hundred pounds. Maybe a little less.' People thought we'd got into tarpon. I said, 'You'll see. We got everything on film.'

"At the cocktail hour we shared the video, and I thought the whole crowd was going to pee its pants with laughter."

George Anderson began his professional fly-fishing career managing a tackle shop in West Yellowstone during college summers. After graduation he worked for six years with Dan Bailey's Fly Shop, leaving to open the Yellowstone Angler in 1980. George has authored many articles over the years that have appeared in *Flyfisherman, Trout, Big Sky Journal,* and *Saltwater Fly Fishing*. He has appeared as a guest angler on ESPN's *Fly Fishing the World*, and ESPN 2's *Spanish Fly*. George won individual honors at the Jackson Hole One-Fly in the only two years he fished in the event, 1989 and 1990.

THE AMERICAN CROCODILE

Flats fly rodders casting for finned rather than scaled prey over the waters of the Caribbean have a small chance of encountering saltwater crocodiles. If you have the thrill of seeing a croc at a comfortable distance, you're probably seeing an American crocodile (*Crocodylus acutus*). American crocodiles range from the Florida Keys south to Venezuela and even Peru, and east to Haiti and the Dominican Republic. They average about 12 feet in length at maturity and can grow as large as 23 feet. While they generally prefer saltwater habitat around swamps and marshes, they will occasionally make forays to more open water and can survive in fresh water. Though they greatly resemble alligators in appearance, American crocodiles can be differentiated by their longer, more slender snouts. American crocodiles are catholic carnivores, feeding on small mammals, birds, fish, crabs, carcasses, and—given the chance—younger crocodiles. They can live as long as sixty years.

THE MAYOR OF DULAC IS WAITING

Wandering along an Atlantic salmon river in New Brunswick or a trout stream in Idaho, no one thinks twice to come upon the loop of a fly line unfurling across the water. Yet there are other places where fly fishing is not the commonly accepted means of angling, and would-be fly fishers are required to make a leap of faith and imagination.

Such as Louisiana.

"Down in Louisiana, if you say fly fishing, most people look at you kind of funny," Captain Dan Ayo began. "I suppose that people associate fly fishing with trout fishing, and since there are no trout down here people don't think about fly rods. I'd been fishing all my life, but one day I convinced myself that I wanted to try fly fishing. I went into Jones Sporting Goods store in Houma and there was a fellow working there from up north. When I said 'fly rod,' he understood what I was talking about, and he set me up with an outfit that cost one hundred dollars for the rod, line, and reel. I thought I had a state-of-the-art setup. I was planning to fish for perch. As we were finishing up the transaction, he said, 'I want you to take this fly.' It was a Keys-style tarpon fly. He said, 'You get good with perch, you can try redfish.' I was thinking that there's no way you can catch redfish on a fly rod, but I took the fly and thanked him.

"I'm pretty obsessive about things, and once I got hooked on fly fishing I spent a lot of time with it. I got pretty good at catching perch with a fly rod, and thought back to that fellow in the store and the talk about redfish. From my conventional-gear days, I had some idea of where I could find 'em in the marshes, so I decided to give it a try. It was slow going for a number of years. If I caught one or two fish in a day, it was a fantastic trip. Sometimes we'd come upon big groups of tailing fish, but we'd have trouble getting to them, as the water was too shallow to take a boat in. We'd stalk them on foot and try to make monster casts. Fishing like this certainly improved my casting! Other times, we'd be right on the fish but the flies we had weren't quite right. I realized I might have to go outside of Louisiana to get some new insights into fly fishing for reds, and I saw there would be a Federation of Fly Fishermen conclave in Asheville, Tennessee. I attended and met a fellow who belonged to a fly fisher's club in Baton Rouge. The following year I attended a conclave where John Cave was giving a slide show that included tying instructions for the Cave's Wobbler, which is really the grandfather of the spoon flies that most redfish fly anglers use today. I'd been trying to tie a fly that would copy the Johnson spoon, a productive lure for redfish, with no success. Learning about the Cave's Wobbler was a revelation, and my efforts improved.

"It was at this conclave, in Haines City, Florida, that someone suggested I book a trip with John Kumiski—author of *Fly Fishing for Redfish*—who guides out of the Mosquito Lagoon region. Fishing with someone like John, I learned that there were many ways to catch redfish on a fly and that I could do a lot better than I had been doing. Some years later John said to me, 'Danny, you're so passionate about this. Why don't you become a charter captain?' I replied, 'I can't do that. It would be moon to moon every day.' John explained that charter fishing is an eight-hour day, and I thought, 'I can do that.'

"When I first started getting serious about fly fishing for redfish, I would catch 'em any way I could. But as I learned more about it I realized that sight-fishing could be extremely effective. And it sure is fun. When I'm sight-fishing, I can see everything and gauge how the fish reacts to our presentation. Every day I go out, there's a chance to learn more about Mr. Redfish and what makes him tick. Anyway, my big boat wasn't doing the trick in terms of getting back into the real shallow water where you'll often find the fish in the marshes, so I decided to build my own. I wanted something that I could pole easy and could get into four inches of water. I bought a welding machine, but when I looked for instructions for using it there were none. I probably had no business trying to weld, but a buddy came over and helped me set up the machine and showed me a few things about welding. The next week I started building my first boat. It's still floating, and I've built three or four since.

"There's a term people have down here to describe the Cajun character, and it's 'Coon-Ass.' The derivation may have come from those coonskin hats, I'm not sure — but I think it speaks to a simple, good-natured, not necessarily educated but filled with common sense and innovative personality a lot of us seem to have. I think it's a term that suits me pretty well. When I take people out in my boat, I tell them I'm a Coon-Ass, and they don't seem to know what to say. I then repeat that I'm a Coon-Ass, not a 'coon's ass,' and then they laugh. Being a Coon-Ass, I'm not very well traveled. I've never even been on a plane. And while I don't watch much television, I have seen a few outdoors shows where the focus has been guys chasing something called a grand slam in the Bahamas or Florida Keys or some other exotic spot that I'll likely never see. Their grand slam is catching a bonefish, a tarpon, and a permit in one day. Once I had been guiding for a while, I got the idea that I could do a grand

OPPOSITE:
Casting amongst the marshes of southwestern Louisiana to redfish on the feed.

slam of my own. A Cajun grand slam: a redfish, a black drum, and a sheepshead. A lot of folks already call redfish the poor man's bonefish. If that is the case, then the black drum could be the tarpon, and the sheepshead—because they can be very finicky—would be the permit. I like to tell people that the best sheepshead technique is to fish from your knees, because you've gotta pray a lot.

"I can't say that we get a Cajun grand slam every time we go out—and I'll admit there are some people who would just as soon not even bother with sheepshead if the redfishing is hot. Nonetheless, I believe that we score our grand slams a little more often than the guys in the Keys. Any grand slam is worthy of celebration. I like to pull clients' legs a bit if they happen to get close to the Cajun slam. I tell them that I have the number of the mayor of Dulac [a town of 2,500 in the Terrobonne Parish] on the speed dial of my cell phone. If an angler gets the coveted Cajun slam, I will make the call to arrange the gala ceremony where the mayor of Dulac himself will present the lucky angler with a seafood platter and the official title Honorary Coon-Ass.

"Tuxedoes are optional."

Captain Dan Ayo was born in Cajun territory. Like other Cajuns, fishing and hunting was a way of life from his early years and continues to the present. Bored with conventional tackle, he underwent a full conversion to fly fishing in the mid-1980s. Sight-fishing is his passion and he'll tell you in a heartbeat, "I'm a hunter, not a fisherman." After honing his skills and catching many fish with the prescribed fly tackle, he adopted the mentality *Why be normal*. Leaving the ranks of normal fly-fishing, Dan started reducing his line weight. When this insanity finally came to full bloom he was sight fishing to large redfish with a 1-weight and size 24 flies! When others ask "Why?" the Captain says "Why Not?" Dan runs a charter service out of Houma, Louisiana, called Shallow Minded Guide Service (www.flyfishlouisiana.com) and is considered by many to be a pioneer of shallow-water sight-fishing in Louisiana. He designed and built several custom skiffs and developed many of the techniques and flies used today in the Louisiana marsh. An innovative and inspirational speaker, Dan calls himself "shallow" minded. Once you meet him you'll know why.

UNBLACKENED REDFISH

Redfish is one of the most popular sport fish sought by saltwater anglers in the southern United States. Fished nearly to extinction during the Cajun-cuisine craze fueled by chef

Paul Prudhomme in the late eighties, redfish (a member of the drum family) are now plentiful, spend a good deal of time in shallow water close to shore, and are tenacious fighters. They are distinguished by one or more black spots on the upper flank near the base of the tail; the sight of these spots exposed in the air as fish root for crabs, shrimp, and sand dollars is a cause for great joy among the fly fishers who seek them.

In Texas and Florida anglers pursue redfish on flatslike terrain around bays and estuaries. In Louisiana, redfish will ride the tide into marsh country to feed. The Spanish-moss-draped bayous provide a backdrop that seems at odds with conventional notions of fly fishing. That makes it all the more special.

GARY BORGER

LEARNING TO DRIVE ON THE LEFT

Sometimes the trip to and from the river is as exciting as anything that happens once you arrive. You know it's one harrowing trip when the day in question is filled with 30-inch browns and rainbows and what's remembered years after is the adventure getting out!

"The year was 1982, and I had been corresponding with a fellow named Mike Allen about New Zealand—the great fishing, the great country, and the great people—and I was more than primed to go," Gary Borger began. "When Air New Zealand graced me with a ticket that allowed me to share stories of that lovely land in my writings, I was on the plane before the dust settled. You know the saying, 'You can have this seat when you pry it out of my cold dead fingers.'

"The country and the people were no less astounding than I had heard, but the fishing was off the charts. Mike cautioned me against casting to the 'little' twenty-inchers. It was hard to pass them by at first, but after a week I too considered them little. Now, New Zealand rivers are not overflowing with fish. A river has a limited potential. It may, for instance, hold a thousand one-pound fish or one thousand-pound fish. So when one hits a 'double-digit' river—every fish over ten pounds—the beasts are a bit spread out. It requires a lot of walking and a lot of looking. But that's the thrill of it—fishing in NZ is really hunting, with the fly rod as the weapon of choice.

"At the end of the first week, Mike suggested we fly into the top end of a river that he knew got very little pressure. We were sure to find plenty of fish in the 'smallish'-to-large sizes. And so we scouted the local air services and found one that knew the area well and could put us right where we wanted to be. I was amazed. Just think, an airstrip in the middle of nowhere. Wrong. Well, maybe partially right. A stump-filled field with high grass perched at the edge of a very tall cliff. Alaskan bush pilots could take lessons from these guys. As Mike and I prepared to climb down the cliff, the pilot called out, 'See you right here at seven P.M., mates,' and he was gone. We descended by hanging on to the scrubby trees and brush and by taking some severe chances, but, oh, what a day it was. The first cast put the climb back up the cliff totally out of mind. And the casts that followed did nothing to draw our attention back there either. The big boys were on the fin, and every pool had one or two

OPPOSITE:
Some of New Zealand's very best waters are only accessible by helicopter —or by very long treks.

of them out and looking. Browns and 'Bows to nearly thirty inches, with plenty of the wee two-footers mixed in.

"At six P.M., weary from the long walk, the hot day, and the arm wrestling with wild trout, we turned reluctantly back toward the 'landing strip.' Now the cliff was firmly in mind, and we groaned inwardly at the prospect of ascending it with the rods and gear in our teeth to free up our hands for the mad scramble. But climbing was not in our future—that is, not in Mike's future. About halfway back to the cliff, Mike suddenly fell to the ground in agony. His legs drew up to his chest and his back arched, curving him into a fetal position in an instant. I was more than a little startled. He did not respond to my almost-panic-edged questions but simply rolled around groaning and moaning like death warmed over. Finally he relaxed a bit and smiled weakly. 'Wow,' he said, 'that was some back spasm.' We had been walking over very uneven terrain all day and, as Mike explained, he sometimes got back pains after a day like that. I was really relieved. After a minute or so we set off again. I had the major share of the gear and wondered if I had been Tom Sawyered into the job.

"This was not the case.

"As we approached the cliff, Mike suddenly dropped to the ground as if poleaxed. The performance was a repeat of Act One, but it didn't let up as soon, and when it did the pain was unbearable. Mike couldn't walk, much less climb the cliff. I bundled him in all the spare clothing we had and helped him get comfortable. Then I climbed the cliff with the rest of the gear in my teeth. To tell the truth, I don't remember too much about the climb because I was so worried about Mike. I just climbed.

"The pilot came in right on schedule, and when I explained what was going on he told me to climb back down and stay with Mike and he would send someone to get us. It was a fast descent without gear and with the push of urgency behind me. We could do nothing but wait. Eventually, I heard the faint chop of an engine. It swiftly became *chop, chop, chop*, and I knew the pilot had sent a helicopter to take us out. It was not a medevac unit that came in, however, but the owner of the sheep station at the bottom of the river. Ian Sargenson put the bird down right next to me and yelled, 'Get in.' It was a two-place chopper, so I had to strap in and then wrestle Mike in and onto my lap where I could hold him partially dangling out the door. Although in his sixties at the time, Ian was strong and bright and he knew how to get us downriver fast. It was perhaps the most adventuresome chopper ride I've ever had.

"Our pilot was waiting for us at the airstrip at Sarg's place, and we bundled Mike into the plane and shot back to town. By this time it was one A.M. and I was a bit disoriented. Mike and I were whisked to the local surgery, where the doctor examined him carefully. 'I think he's passing a kidney stone,' he told me, 'but I have to be certain. I'll have to send him to the hospital.' I was greatly relieved when the ambulance pulled up and they loaded Mike in for the forty-mile ride to the hospital. As they closed the rear doors, I yelled, 'Toss me your car keys.'

"Light blinking, the ambulance rushed out of the parking lot and headed off—on the wrong side of the road! But no, it was the right side—I mean the left side—which in NZ is *the right side*. I jumped into the driver's seat and discovered that they had moved the steering wheel to the passenger side. 'What the . . .' By the time I got it all straightened out, got the car started, the seat belt in place, and figured out how to shift with my left hand, the blinking lights of the emergency transport were no more. I pointed the car in the right direction and jammed the accelerator to the floor boards. Now mind, I usually drive that way anyhow, but I do so on the right—I mean, correct—right side of the road and shift with my coordinated right hand. All I can say is that I didn't accidentally shift into reverse, but that gear box got a good testing that night. And there were a couple of panicked moments when other drivers tried to avoid me as I careened wildly after the wildly careening ambulance.

"About halfway there it suddenly all clicked, and I knew I was meant for survival. I tore along in confidence and actually passed a couple of cars as I stayed close behind the flashing lights that tried to leave me in the darkness. Never again would driving on the left feel foreign, but neither would I ever forget the fire in which my skills had been born and tested.

"As for Mike, we got him 'in hospital' and had the X-ray done. It was indeed a kidney stone, and he went to sleep in the bliss of a healthy dose of morphine. Me, I was graciously allowed to sleep in an empty room in the convent next door. Mike went home the next day and I went fishing, driving like a wild man on the left side of the road."

Dr. Gary A. Borger has been a fly fisher since 1955, and since 1972 he has taught classes and lectured internationally on all aspects of fly fishing for trout and salmon. He holds a Ph.D. from the University of Wisconsin–Madison and is professor emeritus at the University of Wisconsin campus in Wausau. His achievements are recognized in *Who's Who in the Midwest*, *Who's Who in Science and Engineering*, *Men of Achievement*, the *Dictionary of International Biography*, *Who's Who Among America's Teachers*, *Outstanding People of the 20th Century*, and *Outstanding People of the Millennium*. A freelance writer and photographer, Gary is also Midwest field editor for *Fly Fisherman* magazine, editor at large for *Virtual Fly Shop*, and fly fishing columnist for *Midwest Fly Fishing*. He has written five best-selling books on fly fishing: *Nymphing, Naturals, The Borger Color System, Designing Trout Flies*, and *Presentation*. Gary pioneered fly-fishing video instruction with his release of *Nymphing* in 1982, and has hosted four videos for the 3M Company. His video production company has produced an additional seventeen internationally acclaimed videos in the Skills of Fly Fishing video series. Gary has been featured in several television programs, including his own TV pilot, *The Tzar's Trout*, which earned him a listing in *Who's Who in Entertainment*. Gary was also a consultant on Robert Redford's 1992 movie *A River Runs through It*. With his award-winning CD/cassette tape, *My Madison*, he pioneered fly-fishing, nature-music audios. Gary has been a design consultant to Cabela's and Thomas & Thomas Rod Company. Currently, he is a consultant to Gudebrod and Targus Fly & Feather and is the designer of the Weinbrenner Ultimate Wading Shoe and many other innovative angling products and unique fly designs. He is a member of the board of governors of the Federation of Fly Fishers Fly Casting Instructor Certification Program, the Order of the Jungle Cock, Trout Unlimited, United Fly Tiers, the Federation of Fly Fishers, the American Museum of Fly Fishing, the Catskill Fly Fishing Center, and other conservation organizations, and was a founding board member of the River Alliance of Wisconsin. Gary is a recipient of the Ross Allen Merigold Complete Angler Memorial Award, the Charles K. Fox Rising Trout Award, and the Joan and Lee Wulff Conservation Award. In recognition of his conservation work, he received the first Lew Jewett Memorial Life Membership in the Federation of Fly Fishers in 1979.

TAKING FLIGHT

For anglers hoping to reach out-of-the-way places, access to a floatplane or helicopter can be the difference between great fishing or no fishing at all. The use of floatplanes to reach distant waters was popularized by angling master Lee Wulff, who also helped introduce the notion of catch-and-release angling. Wulff established several outpost camps adjoining great brook trout and Atlantic salmon fisheries in coastal Newfoundland in the 1940s and 1950s, but he soon realized that getting visitors to the camps by boat was impractical. Using his clout as a celebrated angling writer, Wulff made an arrangement with Piper Aircraft that gave him access to a J3 Cub that was fitted with floats in exchange for promotional films that would show the plane and Wulff's camps in their best light. Wulff's exploits in the air are wonderfully chronicled in his book *Bush Pilot Angler*.

SHARK 911

Anglers are prone to a special form of exaggeration that renders their prey as more malevolent than it actually might be. A 3-pound brown trout in a spring creek is "a monster." A 32-inch striped bass in the surf is "a whale." But what about a fly-rod species whose ill portent requires no hyperbole, a creature that has the potential to cause mayhem, even take a human life?

That is, more specifically, the mako shark.

Conway Bowman grew up in the San Diego area, traveling to Silver Creek in Idaho in the summer months to fly fish with his dad. Winters there was bass fishing and little else. In the early nineties, he discovered saltwater fly fishing and soon learned that sharks were among the most plentiful sport fish off the coast of southern California. He bought a seventeen-foot aluminum boat and began pursuing Chondrichthyes (cartilaginous fish) in earnest. "After catching twenty-five blue sharks on my first day of fly fishing for sharks, I realized I was on to something," Conway said. "It took me two years longer to figure out how to get the makos to take the fly, but once I did it became a lot easier."

This story relates how Conway's expertise—and advances in telecommunications technology—helped one Ahab-type character conquer his Moby Dick.

"It was 1997," Conway began, "and I had been guiding for sharks with fly tackle for three years. Ken High, who owns Dr. Slick [a company that manufactures fly-tying tools], had booked me for five days. It was the third year he'd come out, and he'd brought along a friend named Lauren. It had been a fairly terrible week of fishing, as the water had turned over. We'd hooked just one or two fish. It was the last day, and I could see that Ken and Lauren were worn out. In fact, they were napping. They had a plane to catch later that afternoon. When they stirred I said, 'Look, I've got one more place I want to check out.' I pulled in close to shore—we were in two hundred feet of water, just two miles off shore. Though there were some birds around, I was thinking that it wasn't going to happen. Still, I set up a chum slick. Not long after, I saw this big black eye creep around the back of the boat. The glare was terrible in the water and I couldn't make it out terribly clearly. I was wondering, 'Could it have been a mako?'

"A couple minutes passed and I had a weird feeling, like I was being watched. I looked in the water and there was the shark, right on the surface. It was huge—two hundred fifty to three hundred pounds. I woke Ken and said, 'There's a big one. Get ready.' I've gotten to be pretty mellow about big fish, or at least my voice didn't give away how excited I was. Ken asked, 'How big?' I said, 'Pretty big.' Ken jumped up and threw the fly in back of the boat. The shark swiped at it and missed. I couldn't contain my excitement anymore and said, 'I think it's the biggest mako I've ever cast to!'

"Ken made another cast and a big strip, and the fly whipped across the surface. The mako's head came out of the water with his mouth open. I could see his eyes on the fly. Ken said, 'Holy s***!' and the shark was on. In ten seconds, it had taken out two hundred yards of line, making these tremendous jumps, some that were twenty feet into the air. Ken just kept repeating 'Oh my God, oh my God!' Lauren reminded him that they had a plane to catch, and Ken replied, 'There's a life jacket. You can swim back!' I started the motor and we began the chase into the swell. Ken was on the bow, Lauren was scrambling around for his camera. Then the fish made this tremendous jump—it seemed like the hang time was forever. When it came down the shark's tail sawed the line in two and the fish was gone. Ken was despondent. He knew quite well that this was a life fish. I reassured him that he'd done everything right, that these things sometimes happened.

"Ken came back several years thereafter and we went looking for that big fish, but we never got another shot. I couldn't help but think that he was rather Ahab-like in his quest.

"A few years back, I got a gig doing a television show called *In Search of Fly-Water* for ESPN. As it turned out, the week that Ken and Lauren were slated to come out I was going to be back in Pennsylvania on Spruce Creek filming a segment. I called Captain Dave Trimble, who does some guiding with me, and told him that he'd have to take them out, and that they wanted a big fish. I could hear him groan. 'It's okay,' I reassured him. 'He's a good angler.' I explained the history and hung up.

"A few days later we were filming on Spruce Creek. I'd just released a trout and my cell phone went off. It was Dave and he was on the fifth day of five days fishing with Ken.

'Conway, you won't believe what's around the boat,' he said. 'It's the biggest mako I've ever seen. Ten feet, at least. It's circling the boat. The fish bumped the engine and knocked me down.' Ken and Lauren were sleeping when the fish showed up. It was a nearly identical scenario to our first experience with the big shark. In the background, I could hear Ken and Lauren saying 'Holy s***!' I could hear how frantic things were on the boat. Dave, who's a

OPPOSITE: Sharks can make for tremendous fly rod prey.

seasoned captain, seemed flustered. 'What should I do?' he asked. I said, 'Put on the biggest fly you've got and hook the fish. Ken wants this bad.'

"About thirty minutes later I got another call. The shark had jumped and rammed the boat. Ken had then hooked it, but the fish jumped six times and came off. Remarkably enough, the shark had come back and Ken had hooked it again. Forty-five minutes later, Dave called again. They still had the fish on and had chased it two miles. Obviously, Dave didn't have lots of time to talk. A half hour later I had the fourth call. 'We've got the fish to the boat, but we can't move it,' Dave said. 'It's so big, I had to stand up on the center console to get the fish in the frame of the camera.' Then Dave swore—the fish had gone under the boat and busted off. But Dave had the tippet in hand, so it was considered caught.

"Ken got his holy grail fish. And I got to take part almost a continent away, thanks to my cell phone."

Conway Bowman is the owner/operator of Bowman Bluewater and a native San Diegan. He began fly fishing in Idaho at eight. Since then, he's mastered the river, lake, and sea. His extensive saltwater experience includes Baja California plus inshore and blue water up and down the West Coast. He also hosts ESPN's *In Search of Flywater.* Conway is the current IGFA world record holder of redfish on 20-pound tippet, a 41.65-pound red!

SHARKING ON A FLY ROD

Suffice it to say, fly fishing for mako sharks is not a dainty game. It begins with chumming. Skippers who regularly chase makos prefer a bloody, oily fish-gut soup, hung over the side of the boat in a five-gallon bucket (such as those institutional mayonnaise containers) punched with half-inch holes. Once you're in position, shut off your engine so as not to put off any finicky fish. Sometimes it takes a while for sharks to appear, sometime their visit is almost instantaneous. When a shark shows up in casting range, you'll want to present a large fly—as big as size 6/0—as close to the shark's eyes as possible (these fish have poor eyesight). It's not necessary to strip the fly quickly; a slow retrieve or even dead drift entices strikes. With those choppers—and with makos often weighing over 200 pounds—a heavy wire leader is the order of the day. Be sure that you also carry three hundred yards of backing on the best reel you can afford. Makos can make runs of several hundred yards and have been known to clear the water by twenty feet or more . . . not something you'll soon forget.

WHY I HATE STEELHEADING

Certain species and certain styles of fishing can arouse very strong feelings among anglers. The fly fisher who celebrates casting dry flies on a certain Catskills creek might despise the notion of drifting nymphs through the very same pools and riffles. Someone who pursues hefty redfish on the Louisiana coast might find the idea of casting any fly to a 10-inch trout absurd.

Anadromous fish—particularly Atlantic salmon and steelhead—provoke perhaps the most powerful emotions. Some anglers will fish for nothing else and give their first hookup equal prominence among seminal life experiences such as their nuptials, the birth of their first child, or a Red Sox pennant victory. Journalist, boat builder, and guide Paul Bruun has some definite feelings about the pursuit of steelhead.

They are decidedly negative.

"Back in 1973, I'd read a *Sports Illustrated* story about the North Umpqua River and the Steamboat Inn, over in Oregon," Paul began. "The author described how you'd write down all of your purchases in a notebook with your room number—whether it was an Ashway Intermediate fly line or lunch—and the proprietor, Frank Moore, would make sure it was added to your bill. It also mentioned how some angler had gone out on the river steelhead fishing with a fly rod and had gotten his brains beaten out falling and catching no fish. He got himself some worms and started down toward the Camp Water—a series of famous pools—and Frank Moore tackled him before he could dip his bait and further dissuaded him from doing so. The *SI* piece also mentioned the innovative catch-and-release and barbless hook regulations then instituted on the North Umpqua.

"At the same time, one of my earliest and best friends in Jackson, John Simms, was very enthusiastic about steelhead fishing. John knew about the North Umpqua and Steamboat from his fishery biologist brother-in-law from Oregon. We talked about the story, and he said, 'You've got to go to this place.' So I planned to go. I was curious about this steelhead thing. Just as much, I wanted to learn more about the catch-and-release idea, as I felt the waters around Jackson were getting a lot of pressure and could use some help. So in September of 1974 I drove out there in my '71 Blazer. On the way down, I stopped in central

Oregon and fished on the Metolius River, a well-known spring creek. The river flows cold and I got pretty wet. I slept in my truck that night. I think I was already coming down with a cold, but being wet made things worse and I came down with a sinus infection.

"I pushed down to Moore's place the next day, feeling pretty poor. He set me up with a little cabin, modest but cute. I had never done any steelhead fishing but knew a lot about fishing streamers with shooting heads and was a pretty good caster, so I figured I'd do okay.

"At this point, I should mention that there had been an article that had come out in *Outdoor Life* on the North Umpqua about this time. A Montana novelist named William 'Yatz' Hjortsberg had gone out to the North Umpqua with Johnny Bailey and Russell Chatham, who was very expert at using a lead-core line from his northern California salmon and steelhead experiences. Using the superfast sinking line, Chatham had absolutely mollyhocked the fish, so much so that people were stopping along Highway 138 above the river to watch the show. Needless to say, the lead-core line was somewhat at odds with the ethos of the North Umpqua. It was all greased-line technique among the regulars, the feeling being that this gave the fish a fighting chance. In dire straits, one might use a sink-tip. Any talk of a lead-core line meant warfare. This was also the time when Oregon had developed a reputation as being unwelcoming to newcomers in general, whether they were casting lead-core lines or not casting at all. This was due to a statement that Governor Tom McCall had made in 1971: 'We want you to visit our state of excitement often. But for heaven's sake, don't move here to live.'

"I was getting ready to go out with a guide named Dale that Frank had set me up with, and Dan Callaghan—one of the regulars down on the North Umpqua at the time, a great photographer and conservationist—dropped by and said, 'We're gonna have a cocktail party tonight, we'd like you to come.' I consented. My sinus infection was starting in earnest and I was feeling dizzy. Not a good state to be in for wading the North Umpqua, with all the basalt ledge rock. Frank loaned me his corkers and I went out. We didn't do much in the way of fishing. Hell, we didn't even see a fish. Still, it was interesting to hear all the rigmarole about the traditions and history of each pool.

"After fishing, I went to the cocktail party. Callaghan was there, as was Jack Hemingway—Ernest's son—and a bunch of the other regulars. I overheard someone saying that there was supposed to be a guy from a newspaper attending the party. Of course that was me. Before I could say anything they started lighting into me: 'What are you doing here, you a∗∗hole!' After the story about Chatham and lead-core lines, they didn't want any more

OPPOSITE: While tricky to fish, the North Umpqua is unquestionably one of the most beautiful steelhead rivers in the world.

stories about the North Umpqua. The general consensus was 'Get the f**k out!' It was one of the more hostile environments I'd ever walked into.

"All the while, I was getting sicker and sicker. I needed a trip to the emergency room, so I zigzagged my way to the hospital in Roseburg, about forty miles away. After my treatment, I stopped into a dinky fly shop in Roseburg, owned by a guy named Dennis Black, who eventually started Umpqua Feather Merchants. He said it had been a tough season on the North Umpqua, that I shouldn't be discouraged. 'You should go down to the Rogue for half-pounders,' he advised. [Half-pounders are small steelhead that spend just a few months at sea before returning to their natal rivers; the Rogue is one of the few rivers where half-pounders show up in large numbers.] When I got back to my cabin, Frank Moore suggested the same thing. He loaned me his corkers and drew me a map. Before I took off, he brought me out to spot some fish. Having Frank point them out was like taking batting practice with Ted Williams. I'll never forget his enthusiasm! That night, while I was lying in bed with a heater blasting and a towel over my face, he got me up to see the northern lights.

"As I was taking off for the Rogue the next day, I saw something that really spoke to the experience of being in Oregon—one-log loads coming down the road, with a timber jack wearing a hickory shirt at the wheel. A tractor trailer hauling one huge tree. It spoke to all the traditions that the surrounding forest lands encompassed.

"I drove down these narrow back roads to get to the Rogue. I was dizzy, having trouble breathing, and all of these logging trucks were whizzing by, trying to run me off the road. In the haze of my drive, somewhere around Coquille, I saw a large mailbox that read 'Stamper' and realized that this must have been where Ken Kesey got the name for the protagonists in his novel *Sometimes a Great Notion*. I got to the campground that Frank had described and set up my tent near the river. The fish were busting and rolling and carrying on. I had a fiberglass rod that Curt Gowdy had given me, a Berkeley Parabolic, and an old Medalist reel. I put on a Red Ant fly and staggered down to the river. Pretty soon I'd hooked two steelhead. I felt so lousy I didn't even play them. I just reefed them in. I thought, 'Okay. I've caught a steelhead now. Big deal.' I went back to my tent and lay down. My head felt like it was part of the timpani near the finale of the *1812 Overture*. That night, I wound up in the Gold Beach hospital and spent the rest of my vacation there, watching the World Series on TV. I was so sick that a girlfriend of mine at the time who was down in San Francisco at a Forest Service meeting had to come up and drive me back home to Jackson. It was well into the fall before I felt better.

"On the way home, we stopped at Steamboat so I could drop off Frank's corkers. Jack Hemingway was there, and he took me aside and said, 'You know, you seem like a pretty good fellow, I'm sorry how we treated you.' A few years later, Dan Callaghan also apologized for the group. Still, it had really rubbed me the wrong way.

"When I got home, I told my friend Simms that he could take Tom McCall, the North Umpqua, and all of Oregon and stuff it. He said, 'No, no, no! You just had a bad experience, we'll change that.'

"'And as far as steelhead are concerned,' I continued, 'I don't care if I ever see another one, let alone catch one.'

"In the last three decades I've been dragged out steelhead fishing a few more times, on the Salmon in Idaho, on the Deschutes in Oregon, and up in BC on the Babine and Morice. In the process, I realized that steelhead fishing was the fishing equivalent of my mom going shopping. She went shopping a good deal but didn't do any buying. Steelheaders never do any catching. After getting one nice fish on the Morice, a fish Simms actually got a picture of, I said, 'If you really want to punish me, take me steelhead fishing.'"

Paul Bruun arrived in Jackson Hole, Wyoming, in 1973 and since that time has pursued many vocations: newspaperman, fishing guide, boat designer, and traveling angler. Among many other achievements, he launched the *Jackson Hole Daily* and started South Fork Skiff, a drift-boat company specializing in high-performance, low-profile fiberglass craft. Paul has also consulted on outdoor product lines for Simms, Life Link INTL, Orvis, and Patagonia. While he has stepped back from South Fork Skiff and his consulting activities, Paul still guides on the Snake River in Jackson and has a weekly outdoor-life column that appears in the *Jackson Hole News & Guide*. When he's not fishing or writing, Paul enjoys traveling, bird hunting, and cooking. His favorite species are smallmouth and snook; *he vows to avoid steelhead forever and at all costs.*

STEAMBOAT CREEK FISH WATCHER

While perhaps at times standoffish to outsiders, the caretakers of the North Umpqua have been at the forefront of conservation efforts, creating one of the first and largest (thirty-three miles) stretches of fly-fishing-only water. Innovative management techniques continue today, with the Steamboat Creek Fish Watcher program. Steamboat Creek, a tributary that enters the North Umpqua just above Steamboat Inn, accounts for up to 35 percent of the wild steelhead that spawn in the system. In the summer and early fall, as many as five hundred adult fish will gather in the Big Bend pool, eleven miles up the creek. These fish historically have been extremely vulnerable to poachers. An act of vandalism on such a pool (such as some hooligan throwing a stick of dynamite, which has happened in the past) could devastate the North Umpqua wild steelhead population. To offset such a disaster, the North Umpqua Foundation has retained fish watcher Lee Spencer to guard the fish. From early summer until the rains of late fall usher the steelhead farther upstream to spawn, Spencer lives in a small trailer above the pool with his dog Sis. When he's not discouraging potential poachers, he educates visitors on the life cycle of the steelhead and keeps an extensive journal of his observations—some of which are published at www.northumpqua.org.

RIGHT–HAND–REACH MEND

Many anglers are quite content to fish the same fly patterns on the same river year after year, but some fly fishers are constantly pushing new boundaries. They are exploring new waters, experimenting with new techniques, striving to get a better understanding of the insects that call their local stream home. The inquisitiveness the pastime can arouse is one of its great attractions. Indeed, some anglers I know would say that the day they stop learning new things on the water is the day they'll cease fly fishing.

A good angler is always ready to expand his or her horizons. Doing so can sometimes lead to immediate gratification, as New Zealand's Chappie Chapman explains.

"I once had a client named Stewart Merrill, an attorney from Anchorage, Alaska," Chappie began. "He came down to the South Island to fish with me for a few days. Stew is a good fisherman and he did pretty well, though we didn't get any extraordinary trout. Before the last day that we had to fish together, Stew said, 'Chappie, I want a chance to catch a trophy trout.' I told him that to get a trophy fish, our best bet would be to take a helicopter trip into one of the lesser-trafficked streams I know that holds large trout. He was all right with that, so we booked a 'copter and the next morning we flew off after breakfast. In New Zealand the fishing doesn't really start until after nine A.M. The water is too cold before for much insect life to be stirring about, and the sun is not high enough to get your polarized glasses to work properly. We fish 'banker's hours,' very civilized. And very appropriate when you're going after brown trout, the great gentleman of the river.

"The helicopter set us down near a spot I like called the Rock Pool on this particular river, and he took off, planning to pick us up around five-thirty. The river I chose that day flows gin clear and is very isolated, though just a short flight from town. It's always very special to be there. I have a routine when I'm guiding. At the start of each day, I rig the client's gear and set them down on a piece of water where I'm reasonably sure there aren't any fish so they can get into a rhythm of casting. It's the same routine for seasoned anglers and beginners alike. On this day, the routine was no different. After getting Stew set up, I had him start making some casts while I searched the river for signs of any insects hatching. There still wasn't enough light to really scan the pool for fish. As my eyes were wandering over the

water I did a double take. In front of a large rock on the other side of the pool I saw a nose break the surface. I thought that perhaps it was just a single rise, but the nose came up again, and it was evident that it was a large fish. I said, 'Stew, there's a fish over there.' 'That's going to be a hard cast,' Stew observed, and he was spot-on. He would have to negate the irregular current flow created by a large rock across the river. The presentation was further exacerbated by a rock that rested between us and the fish. There was no place where we could cross the river and effectively cast upstream to the fish. The only way he might be able to get the proper drift would be with a right-hand-reach mend, plus another mend on top of that. I suggested this and he said, 'I don't know the right-hand reach mend.' So I led him downstream to show him.

OPPOSITE: The streams of New Zealand's South Island are home to many big trout, but it takes cunning and skill to catch them.

"As I mentioned before, Stew is an excellent angler. Despite this, he had no compunctions about admitting he didn't know something, and he was quite willing to learn a new technique. This is a quality I've seen again and again in anglers who visit New Zealand. They come here at least in part to learn. If you come with an open mind, you're going to learn more than you ever thought possible about trout fishing. The people who think they know it all don't catch many fish in New Zealand.

"We walked a hundred yards or so downstream and rehearsed the cast a few times. It didn't take long for Stew to get the hang of it. Then we returned to the Rock Pool. I tied on a small black caddis pattern and Stew began. It was a reasonably long cast—fifty to fifty-five feet—that he had to make, plus the series of mends. It took quite a while to get it just right. Much to Stew's credit he didn't spook the fish, despite the many attempts he made. After forty-five minutes, he got the right cast and the right mend in there. I saw the nose come up and and whispered, 'Go Stewie!' The fish was on. Coming from Alaska, Stew is quite comfortable playing big fish. After twenty minutes, he gave me a shot with the net, and I came up with a gigantic brown—ten and a half pounds. Stew was excited, to say the least. After we released the fish, he said, 'I don't want to fish anymore.' I reminded him that it was just ten o'clock, and that the 'copter wasn't coming back for seven hours. I gave him a snack and he suggested that I fish. I said, 'It's your day. You fish.' He finally consented. We stood up. As I was swinging my pack onto my shoulder I looked out at the rock. Right there in the same spot I saw another nose. It was a different fish but would demand the same cast. I said, 'Stew, you can make that cast. Have another go.'

"Stew stripped some line off, made a few false casts, and then dropped it in there perfectly. As the fly drifted down, the nose came up and I said, 'Go, Stewie!' The line came up tight on the fish and we were off again. I couldn't help but say, 'Oh God, Stewie, that's a big fish!' 'Bigger than the other one?' he asked. 'Can't tell until we get him to the net.' Soon enough, Stewie did just that. This fish—another mammoth brown—was eleven and a half pounds.

"In my twenty years of guiding I've had a number of occasions when I've had clients

An angler charts a possible descent to a remote South Island stream.

catch double-digit fish. I've had a few occasions when an angler has caught two such fish in a day. But I'd never had a client catch two ten-pound-plus fish on two consecutive casts. After landing the second brown Stewie was silent. He walked thirty or forty yards away from me and just looked at the river. He understood that what he'd done was something very special. And he wanted to savor it."

Chappie Chapman (www.chappie.co.nz) caught his first fish at age six and discovered fly fishing at thirteen. He learned his craft fishing the many small streams that flowed off the mountain near his home. In the mid 1970s he quit his job, bought a 4WD vehicle and a caravan, and went fishing for the next three and a half years. This led to a life of guiding, and Chappie has been sharing his expertise with anglers for more than twenty years. When he guided part-time, he spent a number of years in the fishing tackle industry, at both whole-sale and retail, where he had the opportunity to be involved with design and development of some of the more popular brands of fly-fishing tackle on the market today. Chappie also runs fly-fishing schools, for introductory, mid-level, and advanced anglers.

A PH.D. IN TROUT

Fishing the intimate, clear streams of New Zealand provides anglers with an opportunity to pursue an advanced education in trouting techniques. The fish—browns and rainbows that average 4.5 pounds and often reach double-digit weights—are big enough to give the most traveled angler a taste of buck fever. While quite large, the fish are not numerous and it's often necessary to hike a good deal of stream before a fish is spotted . . . if you can spot the fish, which blend into their environment notoriously well. Once spotted, these wary crea-tures will bolt at the slightest miscue on the fly fisher's part, and you'll be left with another hike to find your next fish. At least the scenery is beautiful! "Trout are the great leveler," Chappie Chapman says. "They remind us that we all get into our pants one leg at a time. Trout don't care about your affluence, religion, mental health, politics. All they know is that if the fly doesn't look right they're not going to eat it."

LAUGHTER IN THE CANYON

Sometimes the greatest gift you can offer a loved one is the education they will need to enjoy a pastime that will stay with them through the course of a lifetime. Other times, the greatest gift you can give is a willingness to be educated. This was a gift that Mike Copithorne received from his father on the Upper Sacramento River shortly before his father's death.

OPPOSITE: Castle Crags rise above the intimate Upper Sac near the town of Dunsmuir, California.

"Growing up in the hills of northern California, I developed a love of the outdoors early in my life," Mike began. "From the time when I was quite young, I was ever ready to grab a bucket and pole or a BB gun and charge into the woods. The call of the wild, as it were, only strengthened over the years. My parents shared my love of the outdoors, though it was my mom who was always planning the camping and hiking trips that so often included a fishing rod. My dad enjoyed getting outside but wasn't quite as motivated. This lack of enthusiasm especially extended to fishing. I remember him saying that in his youth, fishing had been a mindless pursuit involving a lawn chair, chips, beer, worms, and a bobber. This memory undoubtedly influenced his indifference to angling. I could count on one hand all the times when he'd accompanied me to the water.

"Given his ambiguity, I was very surprised one day when I received a call from my dad, requesting that I teach him to fly cast. I stammered, 'Shhhure . . . yeah . . . okay!' Later, he explained that fly fishing seemed much more 'engaging' than the worm and bobber stuff, though I believe that he was simply seeking a way for us to spend more quality time together. Our first casting practice went unusually well. My dad's hand, trained by years as a dentist, took quickly to the rhythmic motion of casting. As we cast, I found myself daydreaming of connecting him to one of those silver shimmers I'd grown so fond of pursuing. But I knew that the day I imagined, a day with free-rising trout willing to take any offerings, could just as easily end up as a day of lost flies, frayed tempers, and a sense of helplessness. It would take the perfect spot, where our quarry would be plentiful and willing, and the obstacles relatively few for my dad to negotiate. I believed I knew of such a spot on the Upper Sacramento River.

"We arrived at the spot on a fall day as the sun illuminated the fall colors on the opposite bank. As usual, the sound of the stream gave my tired limbs new energy, and I bounded down the trail. I soon noticed that my dad was falling behind a bit, and I paused, saying a small prayer that the river would yield at least one fish, not for me but for my dad. The colors were just fantastic that day, the oranges and yellow of the trees mixing with the burnt red color of the soil along the railroad tracks that followed the stream, and contrasting with the greens of moss-covered rocks and the darker greens of the deeper pools of the river. 'Beautiful, isn't it?' I almost whispered. I scanned the air above the river hoping to locate the telltale flutter of caddis wings so common late in the year on the Upper Sac. Finally I saw one, then another. 'Just hope they're eating 'em,' I said to myself.

"I soon found a few fish feeding with obnoxious fervor and decided to focus my pupil on them. I positioned my dad and pointed to the foot of the pool where a rainbow poked his head through the surface film to take a floundering bug. 'Try to work that slick water near the tail out,' I suggested. Dad nodded as if he understood perfectly and began to false cast. His back cast stretched closer and closer to a tree branch and disaster, but finally, with a heave, he sent the line hurling through the air. To my happy surprise, it unfurled gently and lit softly on the water. The fly passed over where the trout was lying, then began to swing down below us in the current. 'That was good,' I said. 'Let's try again.' The next cast was much like the first and it received a hasty reply. The moment it settled on the surface a fish darted toward it. We were both taken by surprise and, not surprisingly, he failed to set the hook. After a dozen more fruitless casts we moved downstream.

"We came to a spot where there was a large boulder in the middle of the stream. I asked my dad to cast down to the boulder and to leave some slack in the line so his fly would dead drift down. His first effort straightened out nicely but came up five feet short. 'That's okay,' I said. 'Just strip out a little more line and make that cast again.' He did so, and the fly settled effortlessly onto the surface. I couldn't help but smile at how well he was taking direction. I wasn't the only one admiring his cast. Perhaps it was the scenery, or the fading light dancing on the surface, but at any rate I failed to notice the shadow that had begun drifting up from the depths to waylay Dad's offering until it was almost too late. The next few moments unfurled in slow motion. The fish neared the surface, broke through it, inhaled Dad's caddis, and returned to its lair. 'Set the hook, *set the hook!*' I stammered. Dad scrambled to retract a few coils of slack line from the surface and sent his rod tip sharply skyward. I waited what seemed like a lifetime and was relieved to see the tip of his rod flex with the weight of a good fish. 'Easy, easy,' I said as his reel came to life. The fish took off downstream, venturing dangerously close to the rocks that bordered the end of the pool. With Dad's coaxing and a little bit of my coaching, the fish soon came within reach. The smile that graced my father's face mirrored my own. He lifted the fish, a beautiful specimen of an Upper Sac rainbow, and I preserved the scene for posterity with the flash of my camera. As the tail slipped gently from his hands we looked at each other and burst into laughter that echoed down the canyon in the growing darkness.

"That was the first and last trout that my dad and I would catch together on a fly. Not long after that picture was taken I suffered an injury while skiing that would prevent me from ever hiking into such a rugged canyon setting again. And my dad suffered a heart attack that took him from this world all too early. The moment of our small triumph is burned on that slip of Kodak paper, but also indelibly upon my memory, burned as one of those moments where life unfurls as close to perfect as humanly possible."

Dr. Copithorne and his memorable Upper Sac rainbow.

Mike Copithorne grew up around Redding, California, where he found a love for solitary sports like kayaking, mountain biking, surfing, snowboarding, and fly fishing. Early in his college career he was introduced to wakeboarding and soon put college on hold to pursue a professional career; in 1998 he was second in the nation and third in the world in the Men's I division (nineteen- to twenty-four-year-olds). While snow skiing in the spring of 2000, Mike fell and broke T-9 and T-10 vertebrae, crushing his spine and leaving him a paraplegic. Mike's close family and friends and his strong Christian faith have enabled him to maintain a positive attitude despite his injury, and he feels that he's been blessed with many opportunities. Since his accident he has continued to travel and fly fish, making angling trips throughout the West and to Florida, Pennsylvania, Virginia, New York, Alaska, Mexico, Costa Rica, and Belize in quest of species ranging from brook trout to sailfish. In addition to his career as a schoolteacher, Mike works in the fly-fishing department of Sweeney's Sports in Napa, California. He is currently working toward his fly casting master's certificate. "Remember to cherish each moment of every day," Mike shared. "Especially those spent fly fishing—and especially those spent fly fishing with loved ones. What else is there?"

THE UPPER SAC

The Upper Sacramento River has been called one of the most productive and beautiful freeway-side trout streams in America. Though I-5 and the Union Pacific railroad line closely parallel the Upper Sac, a broad swath of trees and the freestone river's murmur drown out most of the noise. The Upper Sac is all the more remarkable when its near extinction is considered; in 1991 a rail car carrying thirteen thousand gallons of pesticide derailed near the town of Dunsmuir, spilling its poison into the river and decimating a million fish and virtually all other aquatic life downstream. After vehement debate, the California Fish and Game department decided to forgo stocking and let the river fend for itself. It has done so admirably, with rainbows—mostly natives—returning from Lake Shasta (downstream) to populate the river's pockets, riffles, and pools. The Upper Sac's trout are not nearly as big as the bruisers you'll encounter in the Lower Sac, but they are spunky and prone to acrobatics when hooked.

THE HUNT FOR THE MIGHTY MAHSEER

A lesson we may take away from Eastern religious traditions is the notion that the path is the goal, that reaching a milestone or objective is not nearly as important as how you got there. This is at least one kernel of knowledge that Jeff Currier took away with him after an adventure trip to India in quest of the mighty mahseer.

"My wife, Granny, and I had been in India for three weeks, crossing the northern part of the country by ground," Jeff began. "We saw things many Americans wouldn't believe, from the incredible rituals of the dead in Varanasi to the wonders of the Taj Mahal. India amazed us, scared us, and blew our minds. But after three weeks it was time to go fishing. India has some excellent fishing, even for trout, but we were here for mahseer. The largest member of the carp family, mahseer can attain sizes of over a hundred pounds and have gained the reputation as one of the toughest fighters of all freshwater species. They can get so big that their scales are sometimes used for luggage tags! While populations of mahseer in much of southern Asia have been decimated by overfishing and pollution, several species still thrive in the southern state of Karnataka, in the Cauvery River. And that was where we went. After landing in Bangalore, we taxied directly to the office of Jungle Lodges & Resorts and booked eight days of fishing at two different camps on the river.

"At the first camp, a short man met us by a huge boulder that had a mahseer and the camp name, Galibore, painted upon it. 'We don't get many Americans here,' he said. 'I have begun to think that Americans don't know of the mahseer.' 'They don't, I do, and I want to fly fish for them,' I replied, anticipating the 'you can't catch them on a fly' response I'd received on other occasions when fly fishing and mahseer had been mentioned in the same breath. 'If fly fishing is what I think it is, then you can't catch mahseer that way,' he said. 'They are too big and don't eat bugs.' 'That's fine,' I said. 'But I've got some big rods and I'm planning on trying anyway.' 'Well good for you, I think it would be great if your method works,' our host said. 'I'll have your guide Kariapa pack your tackle. Of course, you can use ours.'

"Within an hour, Kariapa was paddling us away from the banks of the camp down the Cauvery in one of the most interesting boats I'd ever fished from, called a coracle. It was shaped like an upside-down umbrella made from straw and waterproofed by some unknown

fabric. Granny and I sat on its floor while Kariapa sat on a stool, leaned over the tiny boat rim, and pulled us along with his hand-carved paddle. I could quickly tell that Kariapa knew the fishing on the Cauvery. The only drawback was that he didn't speak a word of English.

"We pulled over near the tail-out of a pool and rigged up. Kariapa had two heavy weight spin rods about seven and a half feet long, the same size I've used trolling in the ocean. The spin reels were loaded with line that must have been at least thirty-pound test. I didn't know if he had lures or if this would be a bait-chucking event. I was praying for a lure, because then I would have a definite chance with flies, but out came the hook box. He reached in and grabbed an enormous five-zero hook. Next came a twenty-ounce sinker and a burlap bag the size of a small bag of grass seed. It was full of a pastelike substance, dark brown in color, known in India as *ragi*—millet with seeds and berries, things all carp love. There was no way in hell that I came to India to baitfish, but doing it this first afternoon I could learn about the mahseer—where they live, how they bite, and how they fight, all crucial for success on the fly.

"We fished for three hours and caught a number of catfish. We had stayed in the same spot, but at sunset Kariapa had us cast to a different area of the pool. Granny soon got a rod-ripping bite and this time when she slammed the hook home it was no catfish. The fish took off. Granny let out a groan as the fish peeled off line. I reeled in my rig as fast as I could to help land the fish and ready the camera. The fish worked Granny hard for five minutes before it stopped running and Granny was able to retrieve some line. At last, she landed a seven-pound silver mahseer. After the fight it put up, we expected it to be much bigger. We displayed our delight to Kariapa, but he gave us an 'are you kidding me' look. To him, a seven-pound mahseer was like a five-inch bass. This fish was a baby.

"The next morning we set out again and beached the coracle on a huge rock in the middle of the river. Kariapa set up Granny with the *ragi* and let me do my thing. I strung up my eight-weight and tied on a 4/0 red-and-white Clouser Minnow that was heavy enough to knock me out on impact. Kariapa kept a confused eye on me as I began chucking and ducking, just like streamer fishing at home. We fished many spots from sunrise to noon, and I changed lines several times to cover the water column but to no avail. Meanwhile, Granny racked up a handful of fish, a fabulous species called the pink carp, a catfish, and six mahseer, including one silver mahseer that topped fourteen pounds. When we rolled into camp, a puzzled Kariapa couldn't wait to tell the camp boys about my strange and apparently worthless fishing habits.

OPPOSITE: Jeff's wife, Granny, inspects their boat, which she, Jeff, and their guide, Kariapa, would take down the Cauvery.

"Fishing on my own in front of the camp, I eventually hooked and landed a five-pound fish that looked like a mahseer on a chartreuse Clouser. It turned out to be an olive carp. During the next two days at Galibore, not one giant mahseer—or anything else—took my fly. I was starting to think my olive carp was a fluke, but things would improve upstream.

"Our next four days were spent at a camp called Bheemeshwari. Here the river was much wider, but also shallower, with lots of grassy banks and boulders—great fly water! On our arrival at Bheemeshwari, I was amazed to see rising fish. I scrambled for my five-weight, tied on a Royal Wulff, and fooled the first fish I cast to. I assessed it to be a baby silver mahseer, about twelve inches in length. I was dry-fly fishing in India! Granny and I took turns with the five-weight, landing fifty more smaller fish, with a few beauties close to twenty inches. Before long we had an entourage of camp help and a few other guests watching this fascinating way to fish the local river. It was quite hot, and we occasionally visited the camp watering hole for a cold Kingfisher beer.

"The next morning our new guide, Anthony, rousted us early from our tent. Soon we were in our coracle moving through minor white water. I was casting from the boat as Anthony paddled—it was the closest I'd felt to home in two months! Instead of using the Royal Wulff that had been so successful the night before, Anthony chose a Chernobyl ant. Just like home on the Snake, I cast the tan-bellied Chernobyl toward the bank. Anthony soon got the hang of keeping the boat in position so I could drop my fly in all the prime spots. 'Cast over by that rock!' he said, as we dropped two feet in a miniature rapid. I picked up my cast and, before my fly landed, noticed the rising fish that Anthony had surely seen. The instant the ant landed the fish smacked it with a vengeance. I set the hook and the fight was on. 'Wow! I love it!' Anthony shouted with total delight. I could see it was the same species from the day before, only this was a hawg. Using the current, the fish bolted downstream, and in seconds I saw my backing for the first time in Asia. 'It's a carnatic carp!' Anthony added. The fish fought strongly but eventually came to hand. 'This is a carnatic carp?' I asked. 'It looks like a silver mahseer.' 'Yes. A carnatic carp,' Anthony explained. 'Very similar to the silver mahseer, only this type doesn't get as big, perhaps thirty pounds.'

"Over the next few days, we caught many more carnatic carp on the fly, and a bizarre fish called a snakehead that audibly breathes in air from the surface and attacked my mouse patterns like a white shark taking a seal. I even landed a nineteen-inch Deccan mahseer, my only 'official' mahseer on the fly. I dredged for big mahseer with my ten-weight and those killer Clousers every chance I got but didn't even feel a nibble. During the countless hours

I spent dredging the depths of the Cauvery, I reminisced about the incredible two months we'd had in Nepal and India. While I had wanted very badly to catch a giant mahseer on a fly—had even viewed that as one of the main ambitions for the trip—I came to realize that it didn't really matter. The adventures we'd had on the way to *not catching* a mahseer were irreplaceable."

Jeff poses with a snakehead, taken on a deer hair mouse.

Jeff Currier has worked at the Jack Dennis Fly Shop in Jackson, Wyoming, for nineteen years; he presently manages all fishing operations. Jeff has taught the skills of fly fishing, guided fly fishers throughout Wyoming and Yellowstone National Park, and escorted anglers to fishing destinations throughout the world. He has made several television appearances, including on *Fishing the West*, *Fly Fishing the World*, and *Ultimate Fly Fishing*. His articles, photographs, and artwork have graced the pages of magazines, catalogs, brochures, and books. Jeff is the author of the *Currier's Quick and Easy Guide to Saltwater Fly Fishing* and *Currier's Quick and Easy Guide to Warmwater Fly Fishing* guidebooks.

These books have become the standard introductions to saltwater and warmwater fly fishing. Jeff became a member of Fly Fishing Team USA in 1998 when he competed in Zakopane, Poland. It was there that he led the team to one of its best ever finishes with his staggering mix of 128 trout and grayling in just five sessions. He has since remained on the team, adding his vast knowledge of all aspects of fishing, familiarity in many world-wide destinations, and true team spirit. In 2003 at the World Fly Fishing Championships in Spain, Jeff earned a bronze medal for individual performance among his international peers. During the winter months, Jeff can be found lecturing throughout the United States on nearly every aspect of fly fishing. He demonstrates fly casting and teaches seminars on the basic to advanced skills of fly fishing as well as many fly-fishing destination programs, ranging from his home waters in the Rockies to the most remote corners of the globe.

FISHING IN INDIA

India is not synonymous with sportfishing in the way that, say, British Columbia or Maine might be. Yet with more than thirty thousand miles of rivers and streams and another almost two thousand miles of coastline, opportunities do abound. The mahseer is the signature game fish of India, sometimes reaching one hundred pounds and more, and is renowned for its incredible strength. In addition to other endemic game species such as carnatic and olive carp and snakehead, India boasts some healthy trout populations in its Himalayan regions, where browns and rainbows were introduced by the British as early as 1880. Several rivers come well recommended, including the well-stocked Baspa, which begins along the Tibetan border and forms the Baspa Valley.

FLY FISHING 3,000 FEET UNDER THE EARTH

For the past fifty years or so, adventurers and entrepreneurs have advanced the borders of fly fishing far beyond trout and salmon in North America and Europe. First came saltwater fly fishing for bonefish, tarpon, and striped bass. Then the waters of Patagonia and New Zealand became hotbeds for adventurous troutists. Billy Pate and a handful of others realized one could tempt billfish with a fly. Soon after, salmon anglers discovered the Kola Peninsula, steelheaders the rich waters of Kamchatka. And a host of fish—from roosterfish to peacock bass to taimen—came to be viewed as legitimate fly-rod species.

It's safe to say that with a recent trip to Borneo, Ralph Cutter has pushed the boundaries of fly-fishing travel to a whole different level. A much lower level.

"I was part of an expedition that went to Borneo to explore Gunung Buda, a massive block of jungle-cloaked limestone that rises more than three thousand feet into a ceiling of clouds that drench the area in three hundred inches of rain each year. Known by geologists as a karst formation, Buda has been assaulted by hundreds of thousands of years' worth of rain that has carved deep fissures into its limestone flanks. From a caver's perspective, Gunung Buda may hold the crown jewels of Borneo, and on the global level Borneo's caves are on a scale unto themselves. As an example: two ranges south of Gunung Buda at Gunung Mulu there is the Sarawak chamber, a staggering cavern three times larger than the Superdome where a seven-forty-seven could fly laps between its stalactites.

"This expedition was going to be the third try at cracking Buda's secrets. The first was a brief scouting foray by John Lane and George Prest. With a minimum of time and equipment they found tantalizing leads hidden behind the massive piles of rockfall at Buda's northern base. Lane and Prest returned two years later with a team of hard-core cavers and discovered an astounding three dozen world-class caves almost immediately. Unfortunately the close quarters, miserable tropical conditions, and driven personalities of the team combined to cause the expedition to implode in less than a month. Despite the social fallout, valuable data were logged and the discoveries set the stage for our expedition. For this expedition, John scoured the world for cavers with specialties outside of the strictly subterranean realm. I joined the team as its paramedic, herpetologist, and fish biologist.

Ralph Cutter prepares to descend into the subterranean world of Gunung Buda.

"One day early in our expedition, one of the team, Chris Andrews—our cave cartographer—stumbled into camp caked with mud and guano. He described a cave that twisted and corkscrewed downward until it ran out of limestone and collided with the sandstone roots of Gunung Buda. Water flowing down the passage formed a lake, and in the lake something was moving. Though Chris felt it was a snake or maybe a big fish, the natives said it was probably a crocodile. Being the fish, snake, and crocodile guy, it was my job to catch it. We quickly bundled up a snake hook and a fly rod and clanging with climbing gear we left camp for Chris's cave.

"Chris, Scott Bauman—a gastropod expert from Guam—and I navigated the twisting passage into the bowels of the mountain. Guided by flickering cap lamps we rapped from

drop to drop, down-climbed on slimy limestone knobs, and belly-crawled through greasy chutes, all the while descending deeper and deeper into the earth. Flickering in our lamps, dazzling white forests of stalactites were revealed, some as tiny as sewing needles and others as large as trees hanging from the ceilings. Each had its own life-giving drop of water suspended from its tip. As the drips drop, a corresponding stalagmite grows from the floor. Where the mites meet, columns are created and the forest metaphor is complete. Helectites, bizarre twisted calcite formations, looked like the bones of something dead reaching out to us from the cave walls. Differences in air pressure throughout the cave system created puffs and streams of wind. As the winds pass the decorations and chambers, a music is made. It sounds for all the world as if Gollum, in some hall hidden far below, is playing the pan flute. We were the first humans ever to enter this realm and he is playing just for us, beckoning us ever deeper.

"Thousands of feet beneath the summit of Buda the cave sumps at a lake. The water had receded a few feet to reveal a mouse-hole-shaped opening just at the waterline. Deep claw marks in the mud indicated that perhaps a crocodile really did live there. We swam across the cold black water and ducked into the mouse hole. We found ourselves inside a passage where the water was chin deep, and often the ceiling was so low we were forced to duck beneath the water to continue onward. The roof was cov-

Cave fly fishing gives new meaning to the phrase "limited back-casting space." Bats pose additional challenges.

ered with dripping, muddy slime that told of frequent and recent flooding. A quarter of a mile inside the passage Chris stopped suddenly and hissed, 'I hear moving water.' Chris is a wonderful guy, one of my dearest friends and an extraordinarily talented caver but at his mellowest looks like Kevin Bacon on nitroglycerin. When he gets excited you get the distinct impression he might explode. Right now his fuse was lit.

"Fears of being eaten by subterranean crocs were replaced by the more immediate possibility of being trapped by rising water. More cavers die by drowning than any other cause. Knowing there were no air chambers behind us, we rapidly pushed forward hoping to find refuge. We abruptly broke out into a massive subway cave with a crystal-clear river flowing through it. This was our sound of moving water. The cave was seething with life. Thick mounds of guano nourished centipedes, crabs, and thousands of mole crickets. Menacing huntsman spiders the size of Frisbees scuttled along the walls searching for bats to eat. Cave racer snakes slithered along the floor looking for baby bats or swiftlets fallen from the ceiling. The river was teeming with pale shrimp, crayfish, and some unknown type of isopod. Fish finned in the current and held in seams, just like they would in a trout stream. I rigged my fly rod with a five-weight line and tied on a grasshopper pattern, figuring it would be close enough to a mole cricket.

Ralph Cutter proudly displays his catch.

"Casting between the stalactites was tricky enough, but even more troublesome were the bats who wanted to eat the fly. With each cast, bats dropped from the ceiling and wheeled and twisted between the stalactites to catch the fly. We quickly became adept at catch-and-release bat fishing. On the first few drifts the fly passed right over the nose of a catfish patrolling the shallows. The fish did nothing until I gave the fly a little flick. With one strong stroke of its tail the catfish torpedoed the fly and rolled on it like a cat on a mouse. The fish was tough. It ran up the creek and then doubled back downstream, where it dove under a large chunk of ceiling breakdown. We pounded down the shoreline after it, splashing water and throwing wicked shadows from our helmet flames. Our whoops and hollers echoed down the passage and flushed clouds of bats off the roof to swirl in squeaking confusion. It was utter chaos.

"We caught a dozen or so of the powerful, long-whiskered fish. Aside from the fact that they don't have functional eyes, these catfish were remarkably unremarkable. Though the fish can't see, they are acutely aware of any disturbance in the water and the slightest movement of the fly triggered an immediate and aggressive response. Many times two or more fish hit the fly simultaneously, and at other times fish completely beached themselves as they launched at the hopper pattern.

"We saw smaller fish of a different species lurking in the deeper water, so I tied on a tiny bird's-nest nymph and fished it beneath a split shot. Jigging the fly in front of the small fish was reminiscent of fishing for bluegills as a kid. The small, white fish darted forward to inhale, then, just as quickly, exhaled the nymph. Over time, however, we caught two types of the deeper-dwelling fish—a barb and a chub. Both fish had pale skin and opalescent pink eyes, and both were likely new species. We preserved samples of all three fishes in formaldehyde and sent them on to a museum in Kuching for proper identification.

"I'm happy to report that the work from our expedition resulted in the creation of a large national park to protect and preserve the Gunung Buda mountains of Sarawak, Borneo."

Ralph Cutter is the author of *Sierra Trout Guide*, has contributed his writing and photography to a dozen other books, and is a frequent contributor to environmental and outdoor publications. Along with his wife, Lisa, he runs the California School of Flyfishing (www. flyline.com) out of Nevada City, California. It's one of the most respected fly-fishing schools in the country and has been featured in such diverse publications as *National Geographic Adventure*, the *Los Angeles Times, Outside, Adventure West,* the *Wall Street Journal, Sunset*, and *Playboy*. Ralph and Lisa were both inducted into the Northern California Federation of Fly Fishers Hall of Fame, and Ralph is a recipient of the prestigious Order of the Mayfly award. Both Cutters are fully certified FFF casting instructors.

CAVE-DWELLING FISH

Fish that reside in caves, such as the catfish that Ralph Cutter encountered in Borneo, have evolved in darkness and thus have no use for eyes. Instead, they hunt with the help of sensory organs located all over their bodies. These organs help them detect movement and chemical changes in the water, either of which can be an indicator of the presence of food. Life for cave-dwelling fish—and, for that matter, for other cave inhabitants—is largely dependent on the coming and going of resident bats, who import nutrients from the outside world and distribute it liberally throughout the cave in the form of guano. The guano sustains aquatic invertebrates and a plethora of other small creatures that in turn provide fodder for the fish.

OF COFFEE CANS AND KIWIS

It would seem that traveling the world to fish exotic venues and then appearing on television as you release trophy after trophy would be a pretty relaxing gig. That is, unless the weather goes south. The rivers go out. The electricity goes down. The roads go unplowed. And you HAVE to produce a big fish to salvage thousands of dollars of production costs.

So goes Jack Dennis's quest for trout in Patagonian Chile.

"A friend of mine had business interests in Argentina, and we both happened to know the country's U.S. Ambassador," Jack began. "This friend invited me to go fishing down there, right after the Falklands War. We fished many of Patagonia's famous rivers. Toward the end of the trip, we received a tip that there was a lake in the Esquel region that we couldn't miss. We went, and I had one of my best lake fishing days ever. I made fast friends with the outfitter there, a fellow named Coco Hasan. It was Coco's dream to get an outfit like Frontiers to book trips to his lake. I made several subsequent trips down there, and took some video. I brought it to Frontiers. They were interested, but not quite ready to commit. I was appearing as a frequent guest on a national television show called *Fishing the West* with Larry Schoenborn, and I believed that if we got the lake on the show it would seal the deal.

"To justify the cost of filming in South America, we'd have to get enough footage to put together several shows. The political climate in neighboring Chile was moving in a positive direction for tourism, and it seemed that the timing might be right to visit there. We assembled an itinerary that included Coco's lake in Esquel and a drive through Patagonia to Chile. The fishing on the lake—which was like fishing a giant, slow-moving spring creek—was fantastic. I'd brought some bigger rods, 6- and 7-weights, which I gave to our guides at the end of our stay as a thank you. I had two 5-weights left, which I thought would be fine for the Chilean spring creeks that awaited us.

"After an extensive search at the border by forty soldiers with machine guns, our voyage began. We had a government-assigned escort named Carlos Meñoz who made it very clear he was part of the new government, not a Pinochet man. It was all gravel roads. There were no bridges; we had to take barges to cross the rivers. We traveled through pampas, tropical rainforests—very diverse and beautiful country. After two days and 1,200 miles, we

OPPOSITE:
Patagonian Chile is a much sought after fly-fishing destination, as much for its relaxed setting as its excellent trout fishing.

reached a pretty little lodge along the Rio Simpson, just as the sun was going down. The next morning we woke up and there was three feet of snow on the ground. All the rivers were blown out, and the snow was expected to continue for three days. We desperately needed to get more footage, and had only a few days left—was there any place else we could go? Carlos had an idea; there was a lake down south that had several rivers that flowed into it; there were rumors of very large brown trout. Soon we were off again. Luckily, we had four-wheel drive vehicles that the government had provided. We passed many peasants walking through the driving snow, dodging stalled vehicles and cows seeking shelter. The conditions didn't seem to trouble them at all as they sang and drank their matte from silver cups, grinning and laughing as a near miss occurred.

"We drove all day, 350 miles, eventually reaching the little port town of Puerto Anglos near the Argentine border. The snow had knocked out all the power into the town, leaving us no way to recharge our cameras. We had enough battery power left for one, maybe two days of filming. It's been my experience that trips that start out bad often end up well, so I kept a positive outlook. The next day we headed out to Rio Ibañez. We soon learned that the fishing season in this region of Chile was to end in two days, so our lack of camera power really didn't matter. It was slowly becoming apparent that Carlos, our guide, knew less about this region than he'd let on. He was a good talker, but I don't think he'd ever been to this spot. Rio Ibañez was not the gentle creek he had described. It was the size of the Deschutes in Oregon, and very off-color. I had only my 5-weight and a floating line. Larry loaned me a Teeny 200 sinking line and some big Alaskan flies. I'd fished for sea-run browns before in New Zealand with nymphs and dries and had an idea of how to go after them (though these fish migrated from the lake to the river, their lifecycle was similar). It was raining and sleeting and blowing, and the fishing was terrible. Larry and I beat the water until it was black and blue and we were exhausted. Larry landed one fish, an eight-pound brown trout. We shot the hell out of this from every angle, but one fish would not make a show. That night, huddled around our propane stove, Larry and his crew were despondent. 'This show is going down the tubes fast,' one crew member bemoaned. 'Any ideas?' I had no ideas, and time was running out. I said 'All we can do is keep fishing.' The director said only one more big fish and we would have a program. Larry agreed that another fish would save the show. I love a challenge and looked forward to the next day.

"The following day we went out again, and our luck was no better. Late in the afternoon our spirits had sunk as not one strike had occurred. Then about 4 P.M., something strange happened—out of nowhere, two poor peasants holding coffee cans filled with monofilament came up. We hadn't seen a soul in two days. They had handmade lures that were fashioned from Chilean coins. One of the fellows walked up to this riffle, and began swinging his lure out there. We had ignored the riffle, as it seemed too shallow and fast to hold fish. He'd let his lure swing through, and then give a little action by flexing his fingers on the monofilament at the end of the swing. On his third or fourth cast, he got a big brown, about 10 pounds. To land it, he simply ran up the hill until the fish was on the bank. He put the fish in a gunny sack; he was laying in fish for the coming winter. Soon after, he nailed a 12-pound fish. Then another. The coffee-can angler then walked over and tried to give this fish to me. Through Carlos, I understood that he wanted to put it on my hook so I could act as if I'd caught it for the camera. I declined, hoping it wouldn't come to that.

"I knew that Larry could be forced into doing this, but I wanted no part of it and sent the fellow downstream to Larry. Before he left, I asked Carlos to ask the peasant to look in my fly boxes and see if there was anything he liked. Carlos told me he had never seen a fly fisher before but liked the looks of my flies. He quickly pointed to a big off-orange Muddler Minnow that we called the Kiwi Muddler. I think he liked the fly's coppery color as it matched his lures. I'd never caught anything on that fly; I kept it in my box almost as a joke. It had been in my box for at least ten years and every time I fished, the fly it never got even a bump. I quickly asked him to pick another fly. With a shrug, he pointed to a black Wooly Bugger.

"By the time we'd decided on the flies, it was almost five o'clock and snow had begun falling. We'd have light until six. I pulled on my old Jackson Hole red ski hat, as it was freezing. One of the cameramen said it looked dumb, and that I'd have to take it off if I caught a fish. The way the hat looked was the least of my worries. I went up to the riffle with the size two Orange Kiwi, and the black Wooly Bugger tied off the back of the Kiwi. I would have to sling two big flies on a five weight. I chucked and ducked my way to a short cast and let the flies swing through the fast water. The line immediately went tight, and I thought 'Alright!' It was the bottom. I started to pull to break it off; I really didn't care if I lost that orange fly. The rig came loose. I made the same cast, giving the fly the same action the coffee angler did, and the line went tight again. 'Not again!' I thought. I gave a big pull with both hands, figuring I'd get rid of that damn fly for sure this time, and something jerked back hard and the line started moving. I started screaming bloody murder to Larry: 'I've got a fish!'

"Immediately I had the crew around me. I was fighting the fish, and the director got right in my face and softly said 'No pressure, Jack. You lose that fish, it will only cost us twenty grand.' I knew that we were running low on juice for the cameras, and I told the guys that this fish wasn't going to come to hand in ten minutes, so they better conserve their power. Everything seemed to go wrong. I backed up and fell backward over a log. The line went slack and my heart sank, but the fish was still on. In a half hour I started to tire. I alternated playing him with both hands as I felt my arms going numb. Finally, I had him in close—it was the biggest trout I'd ever hooked. I was beginning to think that I had a chance to land him, 5-weight and all. Then I saw Larry off to the side, sneaking up on the fish. Suddenly, inexplicably, he pounced on the fish, literally leaped on it—and worse yet, he missed it.

"To this day, I don't know what he was thinking! The fish screamed off, made a big 360 degree leap, and I went racing downstream in pursuit. I figured that was it. The fish took me to the very end of my backing—I had only three wraps left. It was way on the other side of the river. Then it stopped. I began gaining on him by pumping the rod hard and pulling against the current. Soon I had the fish back on my side and close to the surface, a sign that the fish was tiring. I looked over at a despondent Larry. I had given him a few choice words after the leaping incident, and he looked bruised. Suddenly the fish rolled and tangled with the other fly and wrapped himself in the leader. Quickly I shouted, 'Larry, I need you, buddy. Can you slip behind the fish and get him before he breaks the leader? Our net is way too small! Tail him like a salmon!' I held my breath as he charged into action and skillfully tailed the twenty-pound brown, one of the most beautiful fish I'd ever caught and still the largest trout of my life. We had just enough power left in the camera and light in the sky to get the final minutes but the hour-long fight went largely unfilmed. In the corner of the mouth was the bright orange Kiwi. This was the only fish that fly would catch. After I released the fish, one of the camera crew went up to the riffle with my outfit and lost the Kiwi on the first cast. That fish and fly were destined for each other.

"A friend of mine named Simon Dickey (who started the Poronui Ranch fly-fishing lodge in New Zealand) won a gold medal for rowing in the Mexico City Olympics in 1968. When I asked him how it felt to win that medal, he said that there was no way he could describe it. After landing that brown, I understood what he meant. Having the footage of that fish and being able to relive it has been my gold medal.

"It turned out that that episode of *Fishing the West* was one of Larry's top shows. He re-ran it for years. At times I play the episode for fly-fishing clubs and tell them the story of my biggest trout and give the credit to a Chilean fishing peasant who gave me a fishing lesson on a faraway river. A few years later I was down in Chile again, and planned another visit to Rio

Ibañez. The pilot we hired to fly us there told us that a volcano had erupted, and obliterated the riverbed. There would be no more fishing on the Rio Ibañez in our lifetime."

TALE 10

Jack Dennis began his professional fishing career at the age of twelve when he sold his first flies. He started guiding visiting anglers at the age of fourteen. At nineteen, Jack opened his first fishing tackle business in Jackson, Wyoming, which has become a well-known fly-fishing emporium (www.jackdennis.com). Jack's books, *Western Trout Fly Tying Manual,* volumes one and two, have sold over 300,000 copies, making it one of the best-known fly-fishing books in the world. Jack has also produced twenty fly-fishing videos, winning several Video of the Year awards. His newest book*, Tying Flies with Jack Dennis and Friends*, has been a bestseller. Jack's clients have included Tom Selleck, Don Johnson, Harrison Ford, Vice President Dick Cheney, Richard Pryor, Woody Harrelson, Arnold Palmer, Don Meredith, and "Dr. J." Jack has appeared in four ABC television *American Sportsmen* shows and been a guest on almost all the TV fishing shows. The Federation of Fly Fishers has presented him with their International Ambassador and their "Legend of Fly Fishing" award. Jack is a great ambassador of fly fishing, advising the governments of New Zealand, Australia, Chile, Argentina, and many Western states on fly-fishing tourism. Companies such as Cortland Line Company and Thomas & Thomas Rod Company have appointed him their fly-fishing spokesman; Jack has also been involved for years with the development of tackle and consulting for companies such as Abel Reels, Simms, Action Optics, Umpqua, Clacka Craft Drift Boats, and Frontiers Travel.

FISHING THE ESQUEL

The Esquel region is in the Argentine Patagonia, in the southernmost region of this vast and wonderful country. With backdrops of snowcapped mountains, an abundance of crystal-clear lakes, and streams teeming with brown and rainbow trout, Esquel brings to mind the American west of 100 years ago—the time, roughly, when the trout were introduced. There are many renowned waters here—Rio Carrileufu, Rio Rivadavia, Rio Arrayanes, Rio Grande, and Rio Futaleufu, to name just a few. Fine fishing for consistently large and robust wild trout is only the beginning; excellent horseback riding and birding await, along with the legendary Argentine hospitality. If you stay at one of the fine lodges that serve visiting anglers, you'll likely be treated to a genuine *asado* (barbecue) of lamb or beef.

THE 2X POOL

As anyone who's ever tried it can attest, catching a steelhead on a fly can be a tricky business. First, one must cover miles of water to find where the fish might be resting. Next, one must entice them—out of anger, curiosity, or Lord-knows-what—to take the fly. Then one must resist the temptation to pull the fly away when the fish begins to grab it. And, finally, one must play the fish gingerly to prevent it breaking off during one of the searing runs typical of steelhead.

Given all this, one can appreciate the accomplishment of hooking and landing a steelhead. But how about catching it twice? This is what outfitter John Ecklund once witnessed while guiding advertising guru Hal Riney on the beautiful Grande Ronde River in far northeastern Oregon.

"It was a morning in October of 1989," John began, "a wonderful time to be out in eastern Oregon as it's cold enough at night to bring on the foliage and bring the elk down into the valley, but warm enough in the day to be pleasant. I was fishing with Hal Riney. He would come up from San Francisco from time to time and hire me. He didn't want a guide per se, just someone to show him likely runs, as he was an accomplished angler and could cover the water fine on his own. I put him in a run and I went above him. I made a few casts and was watching him out of the corner of my eye. After a while, I could see by the way he was acting that he'd hooked up. I began retrieving my line so I could go down and help him land the fish. Then I noticed that he had his rod down and was walking up the bank, toward the road that borders the river for a time near the Oregon–Washington border.

"I went down to where Hal was just as the cook for the lodge, Stephen Cary, arrived. Stephen, incidentally, is now the winemaker at Yamhill Valley Vineyards. At that time, the program was that someone would come down and meet the early anglers on the river with coffee and cinnamon rolls, and Stephen was right on time. I asked Hal what happened, and he said, 'Right where you said the fish would be laying, I hooked one. I'm using a new reel, and I guess the guys at the shop didn't attach things right.' The fish took off and the line pulled away from the backing. That was that.

"Hal stepped away for a moment and Stephen took me aside and described how the same thing had happened to him once in New Zealand, and that later in the day he found the fly line—though, of course, the fish was long gone. For a fifty-dollar fly line, we figured it would be worth a shot. So we suggested to Hal that we head downstream to fish another run. He wasn't so sure about the idea but said he would come down later. I drove down in my Suburban, and Stephen drove down in his station wagon. It's not too far from where we started, a half mile or so. As I walked down to the river, Stephen jumped up on the roof of his station wagon with a pair of binoculars. 'There's the fly line,' he said after a moment, 'and it's coming right toward you. And you won't believe it, but it looks like the fish is still on!'

"I had waded in by this time, and returned to the bank to take off my shirt. I was ready to swim for it. I couldn't see the fish but I could see the fly line going up and down the run. I waded out to my midsection, reached down, and grabbed the line. Just at that moment Stephen called out, 'Here comes Hal. Let's play a trick on him.'

"Stephen tells Hal, 'Hey, good news, John's got your fly line.' Hal walked down the bank and pulled his backing through the guides of his rod. I was trying to be cool and not give things away. I was praying that the fish wouldn't feel any tension in the line and make a big run. Hal handed me the backing and I tied a down-and-dirty overhand knot—not very pretty but strong enough—I hoped—to hold together. I handed the rod to Hal, and he began cranking in the line. Just as he began reeling, the fish jumped. Hal played the fish in, a native hen, still full of spunk. Then we let Hal in on the joke. From the time

John Ecklund snaps a photo of ad man Hal Riney and his twice-caught steelhead.

he hooked the fish and lost the line to the time we recovered the line and landed the fish, a total of twenty minutes had elapsed.

"When we began fishing that pool in the early eighties, it didn't have a name. Very few of the pools and runs on the Grande Ronde did. It just wasn't a terribly well known fishery. That's certainly changed. In honor of Hal's catch, loss, and catch, we dubbed it the '2x Pool'—for twice caught."

John Ecklund cashed in his day job more than twenty years ago and founded the premier fly-fishing guide service in eastern Oregon. As the owner of Little Creek Outfitters, John explored and developed a variety of fishing programs that have become the fly-fishing standards. An explorer at heart, John has traveled extensively in Cuba, Baja, Venezuela, Argentina, and Chile. These travels led to the creation of Rivers to Reefs Excursions and to the development of the Mendoza Wine Experience. John has extensive experience in the lodging and food industry, having owned and operated Grande Ronde Lodge, and as current owner of a successful restaurant, Foley Station, in La Grande, Oregon. He also owns and operates Hells Canyon Whitewater Co., a whitewater rafting and fly-fishing service on the Snake River. John now splits his time between his estancia in the Mendoza region of Argentina ("It's a small estancia by Argentinian standards," he says) and eastern Oregon. When John is not holding a wineglass, odds are he has a set of oars in his hands. An accomplished photographer, John's pictures have appeared in Patagonia sales catalogs, *NW Steelheader* magazine, various Oregon tourism publications, and Randall Kaufman's acclaimed book *Bonefishing*. He may best be remembered for his *mojitos*.

SKATING THE GRANDE RONDE

From its headwaters in the Blue Mountains of eastern Oregon, the Grande Ronde flows some two hundred miles, mostly in Oregon, before crossing into Washington and joining the Snake. It's the premier steelhead river in northeastern Oregon, and for good reason—the river's canyons are a remarkably beautiful blend of alpine and high desert environs and the Grande Ronde's steelhead, especially the native A-run fish that return in the early fall, show great proclivity for surface patterns. Skating a Moose Turd or small Bomber across a glassy tail-out and watching the wake of an agitated steelhead while a bull elk bugles in the woods beyond is about as good as it gets for ardent steelheaders. Though ample road access and a copious later run of hatchery fish can make the Grande Ronde a crowded fishery in the later fall and winter, those willing to embark on a multiday float in the river's canyon reaches will find few, if any, other humans.

THE MAGIC CARPET AND THE MUD DAUBER

Fly fish for carp? The most common response to this question is likely "Why?" This may soon change. Carp are beginning to attract attention from serious fly anglers, thanks to the challenge they pose. Like many accomplished guides, Lance Egan loves to fish for carp when he's not out fishing with clients. Though getting to the fish can at times be as challenging as coaxing them to eat a fly, as this tale illustrates . . .

"A buddy named Alex and I decided to head a few hours east of Salt Lake to a place called Starvation Reservoir to fish for carp. We were sight-fishing and picked up a few fish as we walked along the banks. We came to a wash, where water entered the reservoir during heavy rains. At this time, it was dry—or so it seemed. Across the wash there was a bay where we could see some fish tailing. We started across the wash.

"I should mention that I'm about five-eleven, one hundred fifty-five pounds, with a size eleven shoe. Alex is a big guy with a football player build, six-six, close to three hundred pounds, with a size thirteen shoe. In terms of weight displacement, my feet are like snow-shoes. Alex has deer hooves. I waltzed across the wash, sinking in to maybe my shins. Alex began across, tracing my steps. Before he's gone a few feet he's absolutely stuck in the mud, up to his mid-thigh. As he squirmed and struggled, he sunk in a little deeper. As I watched from the bank I couldn't help but laugh. After struggling a bit more, he called out, 'Lance, I really can't get out of here.' I thought he was joking but he had a very serious look on his face. I could tell that he was really beginning to worry if he was ever going to get out of there.

"I tried to stay calm and consider what we need to do to rectify this situation. First, he tossed me his chest pack and rod and I took it up to dry land. He then thrusted a few more times and sunk down to his waist. Every time he moved, the mud in a twelve-foot radius moved. I thought about heading to my truck but remembered that I didn't have any ropes or a shovel. Maybe I can lift him out. I went and tried. It's laughable, I couldn't move him at all. Now, what do we do?

"About this time, another friend, Mark, pulled up. He was supposed to meet us to fish. He parks by my rig. I was hoping that he might have something that could help. Rope, a mat, anything. Mark was rigging up as I explained the situation, and I saw the fishing light leave his eyes. He knows how big Alex is and that it won't be easy. Fortunately, Mark had an emergency pack—a twelve-foot piece of rope, tie-down straps, and a shovel.

"Now the wash had eroded some soil. There was a flat section, then a ridge down to the bottom area where Alex was. We knew we could get a truck onto the flat, but not onto the bottom. I pulled my truck down, busting through some sagebrush and willows. I dropped my back two wheels into the wash and hooked up the tow rope. We're still twenty feet short. Meanwhile, Alex, against everyone's better judgment, has continued squirming and continued sinking. He's past his waist, up to his belly button. His arms are still above the mud, and nothing else seems to be working, so we gave him the shovel and he starts trying to dig himself out. For every three shovelfuls of mud he displaces, he gains only about one. It's beginning to get hot out, and the summer sun in Utah is strong. Mark and I figured that we may as well fish. As we're walking away Alex said, 'What true friends you are!'

"We go over to the bay and make some casts, and about half an hour goes by. As Alex clears the mud in front of him, mud from behind is pressing, buckling his knees. He's losing ground. Finally, he called out, 'Come back.' We finally did and began looking for other options, as it's obvious that he couldn't dig himself out. We attached the tie-down straps to the rope, and that extends the twenty feet down to Alex. We attached him to the truck. Before we even started trying to pull, the buckles were stretched so tight, we're worried they're going to give. We loosened everything up, took the buckles off, and made loop-to-loop connections with the straps. I dropped the truck back down to give it another go. I hit the gas a bit but Alex couldn't hold on. It looked like his shoulders would be pulled out of their sockets before he would get pulled out of the mud.

"While I was trying to pull Alex out, Mark was rummaging around in the back of his truck and he came up with a piece of carpet. The thought was that if we put the carpet in front of Alex, once his weight was on it, it would give a little more traction and help ease Alex out. It would also help disperse his weight so he wouldn't sink down again. We put the carpet in front of Alex, rerigged our lifeline with one more strap, and tied it around Alex's abdomen. I went to the wheel, engaged the clutch, and my wheels just spun. Now my truck was stuck. Mark had to get his truck to pull my truck out of the muck. We got it out but roasted Mark's clutch in the process. I was beginning to think that we'd have to call in the county sheriff and a helicopter to extricate poor Alex.

"We started again. I backed my truck down into a different area so I would't get stuck, we got Alex hooked up, and I began easing forward. I was taking it slow so I wouldn't cut the guy in half. With my front tires up on the flat, and my rear tires dropped into the wash, I gave it a little gas and Alex started yelling, 'We're moving, we're moving.' Finally, he yells, 'Floor it!' There's a popping noise—very audible—and he's out. He landed right on the carpet and we pulled him out of the wash, digging up a trench in the process.

"As you'd imagine, Alex was covered in mud up to his armpits. Mark and I took him over to a little creek we knew of so he could wash up. And then we went back to the reservoir and went fishing. Alex even got a few fish, though we noticed that he walked much softer.

"From that day on, Alex was nicknamed the Mud Dauber."

TALE 12

Lance Egan was born in Salt Lake City, Utah, and has been fly fishing since age twelve. He has worked in fly shops since high school and is currently employed at Cabela's in Lehi, Utah. Once Lance earned his driver's license, he was off fishing every chance he could get. From age sixteen to twenty-one he spent more time on the water than most anglers do in a lifetime. Lance enjoys fishing for carp, bass, or saltwater fish as much (or more) than trout. He is a member of Fly Fishing Team USA, has competed in many distance casting events (sponsored by International Sportsman's Expositions), and has a number of first-place finishes to his credit. In the 2003 ESPN Fly Fishing Challenge, he finished first in the distance event and loop control event, and second in total casting and the fishing event. Lance is the 2003 and 2004 ESPN Great Outdoor Games gold medalist. He also won the 2005 Teva Mountain Games One Fly event. Lance is a member of the Ross Reels Pro Staff, a contract fly tyer for Umpqua Feather Merchants, and a prototype tester for Simms Fishing Products.

FLY FISHING FOR CARP

American fly anglers are beginning to recognize what British fishermen have long understood: *Cyprinus carpio* is wary, will respond to well-presented flies, and is the equal of large steelhead and bonefish when it comes to tearing into your backing. It's the latter comparison that has gained carp the moniker "golden ghost." Carp are catholic feeders—they'll feast on aquatic insects in all life stages, crayfish, baitfish, and even plant matter, such as blackberries. But one shouldn't mistake the carp's broad appetite as license for sloppy presentations. Carp possess highly developed senses of sight, hearing, touch, and smell. This makes them extremely spooky. Like their more glamorous saltwater counterpart, carp often offer the angler just one shot. If you misfire, the fish is gone; if the fish sucks in your offering, hold on.

CRAIG FELLIN

FISHING WITH ED

It's been said that there are five stages in a fly fisherman's evolution. In the first stage, the angler hopes to catch a fish; in the second, to catch the most fish; in the third, to catch the biggest fish; in the fourth, to catch the smartest fish; and in the final stage, simply to be able to get out and fish. Craig Fellin had the thrill and honor to escort a fishing legend on an excursion leading to this last stage.

"It was the second year that I had been running my outfitting business on the Big Hole," Craig began. "We didn't have the main lodge built yet, so accommodating large groups was a challenge, though it wasn't the kind of problem we had to deal with too often at that time. That is, until we booked a big group of guys from the East Coast. There were a couple of outdoors writers in the bunch, including Ed Zern. Like so many outdoors enthusiasts who had come of age in the sixties and seventies, I was a tremendous fan of his 'Exit Laughing' columns in *Field & Stream* and considered him one of the great hunting and fishing writers of the time.

"The group that Ed came with was a lot of fun and had its share of interesting characters. There was one fellow who would dress up like a Native American medicine man, head feathers and all, and would bless everyone's flies each day. I'm not sure how much it helped, as the weather was hot that week, and the fishing was a little tougher than usual. We didn't have a dining room built yet, so we had a bunch of picnic tables set up in the front yard. The first dinner, we didn't lock one of the picnic tables in quite right and it collapsed when six of the guys sat on it. At another meal, my wife and mother cooked meat loaf—five loaves of it. The meat loaf was placed out on the screened porch leading to the front yard as we gathered the rest of the meal. When we came back out, it was gone—my black Lab had eaten it all! Despite these little setbacks everyone was having a good time.

"At the time of his visit, Ed was in his eighties and suffering from Parkinson's disease. He didn't say too much, but he was always smiling. It was quite obvious that he was the patriarch of the group. Much of the fishing we do on the Big Hole is from a raft, simply because it allows us to cover the most water. People were throwing Big Hoppers or Wooly Buggers and catching fish, but a guy in Ed's condition wasn't able to make those long casts and hook

OPPOSITE:
Montana's Big Hole River provides enough Big Sky scenery and top-shelf angling opportunities to bring anglers back year after year.

73

Drifting the Big Hole allows anglers to cover the most water.

the fish quickly enough. By the third day he was pretty frustrated, and I think everyone in his group was hoping that if he went out fishing with the lodge owner, he might be able to do something. I was worried about taking him wade fishing, as he didn't walk well. And I knew that fishing from the boat wouldn't work. Finally, I suggested an alternative strategy. I knew of a spot in the upper river where it flowed through a meadow, where there tended to be a lot of cutthroat. I suggested that we hike in there and Ed was eager to do so.

"It wasn't easy going, especially for an eighty-plus-year-old man. We had to walk through a hundred yards of marsh to get into this one run that had always fished well. The last twenty yards or so we had to crawl, as the fish in that section had always been spooky. Ed didn't mind at all. He still didn't say too much, but a smile said he was enjoying the chance to get out. Once we reached the bank we observed the stream for a while. Soon enough, a couple cutts began showing themselves against the far, undercut bank. They were taking terrestrials. I'd always had pretty good luck with these cutts fishing a Royal Wulff—a good all-around attractor pattern. As you might expect, Ed didn't see all that well at this point, so I put on a larger Wulff than I normally would use, a size twelve. Ed had a little bamboo rod, from another era. Seeing that rod, I imagined how many thousands of casts it must have made in the hands of this angling master.

"We had everything set up and were watching a few fish work against the bank when a much bigger fish bulged. I didn't have to point that one out to Ed. He waited until the fish came up again, then flicked a little cast out there. We were on our knees and he almost toppled over when he cast, but I held on to him to keep him upright. The first cast was a little short, but he let it drift through so as not to disturb the water. The fish continued to rise and Ed made a second cast. This one was flawless, right into the bubble line where the fish was blurping. The fish came right up and inhaled the Wulff. About three seconds later Ed struck—the fish had already spit out the fly. With the Parkinson's, he had no reaction time. I was worried that Ed might be frustrated with himself for missing the fish, but he turned to me with a wonderful twinkle in his eye. 'That was worth the price of admission,' he said. Here was a man who had caught a million fish in his lifetime. He didn't care about catching another trout. He wanted a challenge, the chance to bring up a big fish. It was a magical moment for him to make such a beautiful cast into such a tight spot.

"And it was a magical moment for me."

Craig Fellin has owned and operated Craig Fellin Outfitters and Big Hole Lodge (www.fly-fishinglodge.com) for the past twenty years. Craig has guided in Argentina and fished New Zealand on numerous occasions as well as the Yucatán in Mexico with his son Wade. Over many years as a guide and outfitter, his business philosophy has been very simple: "Try and make each fishing day the best you will ever have."

BIG TIMES ON THE BIG HOLE

The Big Hole River begins in the Beaverhead Mountains near the Idaho border and flows east for 155 miles before emptying into the Jefferson River at the burg of Twin Bridges. The Big Hole is a study in contrasts, flowing through high mountain country, sprawling valleys, and rugged canyons. It also provides great salmonid diversity—brook trout and grayling in the upper river, trophy browns and rainbows in the mid and lower river, and cutthroat scattered throughout. Dry-fly enthusiasts will appreciate the upper sections of the river, which has smaller fish but sees little pressure. Trophy hunters will have the most success fishing subsurface, banging streamers, and nymphing—unless you happen to hit the salmonfly hatch, which generally comes off in early June. Unmitigated by impoundments and rich in Big Sky scenery and wild trout, the Big Hole fulfills the promise that the phrase "Montana trout fishing" holds out.

REELING ON THE ALTA

Fishing the world's most famous Atlantic salmon river for the first time is an awe-inspiring experiencee. On any given cast, you have the chance to tighten up on a forty-pound (or greater!) salmon—a "life fish" for almost anyone. Fighting and landing a large fish on the Alta is a great accomplishment, one the lucky angler may never forget . . . especially if you manage this task without a reel!

"It was my first chance to fish the Alta, and you can imagine that I was a bit nervous," said Mollie Fitzgerald. "Up until this trip, it had been something that the men in the Fitzgerald family did. My dad was lucky enough to get a spot on one of the syndicates that lease rods on the river some years back, but my brother or a friend of his always accompanied him. I was thrilled to be invited. I'd read of the Alta for many years, perusing the journal entries of many anglers that depicted the epic battles they'd waged with the Alta's Atlantics—fish of forty, fifty, even sixty pounds. I'd also spoken to a number of people who had made the pilgrimage there and had many expectations based on these conversations.

"The salmon fishing season on the Alta begins in late June, and my dad's slot on the river is the first week the season is open. Since the river is situated in Finnmark above the Arctic Circle, you have some level of light all night long in the early summer. Atlantic salmon fishing is optimal at low light periods, so the guides fish from eight P.M. to four A.M. This makes for a fairly easy transition for Americans making the trip, as we're basically operating on a regular eastern time zone schedule. Fishing through the night has a special feeling to it—it's mystical. The syndicate my dad belongs to has a group of ten rods, and access to three beats on the river. There's a little lodge for each beat. Generally, groups rotate through the three sections. Most of the fishing is done with spey rods from twenty-eight-foot pine canoes with outboard motors. This is especially true early in the season, when the water is too high to wade. Each canoe has four people: two anglers sharing a rod (that is, one angler casting at a time) and two boatmen. The boatman in the back runs the engine, rows, mans the net, and directs the efforts of the boatman in front, who mostly rows. These fellows speak varying levels of English—generally not too much—but are incredibly adept at maneuvering the boat to maximize your opportunities of presenting your fly over fish. You don't have to cast

OPPOSITE:
Alta anglers
motor to a
new pool in
a trademark
pine canoe.

very far because they get you so close. However, you do need to be accurate and consistent with your casts in order to cover the water.

"The incident in question occurred on the third or fourth night of the trip. I had already hooked and landed my first fish, so much of the pressure was off. We were fishing a pool called Richardholla—pronounced *Rickard's*. It's a classic, lovely little holding pool, at the top of a series of pronounced rapids. It's a very exciting spot to fish, as many salmon that are hooked will immediately head down through the rapids, which means you have quite a ride ahead of you. On this particular evening, I was fishing a sinking line and a tube fly called the Maxoid that was created by a fellow named Max Mamaev, who's a guide on the Ponoi River on the Kola Peninsula in Russia. While on some occasions you'll fish to salmon that you've sighted, on this evening I was blind-casting, while my dad looked on. To get the best swing at Richardholla, you cast into the fast water at the head of the pool and let the current

Mollie Fitzgerald poses with a hefty Alta Atlantic.

bring the fly into the slower water. Takes usually occur there. After each cast and swing, the boatmen drop you down a few feet. At the end of one swing—just before 'the dangle'— there was a huge boil on my fly and a fish was on. When a fish is hooked on Richardholla the boatmen make every effort to move the boat upstream, hoping to discourage the fish from heading downstream into the rapids. On this occasion the fish would have none of it. It made a beeline down into the rapid—it's amazing how quickly the Alta fish can melt line off of the reel. Without further ado, we were all on our knees in the canoe—you ride through rapids on your knees to keep the canoe stable—to give chase.

"Now it's always chaotic when you go through the rapids at Richardholla in pursuit of a fish. The canoe goes through backward, and the angler who's playing the fish is struggling to keep the line free of the rocks while simultaneously keeping it tight so the fish can't throw the hook. This occasion was no different, except that my reel, a beautiful Bogdan that I'd just purchased, fell right off the reel seat! As we bounced through the rapids, the reel was clattering around on the bottom of the canoe, line still screaming off, while I tried to keep my composure and still maintain some pressure on the fish. As the boatmen were busy trying to get us through the rapids and I was trying to keep some control over the line, the task of retrieving the reel fell to my dad. My dad is a big guy and doesn't like moving around in the canoe very much, but for his daughter, the big salmon that was on—and because he was closest—he stepped up to the plate and snatched it up. Soon we had the reel back on. I keep several hundred yards of backing on the reel. Most of it is white, but the last fifty yards or so is yellow. When I get into the yellow, I know we're getting close to a panic situation. By the time the reel was attached I was well into the yellow.

"I began reeling line in frantically. There was so much line out, I couldn't feel any tension, and wasn't sure the fish was even still on. After what seemed like an eternity, I felt the weight of the fish. We were through the rapids and into some calmer water. I began to feel like I was back in control. The salmon made two more great runs into the backing but I felt like we had the upper hand. Eventually we reached a beach area downstream from Richardholla and I brought the fish to hand. The entire fight had taken forty-five minutes. We estimated the fish's size at thirty-five pounds.

"I have to say that this experience has changed the way I fish forever," Mollie concluded. "Now, after every third cast, I check to make sure that my reel is on."

Mollie Fitzgerald is co-owner of Frontiers International Travel. A cum laude graduate of Duke University, she grew up in the travel business as the daughter of Frontiers' founders, Mike and Susie Fitzgerald. Now in her twentieth year with the company, Mollie looks after the Elegant Journeys, Safaris, Air, and Atlantic Salmon Fishing departments at Frontiers. Equally at home in the wilds of the great outdoors and the world's most sophisticated capital cities, her destination knowledge spans the globe and fuels her ongoing passion for travel. Particular areas of interest and expertise include western Europe, India, Southeast Asia, South America and the Galápagos Islands, and Africa. Mollie enjoys fly fishing for Atlantic salmon, photography, gourmet cuisine, wines, and travel with her twelve-year-old daughter and often draws upon her own experiences in planning itineraries. She serves on the advisory board of Abercrombie & Kent and *Condé Nast Traveler* magazine and is a director of the Atlantic Salmon Federation. She has been identified by *Condé Nast Traveler* as one of the "130 Top Travel Specialists" (since the inception of the list six years ago).

FISHING THE ALTA

Most will agree that Norway's Alta River is the queen of all Atlantic salmon rivers, the world's most prolific producer of fish in the forty- or fifty-pound class. It's also the world's most exclusive salmon fishery. Getting a rod in the Alta can take many years, as the upper river beats are closely held by English and Norwegian nobility and by private syndicates that often have openings only when a member dies. When a spot does open up, there's a long line of prospects eager to pay the $15,000 to $20,000 it costs for a week of fishing. Atlantic salmon aficionados will insist that this is a small price to pay for the fish of a lifetime.

TWO MEN OUT, HATCH ON FIRST

For baseball fans, the postseason excitement of October holds a special appeal—especially if your team hasn't won the World Series for a very long time, and it suddenly looks like they're on the cusp of an appearance. As fate would have it, late October can also be a wonderful time to go trout fishing in northern climes. The crowds are gone, the fish are aggressively feeding in preparation for the long winter that lies ahead, and the foliage can be tremendous. What's one to do when a long-planned excursion to fish the big rivers of the West collides with the World Series? If you're Sam Flick, you go fishing—but you let your thoughts drift back to friends and acquaintances whose lives have intertwined with the twin passions of the rod and the bat.

"In my opinion, one of the best do-it-yourself trips you'll find anywhere is fishing western Montana in the late fall," Sam began. "You have all of these blue-ribbon rivers available and hardly anyone is around. The tourists are gone, and many local anglers are either hunting or steelhead fishing over in Idaho and Oregon. There's one section of the Missouri that we like to fish that will have fifty boats at the height of the summer season. When we've visited in late October there's not another soul there. There are a few other benefits to fishing this time of year. First, since most of the rivers we fish are tailwaters, the water never gets frigidly cold. It's usually around fifty degrees, which by Maine standards is pretty balmy. Second, the fishing isn't too taxing. We either look for pods of trout feeding on midges where a Griffith's Gnat will work fine or we throw streamers. You don't need a whole bag of tricks to have success, and this is a pretty relaxing way to fish.

"Now in 2004 I had a few internal struggles as our Western trip came together. By going fishing out West, I was going to lose most of the hunting season back home. Just as important, I was going to lose the baseball playoffs. It had been almost twenty years since the Red Sox had made it to the World Series and, as even people unfamiliar with baseball know, a heckuva lot longer since they had won. I've been a fan for most of my thirty-seven years, and being a Sox fan was made even worse by the fact that my dad was an ardent Yankees fan, and hence had a lot more to boast about than I did. There were times during the first few days of the trip, when we were steelhead fishing over in Idaho and Oregon, that I had doubts about

TALE 15

whether I was doing the right thing—fishing instead of being home watching the games. But then on the day that the Sox beat the Yankees to win the AL playoffs, one of my buddies landed two twenty-pound steelhead on the Clearwater. And on the next day I landed eight steelhead on the Grande Ronde—a World Series steelhead outing for me! I was at peace with my decision.

"On our trips, we usually hit a number of different rivers. As the Sox were approaching the Series, we had to decide on a strategy—should we continue to fish steelhead, should we head to Yellowstone, or should we fish the Missouri. My vote was to fish someplace where we could at least listen to the game. We had found a spot on the Missouri—near Wolf Creek—where I knew from past experience that we could get pretty good radio reception. So that's what we chose to do. We began planning our fishing around the time the games were on, and made sure that we were at the turnout near Wolf Creek when the games were broadcast. There was another decision we had to make—fish until dark or quit when the game started at around five P.M. (mountain time). The fishing tended to reach a climax at dark, and it's always nice to close with a bang. So we opted to fish until it was pitch dark, then tune in to the game as we shed our waders and toasted another great day of fishing.

"There's a lot of time to reflect on things between the time the fly hits the water and the time it has swung below you. With the Red Sox almost sure to win their first World Series in eighty-six years, my thoughts wandered toward three people who had touched me through both baseball and fly fishing. The first person that came to mind was a gentleman who came to one of my casting lessons at Bean's. He was an older fellow who hadn't fished for a long time, as his legs weren't in good shape. He wanted to polish up on his casting so he could cast on the lawn beside the nursing home where he was living. I could tell he was a die-hard fan, as he always wore a Red Sox hat. He explained that when he was able to fish, he loved to go to the Salmon River in New York for steelhead and salmon—though steelhead fishing, which occurred later in the fall, always bothered him, as the Sox were always out of contention by that time. He had a lot of time on his hands, and he'd come into the shop pretty often and we'd talk baseball. He'd go through a fly line every few months, casting on the lawn. I didn't see him for a few years but then he came back again. His health had improved and he had left the nursing home. I think he was lonely, though. 'I miss casting on the lawn, and watching the games with the other folks there,' he said. I told him, 'If the Sox ever get in the Series, you've got to go back to the nursing home and watch with your friends.' As I was chucking streamers in the Missouri, I was wondering if the guy made it back to the nursing

TALE 15

OPPOSITE: Ardent fly fisher (and sometimes slugger) Ted Williams plays a fish.

home, and if he was casting and watching the game with his pals.

"As we scanned the Missouri for pods of slurping rainbows and browns—and as the Sox warmed up for the games that would end the curse of the Bambino—I couldn't help but think of Ted Williams, perhaps the game's greatest hitter and one of the past century's great fly fishermen. When I first began working at Bean, I would sometimes be on the graveyard shift—the store is open twenty-four hours. One night when I was working, a giant of a man walked in my direction, threw some pants at me, and asked if I could sew. It was Williams. He would stop in Freeport en route to the salmon rivers of New Brunswick to pick up supplies and have any gear in need of repair fixed. If it was a matter of sewing on a button, he'd wait. I learned quickly that one didn't ask Ted Williams questions—he dictated dialogue. I think this was a result of playing ball in the Boston market, where the sportswriters could be particularly hard on players. He'd been asked all the questions—at least all the stupid ones—and if he felt like talking, he would ask the questions. Baseball was generally off limits, and so was salmon fishing. Talking about cribbage and bass were okay. On one occasion, he asked me how I liked to fish for bass. I said I liked hair bugs. He said he liked poppers. He proceeded to grab a popper off our fly shelf and said, 'This is a cheap hook.' Then he broke it with his fingers. He asked me to try it, and of course I couldn't do it. This was the only time I ever saw him laugh.

"The last person I thought of as the Sox marched toward the championship was a lady who used to come into the store in December to pick up Christmas gifts for the anglers on her list. We were talking about the Red Sox one day when she came in. As she checked out, she asked, 'Are the Red Sox still playing? Did they win the World Series?' Obviously, she wasn't a big baseball fan. I answered in the negative for both questions, and she asked, 'Will I know when they win?' I laughed and said, 'Yes. You'll see the smoke of Boston burning.' 'That's good to know,' she said. 'My dad passed away a few years ago, and before he died he asked me to come to his grave if and when the Red Sox won the Series.' She paused for a moment. 'You know, I never have much to say to him when I go to his grave. If the Red Sox win, we'll have something to talk about.'

"The day after they won, I had another fine day on the Missouri. And much of the day, I was imagining her sharing the good news at the cemetery."

Sam Flick has worked at LL Bean for nineteen years, with fourteen in the Hunting/Fishing store. He has taught in Bean's Fly Fishing Schools for fifteen years, and has been a

Federation of Fly Fishers certified fly fishing instructor since 1995. Sam grew up fishing for Atlantic salmon in Maine and the Maritimes. During his time at Bean, he has fished in the Florida Keys and Mexico for permit and tarpon, in the West for trout and steelhead, and closer to home for stripers, trout, and bass. "I'm envious of anyone who is just starting out fly fishing," Sam said. "Some of my best memories come from learning and fishing new places. And I believe fly fishing is the best stress management someone can have." Sam lives with his wife, Pam, in North Yarmouth, Maine.

A STAR ON STREAM AND FIELD

Many remember Ted Williams as the slugger who brought scientific principles to the hitting of a baseball, achieving a lifetime batting average of .344 and the status of the last man to bat over .400 (.406 in 1941). Others remember him as a great fly fisherman who also played some ball. Williams was as passionate about fly fishing as he was about baseball— some would say even more so! His casting was long and precise, and his instincts for finding and hooking fish were considered preternatural by his angling contemporaries. While he pursued bonefish and tarpon in the Florida Keys, the Atlantic salmon of the Miramichi River in New Brunswick were his favorite quarry. A committed conservationist, he served on the board of the Miramichi Atlantic Salmon, and was later inducted into both the Hall of Fame at the Atlantic Salmon Museum and the International Game Fish Association's Fishing Hall of Fame. He was also a decorated veteran who flew in two wars. While Williams could be short-tempered with the sporting press and intrusive fans, he had a gentler side. "He was very good with children and people who needed help," recalled his friend Curt Gowdy in an interview with ESPN.com after Williams's death. "I loved the guy."

NATURE'S CALL

The act of fly fishing often involves waders and just about always involves being outside, away from most of the relative conveniences of civilization—such as a restroom. Answering nature's call while "wadered up" in the wilderness can be awkward. First, you must find a suitable spot. A few trees are nice for modesty's sake and, depending on how nature calls, for balance. Next, there are numerous layers to be shed—vest, rain jacket, fleece jacket, the waders themselves, and various skins of insulation. It's best to place these objects out of the wind lest they blow away and safely out of the individual's—well, range. Suspenders can pose a particular problem, as they have a terrible tendency to find their way into nature's path.

On a trip to Alaska a few years back, raconteur and *Gray's Sporting Journal* editor David Foster found something more foreboding on the path to answering nature's call.

"It was the first week in September in 1997, and I was fishing Lower Talarik Creek," David Foster began. "The creek is short and flows into Lake Iliamna. This time of year, the stream is filled with red—sockeye—salmon, but what draws anglers are the big rainbows that come in from the lake to feed on the salmon eggs. Lower Talarik is one of the best creeks in the world for getting a crack at really large trout, and the most famous stretch on the creek is a pool called the Rock. It's only about one hundred yards long and all the guides from the lodges around Lake Iliamna and Bristol Bay want a chance to fish it. There's a settling pond where floatplanes can land below the pool. If you get there around nine or ten A.M., there will be five or six planes parked on the pond. This particular day we got there late for the Rock, so we decided to fish a ways upstream.

"At precisely ten-forty-five, the Lord spoke to me in a warning way. I was going to have to do something personal. I called out to our guide and asked when we'd be heading back to the lodge. He said we'd be departing in ten to fifteen minutes. I figured I could make it. You see, I wasn't eager to use nature's restroom on Lower Talarik Creek. The creek is surrounded by high grass. I knew from past experience that brown bears liked to snack on salmon in the stream and then head up to the tall grass to take a nap. Now there are three ways to get hurt by a brown bear in Alaska: get between a sow and her cub, surprise a bear and fail to give him the right of way, and step on a bear as it sleeps in what Alaskans call a daybed. When I'm in bear country, I carry nothing to protect me other than a very firm belief that a bear is not going to kill me. I make it a point to give them a very wide—*a very wide*—comfort zone.

"Though at ten-forty-five I had determined that I could wait another ten or fifteen minutes to answer the call of nature, at minute six, the Lord spoke to me again and said, 'Now.' I said, 'Please, not *now*.' But the Lord again said, '*Now!*' So I rushed out of the stream to take care of this most personal business. I climbed up on the bank and followed what looked like a trail to ascertain the perfect place, for the Lord had commanded *Now*. There was a little lip of ground, a slight indentation, that I didn't notice. I don't remember stepping off the lip. What I next remember was that I was lying flat on my back, staring up at the azure blue Alaska sky. Two thoughts were going through my head. One, what a beautiful sky and, two, why am I lying here looking at it? Then I heard a *woof, woof.* I looked down my body and sniffing my wading boots was a brown bear. I closed my eyes, terror rising in me like magma in a cauldron. I knew I was a goner and also knew I would be a goner sooner if I did anything other than lie still. A few moments later, I smelled something absolutely wretched. Then a dark shadow slowly loomed up over my face. The shadow belonged to a hairy-ass chin that smelled like rotten salmon. It loomed over my face and made woofing sounds. Ah, crap. A full-grown bear sniffing me and me sniffing him. What the hell? And then it hit me. I must have stepped on a napping bear, a daybed event.

"Now, when an eight-hundred- or nine-hundred-pound bear is looking down at you, time takes on a slightly different dimension. It seemed that the bear looked at me for ten or fifteen years. It was probably more like eight or ten seconds. Having determined that I was not an overly large salmon that had flung myself from the stream and come to present myself as a luncheon treat, the bear made another woofing sound and crashed off into the bush.

"I lay there in that impression in the earth for another thirty or forty seconds. I moved my head. It's not often a man gets a chance to appreciate the air and the sky the way I did at that moment. People think that when a bear kills a human, it grabs you and hugs you to death. In actuality, a bear likes to grab you by the head, lift you up, and shake you. I had been neither shaken, nor lifted, nor dropped . . . or hugged, for that matter. I knew that I was a very fortunate man. I got up and looked at my fly rod, which was still intact, though I had fallen flat on it in the course of my tumble. I thought briefly of the business that had originally driven me into the bush and quickly surmised that I didn't need to worry about that anymore. I went back to the creek and told the guide that we needed to leave now. *Now!* I had so much adrenaline in my system I thought I was going to collapse.

"I should add that it was two days before I had the occasion to perform the task that I had set out to do in the tall grass on the banks of Lower Talarik Creek."

David Foster is editor-in-chief of *Gray's Sporting Journal* and strategic adviser to the National Magazine Group of Communication Channels, LLC, based in Augusta, Georgia. He is also editorial director of *Gray's* as well as *Alaska* magazine, *American Angler*, *Fly Tyer*, and *Saltwater Fly Fishing*. He writes a column in each issue of *Gray's* and contributes to all the Morris magazines as well as other sporting magazines nationwide. He caught his biggest stream-run rainbow ever, 33.5 inches, in Lower Talarik in 1995 at the Rock.

RAINBOWS ON LOWER TALARIK CREEK

Tiny Lower Talarik Creek has an epic reputation for yielding very large rainbow trout to anglers who can work a flesh fly or egg pattern through the throngs of sockeye (in various stages of decay) that come into this Lake Iliamna tributary. The big rainbows are opportunistic feeders, cruising into the creek from the lake in search of an easy meal and sometimes returning to Iliamna just as quickly. Fish here can run as heavy as eighteen pounds, more steelhead-like than trout—well, even bigger than most steelhead! Fish may be present throughout the summer, but September can be an especially magical time here, as the salmon have somewhat thinned out but the bounty of their eggs and flesh is still very present. You won't find yourself alone on Lower Talarik Creek, but most find that the extra company—human and ursine—is a worthwhile trade-off for a very real chance at very large and acrobatic rainbows.

THE FISH THAT COULDN'T BE CAUGHT

Much of the job satisfaction derived by a fly-fishing guide or outfitter comes from watching his or her clients find success—success that the guide has contributed to, in small or large part. Yet there are rare times when despite a guide's best efforts, the prey elude, outwit, or simply outmuscle the clients . . . even if those clients are among the most celebrated anglers in the world.

TALE 17

"I grew up in Hawaii fishing for trevally with conventional gear and learned how tough they were," Rick Gaffney began. "When I started getting into saltwater fly-fishing, I realized this could be a special species on a fly rod. I first encountered giant trevally on the fly at Christmas Island, many years ago. I was there with Big Eddy Corey, who appreciated my interest in GTs. We went hunting for them in the lagoon, driving around in these punts. If we saw a fish, we'd cast a hookless teaser to bring it into casting range, much the way some pursue billfish. We had some luck that way, but my first big fish came in a little canal on the island. GTs would sometimes come into the canal to corral baitfish, and Eddy knew of a good spot there to target them. Eddy spotted some fish for me and I made a cast in. One flick of the fly and it looked like a hand grenade had gone off. The fish went screaming out of the canal at a hundred miles an hour. No one can stop those fish when they're running and I knew I'd have to follow. I went running along the canal, right to the edge of the lagoon. Somehow I got it to hand. It was the first world-record GT on a fly rod, forty-four pounds on twenty-pound tippet.

"It was with this experience in mind that I realized we had a great chance to introduce fly fishermen to this species on Midway Atoll. Midway is a small island in the middle of the Pacific. The air and water are remarkably clear—if you were diving in one hundred fifteen feet of water, you could look up from the bottom and make out the faces of people in the boat looking down. Likewise, you could discern the name of the airline flying overhead to Asia, even though the planes were at thirty-seven thousand feet.

"In the late eighties, the U.S. Navy decided that a presence at Midway was no longer imperative for U.S. defense purposes. In 1993 the air facility was closed and, by 1996, the island was granted National Wildlife Refuge status and put under the control of the Fish

and Wildlife Service. I went there soon after with fishing tackle and a diving expert to explore the potential for establishing a sport fishery there. In 1997 the island opened to sport fishing. It was in an effort to promote this fishery that I invited three renowned anglers to come and experience the fishing, in hopes they'd spread the good word in magazine articles, television programs, and the like. Before these fellows showed up, we fished for GTs every which way. If we didn't know where the fish were, we'd troll hookless teasers until they showed up. We'd sight-fish for them, especially in the inside lagoon. This was perhaps the most exciting fishing method. Outside of the lagoon and the barrier reef, we'd tie up to a float and chum and the GTs would come up in the chum slick. Sharks would generally show up first, sometimes eight or ten of them. If you watched carefully, you'd notice that the sharks would suddenly disappear. That was an indication that the GTs were coming. That says something about the predatory powers of giant trevally and their place in the food chain.

"The first of these legendary anglers—names have been concealed to protect the innocent—arrived with the intention of filming a segment for an outdoors program. This angler hooked seventeen different GTs over five days. The problem was, each of the GTs was over seventy pounds, just about impossible to land on a fly rod, especially at Midway, where there are many caves, nooks, and crannies in the reef where the fish can break off. I felt that if we could get the fish into deeper water, where they couldn't break off on the reef, we'd have a pretty good chance. But I just couldn't locate any reasonably sized fish in the twenty- to forty-pound class to work with. These were the fish that would give us good footage, and hopefully a fish to the boat. Shots of this poor fellow getting beaten up by these huge fish, having his tackle busted, et cetera, may have been fun to shoot, but it wasn't what we were looking for. I think any other angler would've been thrilled to have a chance at one of these fish, but after seventeen tries I think this fellow was just ready to beat a retreat.

"A few weeks later, the second famous angler arrived. Things went even worse for this fellow, a superb caster and truly first-class fisherman. He hooked thirty-one GTs during the course of his stay. He couldn't get a single fish to the boat.

"Our third visitor was another fantastically accomplished big-game fly fisherman. He wanted to bring a group of anglers along and I needed to assure him that the group would have fun. A wonderful facet of fishing at Midway is that there are other species of trevally around, and it's not very difficult to find enough fish in the eight- to twelve-pound class to keep most people happy. Everyone—except the angler in question. Just like the first visitor,

OPPOSITE: Giant trevally are powerful enough to break the nerves— and rods—of anglers who are generally not easily flustered.

TALE 17

he hooked seventeen fish—including one monster that he nearly landed. With this leviathan, angler number three did everything right. We positioned the boat so the fish would run toward the deeper water, and the angler pressured the fish to make him go where we

wanted him to go. The battle lasted until well after dark and took us offshore into extremely rough water. Angler number three waged a heroic battle but, with water crashing over the boat, the fish won.

"The final tally: sixty-five fish hooked, zero landed. I must say that while I was disappointed that these great anglers didn't land a fish, it was a privilege to see these fellows brought to their knees, utterly humbled, by a game fish I've come to love."

Rick Gaffney was born and raised in Hawaii and grew up boating, surfing, fishing, sailing, and diving in island waters. Wanderlust and a navy ROTC scholarship then took him to Oregon State University. After graduating, and duty in the navy, he moved to Kona and obtained his USCG captain's license in the mid seventies. A job opportunity as one of the first Sea Grant Marine Advisory specialists in the Pacific drew Rick to Maui, where he later operated a series of sportfishing charter boats and fished competitively throughout the islands. In 1985 Rick returned to Kona, to be closer to the Pacific's most productive offshore sport fishery. Rick has delivered sportfishing, diving, boating, and travel stories from all over the world for over twenty-five years. His writing career has won him international recognition as a chronicler of game fishing and boating, not to mention two national awards and a marine environmental journalism fellowship. Rick serves as IGFA representative at large for the Central Pacific Islands and holds one of the at-large seats on the Western Pacific Fisheries Management Council as well as the recreational fishing seat on the Northwestern Hawaiian Islands Coral Reef Ecosystem Reserve Council. Rick set the first IGFA world record for giant trevally on a fly, and has landed and released three species of billfish on a fly, in a passion that will last a lifetime. Currently, Rick is president and managing broker of Pacific Boats & Yachts, a boat brokerage company.

*OPPOSITE:
A GT successfully brought to the boat off Christmas Island.*

TALE 17

MIDWAY ATOLL

Midway Atoll is one of the most remote coral atolls (a ringlike coral island) in the world. It's home to some two million birds, including the world's largest population of Laysan albatrosses (a.k.a., gooney birds), spinner dolphins, and Hawaiian monk seals. Like Christmas Island, Midway's past is colored by military activity. In 1942 it was the center of the battle that bears its name. Till the end of the war, it served as an Allied submarine base and continued to play a role as a staging area for American naval forces during the Korean and Vietnam wars. In 1996, the island made the transition from military base to wildlife sanctuary, with limited public access to sport fishers and researchers. Regrettably, access to the island was curtailed in 2002 due to logistical difficulties. At this writing, there is little likelihood that Midway will reopen to tourism anytime soon; anglers will have to travel elsewhere to match wits—and strength—with the muscle-bound giant trevally.

BARBELS AND TIGERS AND HIPPOS, OH MY!

Fly fishing in Africa poses unique challenges. There are the menacing choppers of the tigerfish, the most sought-after prey. There are the ever present crocodiles lurking at every bend, eyeing your fish—and you—as a potential meal. There are elephants and giraffes along the bank that may require a higher than usual backcast. And there are the hippos, which, as Cindy Garrison learned, do not make good fly-rod sport.

"In the fall in the Okavango Delta an amazing thing happens," Cindy began. "The barbel, a species of catfish that can reach up to fifty pounds, begin running up and down the river in huge schools, feeding on baitfish in preparation for spawning. They're in the papyrus reeds, in the side channels, in the main stem of the river—everywhere. And when the barbel are running, the tigerfish are right behind. It's a feeding frenzy for three months. To fish the barbel run, you look for large gatherings of birds. You go past where the birds are and drop anchor. Before you can see anything, you can hear the boiling of the water. The entire river is alive—it's like something out of a horror movie. Pretty soon the boiling mass is upon you. You begin casting whenever you can reach it. It doesn't matter what fly you use—poppers, streamers, anything will work. Whatever you send over there the fish attack it. When a tigerfish hits bait—or your fly—they hit to stun. After one fish has hit the fly, the whole pack—ten or twenty fish—come at the fly at once. After every hit you have to change your fly and leader, their teeth are that sharp. Half the time when you're bringing in a fish, you have a crocodile following along. Other times, a swarm of tigerfish will eat the tiger on your line. In addition to these savage fish and crocodiles, there are hippos everywhere.

"One day, I was out fishing with a few other folks and we were on the barbels. The other anglers in the boat were using poppers, but I was hoping for a bigger fish—a twenty-pounder —and was fishing deeper with a streamer. A twenty-pound fish would be a world record, and for some reason I felt like it was going to be the day. I was stripping in my fly, a pink Lefty's Deceiver, trying to imagine what a twenty-pounder would feel like, when my body almost gets pulled from the boat. My first thought: it's the twenty-pounder! My rod is so bent, the tip is in the water. Everyone on the boat is yelling, and the fish is taking everything off my reel. I was so excited I almost was crying. All of a sudden, the rod goes straight and the line goes slack. Oh no—I'd lost him! At this point, the boat was right next to a sandbank. I started reeling in as fast as I could. Then the rod was bending down again. I yelled, 'Guys, get me on the sandbank,' thinking I could fight it better from there. I'm fighting the thing like mad. Then the line goes slack again. Someone in the boat says, 'Cindy, can't you hold on to that fish?' I remember thinking at the time that it was odd that the fish hadn't jumped at all. Still, sometimes big tigers will just hold on the bottom.

"I'm on the sandbank now, and I see this big wake coming toward me. It's not like the wake of a big fish. It's getting bigger and bigger as it gets closer. I was thinking, 'Croc,' and that I'd better get off the bank. It turns out that it wasn't a crocodile. It's a hippo coming toward me, and he's got a huge pink Lefty's Deceiver stuck in his nose. Everyone in the boat is cracking up. It has to be one of the funniest things that's ever happened to anyone fishing in the Okavango. It's funny, that is, until the hippo looks at me and realizes that I'm the problem. The fly line goes slack and, the next thing I know, a two-ton hippo is running up the sandbank, right at me.

"The hippo was about thirty yards away when he came out of the water. You have to understand that when a hippo is leaving the water it's not very fast, but when they're on land they can move quickly. This hippo wasn't more than ten feet away before I had time to react. Swimming wasn't an option, as he'd come right after me. So I dropped the rod and ran away from the river, through some weeds and brush. I ran hard. It felt like I'd been running for ten minutes, and I was thinking at the time that I'd have a heart attack. The people in the boat called out that it was okay, that the hippo had gone off in a different direction. When I returned to retrieve my rod, it was in six pieces—the hippo had stepped on it. I had three hundred yards of backing on my reel—he took it all. Our guide said that he'd been on the delta for forty-seven years and, in all that time, he'd never seen a human who was able to coax a hippo out of the water. Someone in the boat was able to capture all of this on film.

"There's a little footnote to this story," Cindy continued. "At the time, I was using reels manufactured by J. Reil. While my rod didn't do very well in the encounter with the hippo, the reel survived in perfect condition—minus its line and backing. I went to the fishing show that year with some of the pictures that were taken of the incident and showed them to the company's owner. He ended up using the story in some future advertisements."

Cindy Garrison's professional fly-fishing career began in Alaska in 1993 where she started as an apprentice fly-fishing guide for Kulik Lodge. She soon moved on to a full-time guiding position with Togiak Fishing Adventures in the Bristol Bay region. From there, she guided for the Alaska Sportsman Lodge on the Kvichak River in Iliamna. In 1997 Cindy started her company, Safari Anglers. Based in Anchorage, she focused on guiding float trips on the surrounding rivers as well as booking trips for outfitters in Alaska and around the world. Cindy traveled to Africa in 1998 on her first hunting safari to Zimbabwe and the Okavango Delta of Botswana with Rann Safaris. It was here that she learned of the ferocious tigerfish and organized an exploratory trip to try and fly fish for these fierce predators. The year 1999 saw Cindy teaming up with Jeff Rann and fly-fisher extraordinaire Ed Rice to fly fish Lake Kariba, the Zambezi River, Chobe River, and the Okavango Delta River, in search of tigers. After two weeks of nonstop fly-fishing action beyond belief, Cindy decided to establish a tiger-fishing and game viewing operation in Africa. Cindy has gone on to host *CITGO's In Search of Fly Water* on ESPN2, and a new ESPN2 series, *Get Wild! with Cindy Garrison*, which focuses on hunting and fishing in some of the world's most dangerous and intriguing places.

HUNTING TIGERS

Adventure angler Larry Dahlberg has described the tigerfish as having "the fuselage of a bonefish, the tail of a tarpon, the paint job of a striped bass, teeth like a bull shark and a compound hinged jaw that works like a turbo-powered paper shredder. They may be the most capable and impressive freshwater predator on earth." The Zambezi River in Zambia and the Okavango Delta are two great places to go in pursuit of tigerfish. The Okavango is one of the world's major inland deltas, originating in Angola and spilling back inland to the Kalahari Desert. At high water, the delta encompasses an area of fifteen thousand square kilometers, a maze of islands and channels. Though the fish in the Zambezi may run a bit larger on average than the fish in the Okavango Delta, there are few fishing experiences that match the Okavango's barbel run—and its accompanying mayhem—each fall. Tigerfish are built to prey on creatures up to two-thirds their size, and are not too picky about what they eat. Just about any fly will work, especially when the tigers are on the barbels.

THE QUEEN'S TROUT

Few of us turn to fly fishing as a means of making a financial killing. While there are a few equipment developers and retailers who have forged a handsome *livelihood* from fly fishing, those who work around the sport tend to be in search of a *lifestyle* . . . one that generally involves living in a comely, rural place that provides access to a good deal of fly fishing. It's the rare angler who turns to fly fishing as a means of making ends meet in an urban setting. Jack Gartside, however, has always been an inventive thinker.

"It was in the winter of 1969–70," Jack began, "and I was living in London after graduating from college. I was making ends meet doing odd jobs: driving a mobile radiology unit a few nights a week, sweeping floors in a coffeehouse after closing, anything I could do to earn a little money under the table. I made just enough to pay daily expenses as well as my share of the rent on a flat on the edge of Soho that I was sharing with a couple of medical students.

"Winter in London is cold and dreary as you might expect, and after I lost the driving job when one of my roommates reclaimed it—it was his to begin with—the climate both outside and inside seemed to turn even bleaker. I needed to make more money somehow. The first of the month was coming and I was still a little short on my rent.

"When I first arrived in London some months before, I wandered all over the city, taking in the sights, learning a little history, and always looking out for a bit of adventure. One of the more interesting sights I came across, overlooked in most tourist guides, was the moat that surrounded the ruins of the Old Palace, the original palace of the kings of England in London, which was almost hidden from sight, set back from the main road down by the Houses of Parliament and close to Westminster Abbey. In this moat there were trout, dozens of them. All big and all very fat, being fed by tourists on everything from popcorn to sandwich bread. Throw a piece of popcorn in and they'd swim from the farthest corners to come for it.

"Well, it didn't take me long to figure out that they'd be easy to catch and be a wonderful diversion for a cold and misty English winter day. And so I scouted the place out, especially in the early morning to find out if there was a patrol of any sort—a warden or a bobby on foot or someone else who might have an interest in safeguarding this area. After several mornings of watching and waiting, I learned that there was a London bobby who sometimes patrolled the area around seven-thirty but never before. And so very early one morning, with a two-piece fly rod already rigged up with a fly, I took the tube from Goodge Street Station over to Westminster and walked a few blocks to the moat.

"As I approached the moat I looked this way and that to make sure there was no one around, joined the two pieces of my rod together, and with one flick of my wrist sent the Royal Wulff out into the middle of the moat, where I could see two very large trout swimming slowly about, waiting for the tourists to show up, no doubt. The Royal Wulff must have looked like a piece of bread or something else good to eat and the trout lost no time in coming for it. The smaller trout got there first, inhaled the fly, and I set the hook. It took me around the moat twice before I was able to land it. At least five pounds, I figured. A very nice trout, indeed, which I quickly released.

"Before I set off that morning I had decided to catch only one trout, to not linger but get in and out quickly to avoid detection. If I succeeded this time I could always return. And return I did, at least a few times a week, always in the early morning and always catching and returning one trout. As time went on and winter advanced, tourists became fewer and fewer and I grew bolder, upping my limit to two and lingering longer to add a bit more sunshine to the gray days of winter. All courtesy of the queen, whose trout these were, although she lived some distance away and had probably never seen them and in any case would probably never have allowed me to fish for them.

"Now one of the things I enjoyed doing from time to time while I lived in London was playing pinball at an arcade called the Lots O' Fun. It was on Tottenham Court Road not far from where I lived, and whenever I had a few extra coins I stopped by and played my favorite game, Royal Guard. Because I had gotten quite good at it and frequently won free games, I never had to spend more than a shilling or two for hours of play. Sometimes I would win more than I had the time to play and would give my free games away to one or two of the other regulars, who always appreciated my generosity.

"One of these regulars, as it happened, was a fishmonger, the proprietor of a shop in Soho not far from where I lived, and over time and many pinball competitions we became quite friendly. One day, quite casually, I asked him if he ever bought fish from individuals—like myself—and not just from a wholesaler. Certainly, he said, but only if they were fresh, very fresh. Here, I thought, was the solution to a problem that had been nagging at me—a way to get enough money to pay my next month's rent. And so the next evening I walked into his shop with two very fresh trout, about eight pounds in weight when put on the scale and worth about two pounds, ten shillings each, wholesale.

"Very nice trout, sir,' he said, as he handed over a five-pound note. 'Very nice indeed. They'll make a meal fit for a king.'

"Or a queen, I thought, as I silently thanked the current resident of Buckingham Palace. As the winter wore on we would have further business to conduct."

Jack Gartside got his first fly-tying lesson in 1956 from Ted Williams, the great Boston Red Sox outfielder. He's been tying and fishing ever since—in both freshwater and salt—accumulating an extraordinary range of fishing experience in the United States and throughout the world. Jack was one of the first fly-tyers profiled in *Sports Illustrated* (October 12, 1982). Since then, he has been profiled in *Fly Rod & Reel, Fly Fisherman Magazine, Fly Fishing in Salt Waters, VillmarksLiv* (Norwegian), *La Péche en Mer* (French), *Tight Loop* (Japanese), and other national and international publications. Jack is the author of *Striper Flies*, the first book written specifically on this subject, and *Striper Strategies*, which was described by reviewer Steve Raymond as "one of the most remarkable striper-fishing manuals to see the light of day." His latest books are *Scratching the Surface*, which deals with surface and (slightly) subsurface flies/fly fishing, and *The Flyfisherman's Guide to Boston Harbor*. Other books to Jack's credit include *Fly Patterns for the Adventurous Tyer* (volumes I and II), *Flies for the 21st Century*, and *Soft Hackle Streamer*. He has also authored *Secret Flies* and *More Secret Flies*, two instructional pamphlets featuring designs utilizing a special tying material, Gartside's Secret Stuff (or GSS). Jack has been tying flies for over forty years and is considered to be among the most talented and inventive tyers of the modern era. Among his best-known original patterns are the Sparrow, the Soft Hackle Streamer, the Gartside Pheasant Hopper, and the Gartside Gurgler. For the past twenty-five years Jack has conducted fly-tying seminars and fly-fishing programs in the United States, England, France, Norway, New Zealand, and Japan.

TALE 19

STILLWATER FISHING IN THE UK

Stillwater fishing—be it on lakes, ponds, or moats—is the primary attraction for trout anglers in England. This is because there is a limited number of streams and rivers containing trout, and almost all of that water is private, in the hands of syndicates or the Crown. (Beats on syndicate water can be had on a daily fee basis; fishing Crown waters requires special connections . . . or unusual cunning.) Lakes and reservoirs, on the other hand, are in the public domain. English anglers take a very different approach to lake fishing than do Americans. With the aid of a sea anchor (which resembles an umbrella) attached to the bottom of the boat, they drift broadside, with one angler in the bow and one in the stern. Anglers cast downwind, with a team of three flies. Generally, anglers rig with a weighted damselfly on the point, a buzzer (chironomid) on the middle, and a drowned caddis or mayfly on the uppermost fly. Flies are slowly stripped in, then "dapped" as they get close to the boat so that they flutter near the surface. The fluttering motion is especially seductive for the fish.

A PAIN IN THE NECK

For East Coast anglers of an earlier generation, a voyage to northern Maine in quest of brook trout defined the consummate angling adventure. There, somewhere in the Rangeley Lakes region, in the hinterlands of Aroostook County or above Moosehead Lake, weathered fishing lodges served visiting sports from "downstate," which could mean anywhere from Bangor to Baltimore. Meals were taken in the main lodge along with generous helpings of fish stories; the lodge would be dotted with requisite fish and game mounts. Guests slept in simple log cabins that fanned out around the lodge and fished the ponds, lakes, and creeks that rested within a short paddle of the camp.

Some of these camps remain in operation today, a pleasant backcast to a simpler time. Fathers and sons still come to fish these waters, generation after generation. There's a special camaraderie that develops among visitors to such a fishing camp, a camaraderie that can lead to lasting friendships and often spawn some good-natured ribbing. Sometimes, the object of the ribbing has the opportunity to get the last laugh, as Charles Gauvin discovered some years back.

"It was a bit of a tradition with my father and me to spend a week brook trout fishing in the woods of Maine," Charles began. "We'd stay at one of the old sporting camps there, and most of our fishing would be from boats on a lake or on a hike-in pond, where we would fish from a canoe. One morning during a trip about fifteen years ago, we decided to head out early, before breakfast, to fish a bit. It was fairly early in the season, and when the wind came up it was quite cool. I was in the bow of the boat and my dad was in the stern. I had a Muddler Minnow on, a pretty reliable pattern on those waters. I guess I made a somewhat wild cast. That, combined with the wind, sent the fly astray—more accurately, into my dad's neck. It was in there pretty good, and I asked him if he wanted me to pull it out. He replied, 'No, I'll just cut it out later.' Dad clipped the leader, I affixed a new fly, and we continued fishing a bit longer. I should mention that my dad is a physician, so I trusted his opinion on the matter.

"We soon returned to the lodge for breakfast. As we docked our boat, I asked again if I could help him with the removal of the fly. Once again, he said, 'No, I'll get it out later.' We proceeded to breakfast, my dad sporting my Muddler sprouting from his neck. After a few

TALE 20

moments I could see what was going on. My father was taking great joy in walking from table to table, having other guests ask why there was a fly in his neck, and replying, 'My son, the head of Trout Unlimited, made a bad cast.' This little riposte was the cause of much laughter and gave my dad no small bit of satisfaction. Pretty soon, it seemed that everyone in the camp had asked him about the Muddler Minnow. As he told the story again and again, I got more and more embarrassed. I smiled wanly and filed this all away. There would be more fishing ahead.

"After breakfast he removed the errant Muddler, and we headed back out on the pond. By this time the wind had calmed down and it had become quite warm—in fact, unseasonably warm for that time of year. As the water warmed, the fish became very active. I began peeling off layers and applying sunscreen—not something I had anticipated but a pleasant surprise. We were both fishing with sinking lines and streamers. Having fished the pond on more than one occasion, I knew the water a bit and positioned our boat near a drop-off, where the sun's warming effect on the water stirred the pond's brookies into a subsurface feeding frenzy. I think that I have a little more patience and feeling for this type of subsurface fishing than my dad, and I also had a good sense of where the fish might be foraging. For whatever reason, I was hooking fish after fish while my father cast in vain. This went on for much of the morning. By eleven-forty-five, the sun had become so intense that we had stripped down to our T-shirts. I had brought thirteen brook trout to the canoe to my father's none. The jocularity my dad had shown while displaying my misplaced Muddler at the lodge had been replaced with a decided sullenness. As I landed my fourteenth brookie, I asked my father if the sun was bothering him.

"His terse response was: 'No. My son is bothering me. Let's go in for lunch.'"

Charles Gauvin is the president and CEO of Arlington, Virginia–based Trout Unlimited. He is a leading expert on the Clean Water Act and other environmental legislation and is an attorney with extensive experience in environmental matters, principally water-quality standards and permits under the federal Clean Water Act. Before becoming TU's executive director in 1991, Charles practiced law in the Washington office of Beveridge & Diamond, P.C., where he negotiated and litigated discharge permits and water-quality standards issues on behalf of corporations, municipalities, and environmental organizations. He is a 1978 graduate of Brown University and a 1985 graduate of the University of Pennsylvania Law School. In addition to fly fishing, Charles enjoys upland bird hunting and gardening.

BROOK TROUT IN MAINE

Eastern brook trout (or squaretails, as they are often called downeast) are, along with land-locked salmon, closely associated with the Maine fishing experience. Brook trout are native to the Pinecone State, where rainbows and browns have been introduced in latter years; as you move north, brookies can be found in almost any creek, pond, or lake, ranging in size from six inches to six pounds. (For the record, brook trout are members of the *Salvelinus* or char family.) Brook trout are generally aggressive feeders, foraging on insects in their nymphal and adult stages and on minnows and other baitfish during their short growing season. Casting and stripping one of the classic Maine streamer patterns—say, a Gray or Black Ghost—is one of the rites of passage for brook-trout anglers.

TALE 20

A RISKY SHOT

Being a fly-fishing photographer has its perks. You get to travel to exotic locations around the world on somebody else's dime and all you have to do is snap a few pictures. Right? Truth be told, being on the other side of the lens can have its hardships. A low-pressure system—or some uncooperative fish—can make a carefully planned trip a bust. And more often than not you don't get to fish . . . or at least not as much as you'd like. Getting the shot you really want can require hard work and sacrifice—though the kind of almost-sacrifice that Brian Grossenbacher describes goes beyond the call of duty.

"Back in 2000, a photographer named Andy Anderson and I took a trip to Turneffe Flats Lodge in Belize," Brian began. "We were trying to get a lot of generic flats-fishing shots for Andy's stock library and some shots for LL Bean as well. Before we arrived, Hurricane Keith had blown through. It was a pretty serious storm—we drove through fourteen to eighteen inches of standing water in Belize City—but for the first three days on the water the weather was very cooperative. The flats were a little stirred up after the storm, but we were able to get a lot of the shots that we were hoping for . . . except for one.

"Andy hoped to orchestrate a shot where a bonefish would be visible underwater in the foreground and the angler, making his stealthy approach and cast, would appear in the background. Nowadays, this is a shot you see pretty regularly in the catalogs and magazines. But at the time it really hadn't been done. Andy had bought a special—and very expensive— underwater case specifically to get this shot, as the camera would need to be half in and half out of the water. After day three, we felt like we could take some time to make this shot happen. The remnants of Keith, however, were against us. For the next four days the rain came down, and when it wasn't raining there was flat light, terrible for photography. We were supposed to leave after seven days and really couldn't afford to extend our stay. Craig, the owner of Turneffe Flats Lodge, saw our disappointment and invited us to stay a few extra days to try and get our shots, and they'd cover our expenses.

"On the eighth day of our stay, the weather cleared up beautifully and we were able to get out on the flats to try and get our photo. The trick of the shot, of course, is getting the bonefish to behave. There's simply no way that a photographer is going to be able to get close

TALE 21

OPPOSITE: *The attempt to get a shot like this led to photographer Andy Anderson's close encounter with eunuch-hood.*

enough to a bonefish in the water to get this shot—they're far too skittish. To pull it off, you have to have a fish in your control, and that means you have to catch one. That was my task—in addition to posing for the photo. We were out that day with a guide named Eddy, as intense a guide as I'd ever met and very striking, with dark black skin and white hair and an intrinsic relationship with the Turneffe bonefish. Eddy soon led me to a fish, a fine specimen that was between seven and nine pounds, large by Belizean standards. We had to figure out a way to tether the fish so Andy could get his shot, and we came up with the idea of tying a light piece of tippet to the lip of the fish and attaching the other end to a conch shell.

"Although I have tied knots to hundreds of thousands of flies, I had never attached a piece of tippet to a conch shell. After a few minutes of struggling, Andy impatiently grabbed both shell and tippet from me and tied the knot himself. He then set the shell and bonefish back in the water and stood back to admire his handiwork. 'If you want something done right, you've got to do it yourself,' he said in a mocking tone. His moment of satisfaction was fleeting as the fish swam away without even a nudge of resistance from his failed knot. Andy shoved the camera in my hands and took off running across the flat after the fish. It was a rare moment of comedic brilliance—heavy flats booties, knee-deep water, a body past its prime losing an uphill battle against one of the fleetest fish on the flats. It was a lopsided race with a predetermined finish but Andy, God bless him—he must have kept up with that fish for at least a hundred yards. Eddy and I were doubled over, dripping tears from our violent laughter.

"It was a shame to lose such a wonderful fish, but we figured we could get another one. A half hour later the tide began to come in, breathing new life into the flat. Fish were soon all over and I hooked another one. It wasn't as big as the first fish, but quite serviceable for our purposes. Andy decided that this time he'd hold the tippet in his hands. We got the tippet attached to the fish's lip, and Andy sat down in the water with his legs splayed as wide as he could, as he didn't want to get his flats booties in the frame. It was an awkward and potentially vulnerable position, but that's what the shot required. The water was up to his chest and he had the tippet in the same hand as the camera.

"Eddy, I should mention, didn't have any interest in our photo escapades. He was only interested in fishing. I got into position and began casting. I didn't have a fly attached to my tippet, as it wasn't important for the shot. Eddy was busy ignoring us, looking around the flat, presumably for fish. Suddenly he became very animated and began yelling, 'Permit, permit, permit!' Fifty feet away—and swimming right toward us—was a permit the size of a dinner platter. I quickly forgot about Andy, who was still sitting on the sand with the bonefish, and brought in my line so I could tie on a permit fly. Soon I was setting up to make my cast. Before I could let it go, I heard a bloodcurdling scream. Out of the corner of my eye I saw Andy running in place on top of the water, which was stained red. A shark that Andy estimated at six feet in length had swooped in while Eddy and I were focusing on the permit and devoured the bonefish from between Andy's legs.

"Needless to say, we never did get 'The Shot' on that trip, and we have not attempted it on subsequent trips. 'It has become a cliché and outdated,' Andy retorts whenever I ask him why he doesn't want to revisit 'The Shot.' Cliché, outdated—or fear of being castrated?

"Whatever Andy's reason, I still get plenty of laughs when I see a similar shot in a magazine or catalog."

Brian Grossenbacher has a B.A. from Wabash College and a master's in education from Montana State University. He has published articles in *Fly Fisherman*, *River*, and *Flyfishing Quarterly*. Brian is the author of the *Tying Flies Workstation*, a comprehensive beginner's guide to tying flies, which has sold more than sixty thousand copies to date. He has appeared in the LL Bean, Fly Shop, Dan Baily, and Simms product catalogs, as well as in *Big Sky Journal*, *Gray's Sporting Journal*, and on the cover of *Fly Rod & Reel*. Brian and his wife, Jenny, own and operate Grossenbacher Guides (www.grossenbacherguides.com), a fly-fishing guide service in Bozeman, Montana, and have just completed the *No Nonsense Guide to Flyfishing Montana*.

TURNEFFE ATOLL

Turneffe Atoll is situated some thirty miles east of Belize City and is one of four atolls in the Western Hemisphere (three are off the coast of Belize). It includes more than two hundred mangrove islands and countless creeks, providing a rich ecosystem that sustains a host of game fish. The southern tip of the island features Turneffe's premium flats terrain. Here, on a mix of hard coral and soft grass flats, anglers will encounter large schools of bonefish in the three- to six-pound range, and occasionally solitary fish exceeding ten pounds. Visitors to Turneffe have a very real shot at permit, as significant schools of this holy grail of flats fish stage offshore and frequent the shallows on a rising tide. Juvenile tarpon are available year-round at Turneffe, mostly in the creeks; adult fish appear in the early spring and linger in the region until October.

A GOOD CASE FOR BARBLESS HOOKS

The use of barbless hooks has been widely accepted as a means of limiting mortality for trout (and other species) that anglers plan to release. Quite simply, the lack of a barb expedites release of the fish, limiting the time it is handled and potentially out of the water. The concept of barbless hooks can also work well for people, as Jenny Grossenbacher learned the hard way.

"My husband and I had a couple of guys that had been coming out to fish with us from Michigan for a number of years," Jenny began. "They were actually fierce competitors in business during the workweek, but a couple of times a year they'd forget about the business and come out to Montana to go fishing. Their feeling—at least on those weeks when they knew they were going away—was, 'It doesn't matter who wins, so long as we go fishing!' They came to be one of our favorite sets of clients. They liked to have a few drinks while they were fishing, and told one knee-slapping story after another. I'd heard about their wives—Marnie and Julie—forever, but had never met them.

"One October, the fellows booked a trip—except it was going to be for their wives. They said it was their wives' idea. 'I had to finally come out to meet you, I'm tired of seeing all these pictures of you, my husband, and those big fish,' Julie had joked. Marnie's daughter had come out with her dad earlier in the season and must have given the experience a thumbs-up, so mom and her friend were ready to give it a whirl.

"The day Marnie and Julie came out was brutally cold and miserable. It was supposed to be my last trip of the season, and winter was definitely in the air. We were all layered up for the cold, and I'd even put a propane heater in the boat—something I'd never done before—as I wanted the ladies to be as comfortable as possible. I didn't have to worry about their well-being. Despite the cold, they popped a few beers as soon as we got in the boat, ready to enjoy a day on the Yellowstone. Within fifty yards of the boat launch, Marnie—who'd never fly fished before—was into a good brown. Their husbands, who were hanging around the put-in, could hear their wives howling with amusement. We got that brown to the boat, released it, and in another few casts she was fast to a nice rainbow. We were fishing number six Wooly Buggers—a nice big meal for the fish as they fattened up for the long winter. We landed and released the rainbow, and I was hoping it would soon be Julie's turn.

"Another few strokes of the oars and Julie's rod bent over. I could tell it was a heavier fish than the first two and grabbed the net so I'd be ready to land it. Julie did a great job playing the fish, and as it got closer to the boat I realized it was a whitefish—though a very healthy specimen of whitefish. For trout anglers in Montana, whitefish are second-class citizens, somewhere on the pecking order of game fish just above suckers. But this was Julie's first fish on a fly rod. Whether it was a trout or a whitefish didn't matter to her, and she was excited. I wanted to appreciate it, to treat it with all the wonder that a lunker brown would receive. I paused with the fish in the net so she could get a good look at it. As I leaned over the net, the fish suddenly spit the fly out and it lodged in my right cheek. To this day I don't understand how this happened. There must have been a lot of tension in the line. It was as if the whitefish, sensing how I felt about it, said, 'Take that!' The impact of the fly striking me was so great that it left a bruise. Then there was the matter of the hook. In the excitement of the moment Julie, trying to help—I think!—reared back on her rod, driving the hook deeper into my cheek. A hook that, it soon became apparent, had not been completely debarbed. (I always debarb my hooks, generally crimping down the barb once we've attached the fly to the tippet. Sometimes when you crimp the barb down, you'll break off the hook. On this cold day, I had done an incomplete crimping job. I didn't want to break the hook and have to take my gloves off to attach another fly. I paid for my indiscretion!)

"Lest Julie have any ideas about setting the hook again, my first task was to part the fly from the tippet. This was achieved easily enough with my nippers, but I was then faced with the trickier job of removing the fly from my face. I was trying to remain calm, as the leader—even if you're just the leader of a drift boat—always wants to exude an aura of control. As I was thinking of how the heck I'd get the hook out, my one other hook incident in twelve years of professional guiding flashed through my mind. On that occasion, one of the fellows in my boat had hooked a nice rainbow just a few hundred yards from the takeout on a double-nymph rig. I reached down to remove the hook from the fish's jaw, but as I was doing so the top fly caught on my finger. We were drifting into some faster water, heading straight toward the bank, and I had a very agitated rainbow trout pulling very hard on a hook that was embedded in my index finger. Keeping the oars under my legs, I reached back and grabbed my hemostat. Then I clipped off the end fly and grabbed the oars in what seemed like one motion. When I'd got us to the takeout, I gave the hemostat a big rip on my finger and pulled the fly out and my finger gushed blood. All in all, I felt pretty heroic, and I think my clients felt the same way.

TALE 22

"Oddly enough, the anglers on that trip were with Marnie and Julie's husbands. Reflecting on this earlier experience, I wasn't sure I was up to such heroics when it came to my face.

"We floated about twenty yards after I'd cut the tippet and I dropped the anchor. It was clear that the ladies were not going to be performing any surgery on my behalf. 'Don't you know the trick of how to take it out?' Julie asked tentatively. 'I think I'm going to throw up!' Marnie added. The trick in question was to give the fly a good, quick tug. I didn't have the nerve to do it. I was pulling full force but nothing was happening. The ladies opened another beer, I think to ease their suffering, as they were terribly upset by the whole incident. Then someone had the bright idea to take a close-up picture with a digital camera we had

on board. Once I had a picture to reference, I had a slightly better sense of the path the hook would have to take to come out. The ladies opened a beer for me. Though it's generally a strict policy that we don't drink while guiding, under the circumstances I took a sip from one of their beers and got up the nerve to try the quick-tug approach again. This time, the fly popped right out. It left a nice-size hole in my cheek but didn't bleed too badly. Marnie and Julie wanted me to get off the river to take care of my face but I said, 'We're not going in. The fishing's too good!' I ended up tying that same Wooly Bugger back on to Julie's tippet and she caught a few more good fish on it.

Jenny Grossenbacher models the latest trend in body piercing—the Wooly Bugger.

"Thanks to the ladies' extremely good nature and sense of humor, the great fishing we had, and the hook incident, that experience sticks with me as one of the most amusing guide days I've ever had. A few days after I was hooked, a package arrived from Michigan. Inside was a sixteen-by-twenty-inch poster of my face with the big bugger. I'll never be able to forget that day now."

Jenny Grossenbacher is co-owner of Grossenbacher Guides (www.grossenbacherguides. com) based in Bozeman, Montana, where she and her husband, Brian, lead anglers on trips on many of Montana's blue-ribbon waters. She holds a B.A. in philosophy and a B.S. in fish wildlife biology and has led grizzly bear research projects in both Yellowstone and Glacier National Parks as well as songbird studies throughout southwestern Montana. Jenny has appeared as guest host on *Flyfishing America* and *Gray's Sporting Journal Television*, and was selected as one of twelve international anglers to participate in ESPN's 2001 Great Outdoor Games in Lake Placid, New York, where she competed against some of the best anglers in the world. She has appeared in *Big Sky Journal, Gray's Sporting Journal, Saltwater Sportsman, Women & Fitness, Sporting Classics, Northwest Flyfishing*, and *Outdoor America* magazine, and in several outdoors calendars, including: *2002 Freshwater Fishing, Sportsman's Calendar, 2001 Flyfishing Dream Trips* (fresh & saltwater editions), *Silver Creek Press Daily Calendar, 2000 Angler's, Hooked on Fishing, Silver Creek Press' Sportsman's Calendar*, and *365 Days of Fishing.* Jenny has also appeared in the LL Bean, Dan Baily, and Simms product catalogs. She is currently serving as a board member for the Federation of Fly Fishers, Headwaters chapter.

CATCH AND RELEASE

Fly anglers who've come of age in the past twenty years take catch-and-release regulations for granted; for many, that's all they've known. Fly-fishing historian Glenn Law has pointed out that records show that the concept of catch-and-release angling dates back as far as China's Zhou dynasty (1027–221 B.C.), but the notion did not gain much popular acceptance until perhaps fifty years ago. This was largely thanks to the proselytizing of pioneering angler Lee Wulff, who has been called the "Father of Catch-and-Release Fishing." In 1933 Wulff began releasing the Atlantic salmon he caught, and is remembered for the phrase, "A good game fish is too valuable to be caught only once." The protocols that Wulff advocated found greater voice with the formation of conservation organizations such as Trout Unlimited, which was established on the banks of Michigan's Au Sable River in 1959. TU continues to promote catch-and-release angling to its members and other interested anglers, setting forth the following tenets for successful release:

~ Don't play fish to exhaustion. To prevent a fatal lactic acid buildup, bring fish in quickly and use a landing net.
~ Handle fish with wet hands, grasping them across the back and head.
~ Don't remove swallowed hooks; just cut the line.
~ Don't keep the fish out of the water for more than 10 or 15 seconds.
~ When placing fish back in moving water, face them upstream in their natural position.

TALE 22

ALBIES AND THE APPLE

Young writers, perhaps taken aback at the seeming anonymity and indifference a large city projects upon newcomers, sometimes summon wilderness metaphors when attempting to describe the urban landscape. "City as asphalt jungle" is a common characterization. Is such a characterization cliché or even wildly inaccurate? Perhaps. And perhaps not. Jungle connotes a place where wildlife—not inclusive of a band of bonds salesmen running amok at a Friday happy hour—thrives, a place where the cold, amoral efficiencies of the food chain are borne out. Looking to the sometimes murky waters that surround the island of Manhattan, one will find the cycle of life and death playing itself out again and again, providing sporting opportunity along the way, an opportunity Peter Kaminsky first recognized some twenty years ago.

"I started fishing in and around New York harbor back in 1985 with two fellows named Steve Sautner—now a fellow *New York Times* contibutor—and Joe Shastay," Peter began. "They were partners on a mako-fishing boat and were kind enough to take me along. Most people don't realize that there are more than twelve hundred miles of coastline around New York, myriad crags, crooks, and crannies that make for some great fish habitats. There are fly-fishing opportunities from April to January and we get pretty good species diversity too. First, there are striped bass—some one hundred thirty million in the Hudson on a good year. Bluefish also come in, along with shad and false albacore. When I started fly fishing around New York harbor, I caught many stripers on trout tackle in the flats near Ellis Island. Whether the bite is on or not, getting the water's-eye view of the city is very cool. I especially like the perspective from beneath the Williamsburg Bridge.

"One of my favorite New York angling adventures took me from Governor's Island all the way up the East River to Harlem. It began when Captain Brendan McCarthy, who runs a fly-fishing charter operation around the city, called and said that a buddy of his who kept a boat on the East River had alerted him that the albies were in. We were on the water by the early afternoon. We first fished by an abutment under the Manhattan Bridge, which crosses over to Brooklyn and empties onto Flatbush Avenue. There were no signs of albies around, but in a few casts we came up with some stripers. We drifted with the tide down toward the southern tip of Manhattan and spotted some activity up by the seawall that surrounds Governor's Island. Closer inspection revealed that the commotion was a group of false albacore that had pinned a big school of bay anchovies right up against the seawall. We cast into the melee—epoxy flies developed by Bob Popovics that looked just like the tiny baitfish—and took three fish out of there, eight or nine pounds each. The Statue of Liberty was looking on in the background as the albies sped around us.

"The tide was coming in and the fish were moving up the East River with the tide and we decided to stay with them. We headed up toward the South Street Seaport and nabbed a few fish there. We encountered a few more at the abutments of the Manhattan Bridge. There's a spot we like to fish near the United Nations, but we came up empty there. We kept pushing right up the East River, beyond Roosevelt Island to just below Wards Island and Randalls Island, to a spot called Hell Gate. Hell Gate isn't far from the confluence of the East River and Long Island Sound, so there's often a lot of water ripping through there. Traditionally, it's been great striper grounds. For a short period of time when the tide begins going out—a half hour or so—the area looks like a gigantic riffle, with the water flowing toward Harlem on the west bank of the river. This spot is always marked in my mind by a wonderful Art Deco building there in Harlem, with sculptures of dolphins in bas relief on the side.

TALE 23

"We'd hoped to get to this spot at the time of tidal transition, as bait often gets caught up in the rip. We couldn't have timed it better. Just as we'd hoped, the albies were on the outer edge of the current, against the shore, where they'd corralled the bait. We could make out the telltale slashes as they darted in to stun the baitfish. You could even hear them as they churned the surface, working the bait. We must have taken ten or twelve more fish from this spot before it was time to head home.

"When I think about this afternoon, it still amazes me. We had excellent fishing for a premier saltwater game fish, chasing a blitz for four or five hours with steady action. And we never saw another angler . . . with eight million potential anglers within a twenty-mile radius!"

Peter Kaminsky is the author of *The Moon Pulled Up an Acre of Bass, Fishing for Dummies, Fly-Fishing for Dummies*, and, most recently, *American Waters*. His outdoors column appears regularly in the *New York Times*, and he also has written for *Food & Wine, Field & Stream, Sports Afield*, and *Outdoor Life*. Peter lives in Brooklyn, New York, with his wife and two daughters.

FALSE ALBACORE

Although their name is cause for some confusion, fly anglers express no uncertainty when testifying to the speed, fighting prowess, and pleasure of *Euthynnus alletteratus*—sometimes known as little tunny, Fat Alberts, mackerel tuna, or false albacore. A member of the tuna/mackerel/bonito family, false albacore are marked by a torpedo-shape body, and the presence of three to seven dark spots between the pelvic and pectoral fins. They have a broad range, including the western Atlantic from Maine to Brazil, the Mediterranean, and the Black Sea. Adult false albacore average 32 inches in length and can weigh up to 20 pounds and favor shallower waters, a feature that makes them of great interest to fly anglers. When schools of false albacore are on the feed, it's not hard to find them, as their frenetic surface activity seems to bring large areas of water to a boil. When albies are feeding on herring, sardines, or sand eels, a baitfish pattern (such as a Deceiver or Clouser Minnow) flung into the carnage is almost sure to produce results. Hold on—an albie's first run is like hooking into a passing Boston whaler! Albies arrive around the island of Manhattan in the early fall and can linger into November.

BEGINNERS

Whether you're a toddler trying to take your first steps or a senior citizen seeking to master the intricacies of the Internet, learning something new can be intimidating. It takes guts, especially when that new activity is something so esoteric and cloaked in mystique as fly fishing. Longtime fly fishing instructor Pudge Kleinkauf knows the terrain, and it's with great affection that she shares a few tales of her students as they try to make sense of the pursuit of the long rod.

"I started fly fishing twenty-five years ago, largely because my fly-fishing ex-husband would always outfish me and my spinning rod," Pudge began. "I went with a lady friend to the Russian River and, on my third cast, hooked a sockeye. I was sold on the idea. I asked her if she would teach me the intricacies of the sport and she laughed. 'All I know how to do is flip it out there for sockeyes.' 'Do you know any women instructors?' I asked. She laughed again. A few days later she called and set me up with a male instructor. I took a few lessons and then began fishing like crazy. Oftentimes, I'd go fishing by myself. If I ran into any women on the water, they'd watch me cast awhile and then say, 'I'd love to learn how to do that. Do you know any female teachers?' The ninth or tenth time this happened, the lightbulb above my head flashed on. I rang the fellow who taught me and said, 'I have all these women asking me to teach them how to fly fish. Do you think I'm ready?' He thought I was. I started doing a few little classes here and there. Then I was approached by a woman who ran a business outfitting Alaska visitors for outdoor trips. She asked if I'd be interested in doing some fly-fishing classes for women. I did some classes, then led a few groups on angling trips. I had no idea at the time that this would become my life. Now Women's Fly Fishing has been in operation for twenty years!

"Most of my classes are conducted on the river, in the context of a fishing trip. I do ten adventures each summer, some on Kodiak Island, some around Anchorage, some on the Kenai Peninsula. We go wherever the fishing will be optimized, depending on the time of the summer and the salmon runs. I always loved teaching, so it's no surprise that I specialize in taking beginners. Novice fly fishers are special—everything is new to them. They're just starting to experience the thrill of the pastime. I work with an enormous number of women in their late forties and early fifties. They've never been in the outdoors. Why suddenly fly fishing? It may be a divorce, or an empty-nest response, or single women looking for something more in life than going to work. Whatever the case, I get great satisfaction from turning other women on to this sport that I love, watching them catch their first fish. My favorite thing is hearing them say, 'I can do this!' It's a sense of helping someone spread her wings.

"In the course of working with many newcomers over the years, I've gotten quite a charge from some of my students' reactions to instruction, both in the classroom and out on the river. In my beginner's class, I've noticed that many people are challenged by the rhythm of the casting motion. I always ask, 'Who has seen *A River Runs through It*?' Most hands will go up. I then ask, 'Remember when the dad gets the metronome out to help his sons get the tempo of the casting motion? If you think about the metronome as you move the rod back and forth, you'll get the motion quickly.' Heads generally nod, but the metronome metaphor doesn't always work to strike home the muscle memory message. Sometimes I'll try the hammer metaphor. I'll say, 'Make believe your thumb on the cork of the rod is a hammer. You want to hit the nail in front, hit the nail in back, hit the nail in front, hit the nail in back.' I'll ask the students to say this out loud—'Nail in front, nail in back, nail in front, nail in back.' Other students relate better to the metaphor of the rod positioned at eleven o'clock at the start, one o'clock on the back cast, and eleven o'clock on the forward cast—'eleven o'clock, one o'clock, eleven o'clock, one o'clock.' It's very amusing to walk around a classroom of grown women chanting nonsense phrases.

"I feel that it's very important to give people the right language for a discipline, whatever the discipline might be. The biggest language error newcomers to fly fishing will make is calling a fly rod a pole. Call a fly rod a pole around some male anglers and your credibility is instantly shot. I had a class once where a woman and her daughter kept saying 'pole.' After three or four faux pas, another student suggested, 'Every time you say pole, you have to say rod three times. And every time you say lure, you have to say fly three times.' We all agreed this would be an effective behavioral modification technique. Later in the week, we'd be hiking along a riverbank, and back in the line I'd hear a few of my students repeating, 'Rod, rod, rod. Fly, fly, fly.'

"Of the many students I've had over the years, one of my favorites was this delightful young woman from Texas. I could tell that coming to Alaska to learn to fly fish was going to be one of her first real trips far away from home. She was anxious to come, but her folks were a bit hesitant. Her dad called and asked for my guide license number, insurance company, and five references. I told him that I wished everyone did that and supplied him with all the information he wanted. The woman was given the green light to come out and she was a darling. She had a distinctive southern accent—she called me 'Puhhdge,' we fished with an 'uhhg' pattern for salmon. It was really delightful.

"About a year later, she sent me an email that went something like this: 'Dear Pudge. You don't know how you changed my life. I went out bass fishing a few months back with my fly rod, and met an interesting guy who happened to own a fly shop. We're married now. And I'm part-owner of the shop!'"

Cecilia "Pudge" Kleinkauf, a longtime fly fisher, has owned and operated Women's Fly Fishing (www.womensflyfishing.net) in Anchorage for over fifteen years. She is a regular presenter and fly tyer at outdoor shows in Alaska, California, and Washington, and has been featured in the *Anchorage Daily News* and is one of the special explorers for the *Alaska Magazine* television series on PBS. She is also a contributing editor of *Fish Alaska* magazine and a regular contributor to other fly fishing publications. Pudge is a member of the World-wide Outfitter and Guides Association, Alaska Fly Fishers, Trout Unlimited, Federation of Fly Fishers, and serves on the board of directors of the International Women Fly Fishers. She is a member of the pro staff of Ross Reels, Mustad Hooks, and Patagonia.

TALE 24

BACK TO SCHOOL

While the gravy days of fly-fishing instruction that followed the release of the movie *A River Runs through It* have passed, there are still a number of fly-fishing schools in operation around the country. Many schools take a comprehensive "classical" trout-oriented approach, splitting the allotted time—generally a weekend, though sometimes longer—between casting classes, entomology lessons, knots 101, and a morning or afternoon (or two) on a nearby stream. As the sport has become specialized, more focused schools have appeared. These range from advanced saltwater fly-fishing techniques to crash courses in spey casting to graduate-level trout courses with some of fly fishing's most noted experts. If someone you love wishes to take up the sport, and you suspect that when push comes to shove teaching may take a backseat to fishing when you get them to the river, a fly-fishing school—or a more casual and economical class or two taught at your local fly shop—may be just the trick.

HOOKING UP WITH THE GENERAL

Say what one might about the evils and inequities of the capitalist system, there are perks to being rich. Exorbitant four-figure rates for beats on storied Atlantic salmon rivers are not an issue. Cross-the-world fishing flights to the Seychelles or Tierra del Fuego are far more comfortable in first class—or in the cabin of your own Gulfstream 550. Wealth certainly has its advantages, but political power can yield even better perks. During his reign, Francisco Franco closed all of Spain's trout streams to fishing so that he and his cronies could have exclusive access, whenever and wherever he wished. British nobles have beats on chalkstreams and salmon rivers reserved in perpetuity. And when generals from the ruling junta in Argentina show up to try their hand at fishing for sea-run browns, less connected anglers are expected to surrender the river . . . and to refrain from assaulting its more celebrated guests.

But things don't always work out that way, as Mel Krieger can attest.

"Some years ago, I was visiting Tierra del Fuego and fishing the Rio Grande," Mel began. "I'd gone down for a number of years and fished with a friend of mine there, Bebe Calvo. At the time, Bebe's mother-in-law was holding court at the old Maria Behety Lodge, a very elegant place. Bebe and I had the whole river to ourselves, and the fishing had been very good. This did not make Bebe's mother-in-law very happy, as she had some very important visitors coming—Argentina's minister of economics, and two generals who were effectively running the country. Perhaps lacking an understanding of the vagaries of fly fishing, she expressed real concern that her son-in-law and his American sidekick might be catching all the fish in the river, which would leave her next visitors with no sport. Arguing that it would not be possible to catch all the fish in the river—and that the few fish we had caught had been returned unharmed—would've made little difference to the mother-in-law.

"The minister and the generals were going to be guided on the river by Jorge Donovan, a very famous guide in Argentina at the time who had done a good deal to promote catch-and-release angling in Argentina. While an accomplished angler, Donovan, like more than a few guides, was also a bit of an exaggerator. Apparently, he had convinced the VIPs that he knew the Rio Grande well. He would soon prove otherwise.

"The minister, the generals, and their entourage soon arrived at the Maria Behety Lodge and Bebe and I were compelled to stop fishing. I was asked to leave the lodge, and decamped to the town some distance away. The weather turned upon the VIPs' arrival, and a ceaseless rain began to fall. The river muddied up and the fishing became much more difficult. Under Jorge's guidance, the minister and the generals caught nothing in three days. This must have confirmed the mother-in-law's suspicions about the impact Bebe and I had had upon the river, that with our two rods we had effectively shut down fishing on forty miles of river! Returning from the river on the third day, Jorge had gotten the car stuck in the mud. Perhaps feeling the hauteur that comes with being Argentina's foremost fly-fishing guide, he asked the generals to push the car while he handled the wheel. The generals pushed, the car shot forward, and the generals were covered toes to nose in mud. When Jorge returned to the lodge with the generals coated in mud, the mother-in-law was utterly distraught. Here she had the country's de facto leaders covered in mud and unable to catch a fish, thanks at least in part to a prideful guide. In desperation—and it must have been profound desperation, because she had no particular faith in him—she called Bebe, and begged, well, *commanded* him to take her visitors out and catch them a fish.

The next day, the minister of economics decided to stay at the lodge, so Bebe took the two generals out to find a fish. He had a favorite pool that was on a lower section of the ranch. To get there, you had to drive a ways on two-track roads and then hike about two hundred yards to reach the river. On the walk to the river, you had to cross a ditch with steep banks and water on the bottom. Bebe was a young man then and quite agile, and he ran down one side of the ditch and up the bank on the other and waited for the generals to follow. The generals were much older than Bebe. They staggered down the bank on one side and slowly made their way up the other. One of the generals was having trouble making it up the bank, so Bebe reached the handle of his fly rod down to give the general a boost. Bebe assumed he would grab the cork above the reel seat. Instead, the general grabbed the rod above the cork, where a large hook belonging to a streamer fly was resting in the hook keeper. Bebe pulled and the general screamed, for the hook of the fly was now embedded in his hand. I can't recall the pattern that Bebe had chosen, but I can say with some confidence that it wasn't barbless. So at this point the general, still fishless, had his rod attached to his hand, with the hook forming a bond between the general's flesh and the hook keeper.

"Bebe got the two generals up the bank and back to the lodge and cut the hook keeper, so at least the general was no longer attached to his rod. The general still had a large fly in his

TALE 25

hand, a procedure that would require the medical expertise of a more seasoned practitioner than Bebe. Having impaled the general, Bebe was out of the picture. His brother-in-law, Carlos, happened to be at the lodge when the unhappy fishing party showed up, and the mother-in-law asked him to convey the general to the hospital in town. The roads in Tierra del Fuego are not very good, and they are seldom traveled. Halfway to town the car hit a puddle and stalled out. Carlos tried to hitch a ride, but the few cars that came by wouldn't stop. It was getting past midnight. Carlos, undoubtedly fearing the wrath of his mother more than that of the general, who was very good-natured about the whole thing, finally stood out in the middle of the road and flagged down a car. With the passing motorist's help, they were able to get the general to the hospital and the hook removed. That was it for the general's fishing.

"I don't know if the general and his cohorts ever made it down to the Rio Grande again, or if they ever had the thrill of catching one of the river's great sea-run browns. I do know that, to this day, the mother-in-law has never forgiven Bebe for hooking her guest in the hand."

Mel Krieger has been a devoted fisherman since he fished for black bass as a young man in Louisiana and Texas. In 1964 he moved to San Francisco, where he took up fly casting with a vengeance and became an avid tournament caster. Mel's love for the sport and his competitive zeal paid off when he won a fly-casting tournament in which the first-place prize was a trip to New Zealand. This was his first trip to New Zealand, but his love at first sight for the land and the people inspired him and he created his Angler-to-Angler travel program. From this inspiration he now operates a popular agency for fishing travel to all parts of the world. Mel has taught fly-casting and fly-fishing for over twenty-five years and presently heads the Mel Krieger School of Flyfishing. He has taught in Europe, Asia, South America, Australia, New Zealand, the United States, and Canada. Mel's acclaimed book and videotapes, entitled *The Essence of Flycasting*, and the new video *Beginnings: An Introduction to Flyfishing*, have been used as curriculum for casting schools all over the world. He has written articles for books and magazines published internationally. Mel has been involved in the creation of many innovative programs, such as the Flycasting Certification Program, which is endorsed by the Federation of Fly Fishers and has been functioning both in the United States and abroad. In 1994 Mel was inducted into the Northern California Council/Federation of Fly Fishers Hall of Fame for his contributions in the world of fly fishing.

THE SEA-RUN BROWNS OF TIERRA DEL FUEGO

The Rio Grande runs through the windblown pampas country of southernmost South America. From December through March, anadromous brown trout return to the river to spawn. These fish—which average 8 to 10 pounds but can reach as high as 30 pounds—hold a special allure for anglers, for both their scarcity and their size. Brown trout were introduced to the region in the late 1800s. The fish of the Rio Grande that forage in the sea began to resemble Atlantic salmon in appearance; in fact, they are genetically related to *Salmo salar*. The technique for taking sea-run browns on the Rio Grande bears some similarity to Atlantic salmon angling. Anglers cast across the current and let the fly swing across; takes usually come on the swing. It is not terrifically technical fishing, though the fierce gales that scream off the Strait of Magellan can make even short casts a challenge.

TALE 25

BULLISH ON BULL TROUT

Many anglers, when asked about their favorite quarry, will reply, "It doesn't matter what I fish for, I just like being out there" or "I love them all." For Joel La Follette, there's little hesitation. In fact, bull trout are a part of his fishing heritage.

"My introduction to bull trout came in a story that my grandfather shared with me when I was a boy," Joel began. "He was a passionate fly fisher and loved to spend time on the Metolius River, a picture-perfect spring creek in central Oregon, casting to the river's native rainbow trout. At one spot where he liked to fish, he'd lost three or four rainbows to a much larger fish—then they called them Dolly Vardens, though now we recognize the larger fish in the Metolius system as bull trout. Bull trout in this system can get quite large—thirty-inch fish are encountered with some frequency and most fish I've caught are at least five pounds. My grandfather was getting tired of losing trout to the creature in the pool he was fishing. As he didn't have any large flies with him—and it was obvious this fish liked a big meal—he cut a piece of handkerchief and stuck it on a bare hook. A few casts later, he had a bull trout on the line and soon after on the bank. He promptly slit it open and there were six rainbow trout inside. A fish that could eat six of the trout that my grandfather and I so loved to fish for captured my imagination, and has done so to this day.

"Over the last ten years, I've spent a lot of time on the Metolius chasing bull trout. I've experimented with a number of different flies and techniques and now have pretty consistent results. A lot of people who are targeting bull trout focus on deeper water where there's good cover. Certainly, the fish will hold in those places. But I've found that I have better luck fishing riffles with deep drop-offs. The fish move into these spots looking for food, and if you're observant you can sight-fish them. [Like most spring creeks, the Metolius is remarkably clear.] One of my favorite bull trout flies has been the Barnyard Sculpin, a gigantic pattern that calls for rabbit fur, goat hair, and sheep's wool—hence its name. One day in March a few years back, I took eleven bull trout in the day with the Barnyard Sculpin.

"When fishing the Metolius, I'll usually carry two rods—one lighter rod for rainbows, and one sturdier stick for bull trout. On this one occasion, my wife, Kellie, and I were walking along the shore scouting the water when we came upon a riffle where I could see three

OPPOSITE:
The Metolius maintains a healthy fishery for both native bull and rainbow trout, and is as pretty a stream as you could hope for.

TALE 26

rainbows holding. I made a short cast and drifted a small nymph through, and one of the fish grabbed it. The fish bolted downstream and then stopped. The fish had jammed itself up against a large rock. This was odd behavior, and I stepped into the water to get a different angle on the fish. From the new angle I could see that the rainbow hadn't snuggled in against a rock. It was in the mouth of what I would estimate to be an eight-pound bull trout! The bull trout started moving downstream with the rainbow in tow. I put some pressure on and began gaining ground. Kellie joined me in the river with a landing net at the ready. When the fish were about eight feet away, the bull trout let go. The rainbow was still alive, though I can only imagine what sort of mental state it must have been in. I got it the rest of the way in and was reaching down to remove the nymph when I saw the bull trout swimming behind Kellie, between her and the bank. There's no question in my mind that he was getting in position to finish off the rainbow. Something we did must have spooked the bull trout and he bolted—right into the net! We kept the bull trout in the net as I released the rainbow, hoping this would give him enough of a head start to sip mayflies another day. Sometimes bull trout will have very distinctive markings on their orange pigment, almost like birthmarks. This was such a fish, and I figured I'd recognize him if we met again.

"I got that chance much sooner than I would have expected. That evening, I had my seven-weight out, and was fishing another riffle near where we'd netted the bull trout. I was swinging a Barnyard Sculpin across the riffle when I saw a wake coming toward the fly. When bull trout take a fly, they don't slam it. They just grab it. I felt the grab and the fish was on. As the light was fading I brought the fish to the net. It was the same size as the earlier fish. On closer inspection, I noticed the markings. Sure enough, it was the same fish that we'd met earlier."

Joel La Follette learned the art of fly fishing in the cool pine forest along the banks of the Metolius River at the ripe old age of nine. His grandfather had brought him there to share some of the joys of his childhood fishing the same stream. Since that first outing Joel has fished the wilds of Belize, Mexico, the Bahamas, and Christmas Island for bonefish, tarpon, permit, trevally, and other saltwater fishes. He's traveled the Northeast for brookies, browns, and stripers. In the South he's tried his luck with redfish and giant tarpon. Up north he's chased BC steelhead, but the Metolius has always remained his favorite water. After an adventurous career that has included work as a commercial fisherman, professional photographer, and race car driving instructor, Joel has settled in as the retail manager for Kaufmann's Streamborn in Tigard, Oregon, one of the biggest fly-fishing retailers in the United States. He occasionally guides on the Deschutes on his days off and hosts trips around the globe for Kaufmann's. Joel and his lovely wife, Kellie, live in West Linn in a home they've named Woodsprite Lodge. They share their treetop view with a variety of birds, squirrels, and other woodsy creatures. Joel's fishing reports, short stories, and other musings are updated regularly at www.royaltreatmentflyfishing.com.

BULL TROUT: BELLWETHER OF THE WEST

Bull trout (*Salvelinus confluentus*) are indigenous to western North America. Technically members of the char family, they are frequently confused with the Dolly Varden, as they are quite similar in appearance. No one is sure of the origins of the name "bull trout," though in *Trout and Salmon of North America*, biologist Robert J. Behnke conjectures that the name may apply to the stocky, flat head on larger fish or their aggressive feeding habits. Whatever the source of the moniker, no one will dispute the latter statement; in fact, larger bull trout are predominantly piscivorous, or fish-eating. Bull trout require cold, clean water to thrive and have not fared well with increasing development in the western United States. Indeed, they are listed as an endangered species in many river systems in Oregon, Washington, and Idaho. (Some biologists will monitor bull trout populations to help gauge the overall well-being of a river system.) The Metolius is one river where bull trout still thrive, and where catch-and-release angling (with barbless hooks) is permitted. This is the result of the purity of the Metolius's spring water, as well as the presence of kokanee salmon, which run up the Metolius in the fall from Lake Billy Chinook to spawn, providing a fine protein supplement to the bull trout's diet of rainbows and whitefish.

HOOKED ON FLY FISHING

Some people come to fly fishing with no preconceptions gathered from other styles of fishing. Others come to it after years of spin-fishing or bait-casting, seeking a new challenge or something slightly different. And some come to it only grudgingly, when they're forced to admit that at times it can simply be the most effective way to catch fish.

Over nearly thirty years of outfitting—and a number of guiding years before that—Mike Lawson has gathered up a few good stories. One that stands out for him involves his brother Rick and two clients who were brothers, one a fly fisher and one who would eventually become hooked—as it were—on fly fishing.

"When he was in college, my younger brother Rick worked for me in the summer guiding," Mike began. "He's a CPA now, but he put himself through college in part by guiding. On the day in question, we had two middle-aged brothers sign up for a float trip on the Henry's Fork. One brother was an ardent fly fisher and the other brother was adamantly *not* a fly fisher. We tried to tell him that on the rivers we fish—mostly the Henry's and the Madison—fishing with a spinning rod is not very effective. The lures a spin fisherman can use don't imitate the forage the fish are seeking as well. Just as important, you miss a lot of the best water as you're retrieving your lure back to the boat to cast again. Of course, with a fly rig, you can just lift the fly up once it has drifted through the sweet spot and cast it to the next good water, without missing a beat. He didn't want to hear about it. People want to go with what they're most comfortable with, no matter how good a case you can make for a new approach.

"That day, they were floating the stretch from Osborne Bridge to Riverside Campground. The first few miles of the float go through the heart of Harriman State Park and the fabled Railroad Ranch. They didn't even bother fishing this fabulous water, as it's fly fishing only, and the one brother refused to swap out his spinning rod for a fly rod. Once they got out of the fly-only water they began to fish. As we'd predicted, the brother with the spinner wasn't doing much of anything, while his fly-fishing brother was getting lots of action. After a few hours of this, the spinning brother gave in and took one of Rick's fly rods. Rick's a good teacher and the spinning brother caught on pretty quickly. Rick put him in the front

MIKE LAWSON

OPPOSITE:
*Henry's Fork
of the Snake
River is among
America's most
storied trout
fishing waters.*

of the boat, which is the best casting position, and he was getting the fly out there pretty good and getting some action.

"Pretty soon, they came into a fast stretch of water. Somehow in this stretch he managed to foul-hook a big fish. Rick had given him a lot of instruction on how to cast and present the fly but hadn't talked to him much about what to do once you actually hooked a fish—especially a big fish. As any fly angler knows, having lots of slack line between you and a big fish is probably the quickest way to bid that fish good-bye. The spinning brother had lots of slack line, and while he didn't exactly know what to do with it he knew enough about fishing to understand that this wasn't a good situation. Instead of playing it in by hand until he could take up the slack with his reel, he lifted the rod up in the air and started backing up in the boat. It wasn't too many steps before he went right out of the boat! He came up bobbing in the fast water, still fighting the fish. He didn't seem to care that he was in the river, so long as he had the fish on.

"At this point, I should mention that when the bobbing brother had been using his spinning rod, he'd been bringing the spinner right to the top of the rod, leaving it dangling. When he switched over, he'd set the rod down on the side of the boat. When he'd backed up and fallen out of the boat, the spinner had hooked him right in the butt. As he was bobbing down the river, line was peeling off the spinning reel and the rod was bouncing all over the boat. Out of instinct, the fly-fishing brother grabbed the spinning rod and started playing his brother in. To this day, we're not sure if the fly-fishing brother was trying to help his bobbing brother out or having fun with him. It didn't seem to bother the bobbing brother, who was still playing the big fish.

"As you might expect, my brother was getting in a panic. He didn't want to have to report back to the shop how one of his clients had drowned while catching his first trout on a fly. Soon, my brother got the boat into some shallow water, jumped out, and pulled the bobbing brother out of the water. By some small miracle the fish was still on. The fly-fishing brother got the line reeled up to his brother's behind. Rick helped the no longer bobbing brother land the fish, some pictures were snapped, and the hook was removed from the happy angler's rear end."

Mike Lawson was born and raised in southeastern Idaho. He has fished the local trout streams, and especially the Henry's Fork, all of his life. While teaching junior high school for six years, Mike and his wife, Sheralee, tied flies commercially and did some guiding. In

1977 Mike and Sheralee opened Henry's Fork Anglers in Last Chance, Idaho, a full-service fly-fishing specialty shop and outfitter. Mike's fly-fishing experience is not limited to the Yellowstone region. He has led trips to Alaska, New Zealand, Australia, Tasmania, Christmas Island, Mexico, Belize, and the Florida Keys. In addition to his travels, he has written articles on fly fishing for *Fly Fisherman*, *Fly Fishing for Trout*, *The Fly Fisher*, *Trout* magazine and *The American Angler*. His photographs have also appeared in many of these publications and he has been featured on many of their covers. In 2004 he published his first book, *Spring Creeks*, which received rave reviews. He has also contributed to several books on fly tying, fly fishing, wild turkey hunting, and upland bird hunting. Mike is featured in several fly-fishing videos, including *Tying Western Dry Flies* with Jack Dennis, *Tying and Fishing Caddisflies* with Gary LaFontaine and Jack Dennis, and *Fishing the Golden Ring* by Gordon Eastman. His latest video, *Tying Flies for Spring Creeks and Tailwaters*, was released in 1998. Mike loves turkey hunting as much as fly fishing and has hunted the wary birds extensively throughout the West and Midwest.

THE HENRY'S FORK

For many, Henry's Fork—just southwest of Yellowstone National Park in southeastern Idaho—ranks among the top trout fisheries in the world. A river of many characters—from the pounding rapids of Box Canyon to the placid meadow stretches in Harriman State Park—Henry's offers anglers the opportunity to cast to large, wary rainbows against a backdrop of stunningly beautiful Western scenery. The river, especially the Harriman section —often referred to as the "Railroad Ranch," supports a tremendous diversity of insect life, and this diversity makes selecting the fly necessary for duping the fish a supreme challenge. Anglers willing and able to take their time, study insect activity on the water, find a feeding fish, get slowly into casting position, and make a drag-free presentation over the Henry's swirling microcurrents *may* find some success! Though many leave Harriman scratching their heads, a day spent fishing there is a day most anglers are likely to cherish, no matter what their luck.

TALE 27

HURRICANE HATTER AND TYPHOON LEON

Almost anyone who's traveled to distant locales for a special fishing adventure has experienced the traveling angler's most dreaded nemesis—bad conditions. On an Atlantic salmon river, it could be that the fish haven't returned from the sea when expected. On a Montana trout stream, it could be late runoff from the mountains, turning your blue-ribbon river into a sheath of mud. On bonefish flats, it could be unrelenting gale-force winds. However nature has conspired against you, choices must be made. You pack it in and fly home. You rummage through the lodge library to secure a good book—and perhaps a forgotten bottle of single malt—and hunker down.

Or you accept that you are there to fish and decide to make the best of it.

Scott Leon chose option three.

"Back in December of 2003, Mark Hatter and I traveled to Guatemala. It's peak season for sailfish there and you have an excellent chance to see a hundred sailfish in a day. I had the cockamamie idea that we could get underwater photos of a sailfish for *Fly Fishing in Saltwater*, the magazine I used to edit. Normally the lodges that cater to fly anglers down there are booked solid, but we had no problem finding a space. We'd have five days to fish and hopefully get our shots.

"The first morning, we got down to the dock with enough gear to start a fly shop, plus all of Mark's underwater cameras. Looking east, we could see these tremendous volcanoes. Usually they're masked in clouds. The local folks said this was not a good sign, as the winds that had pushed the clouds away were undoubtedly making for bad weather offshore. We paused for a moment but decided to push ahead.

"To get out to the ocean, you need to go through a little pass—literally the width of a boat. The pass is infamous around this region of Guatemala. Our captain, a New Zealander named Chris Von Leeuwen, who goes by the nickname Kiwi, lined up the boat expertly to run through—you have to catch the waves just right, almost like a surfer. As we gunned through, there were ten-foot rollers in the pass. I was thinking, 'We're gonna die.' We hadn't even begun.

"That first day, we had eight- to ten-foot seas. There were six seconds between rollers.

The only good thing we could say about conditions were that they were consistent. We pushed out to about twenty-five miles offshore and things just weren't improving. Kiwi wanted to console us. 'Don't worry,' he said, 'if it's bad today, it will be fine tomorrow.' Despite the conditions, we put lines out and, sure enough, a sailfish showed up. I took the first shot. Kiwi said, 'You're going to have to be quick with your cast, because I can't watch the fish and keep the boat in current at the same time. I have to keep our bow into the waves so we don't get swamped.' I missed that one, and then went up to have a talk with Kiwi. 'I know we're here to do a story,' I said, 'but if you don't think it's safe, let's go in.' We stayed out, and by the end of the day we had six sailfish to the boat. Not too bad.

"The second day was just as bad as the first day. Kiwi said that they've never seen it this bad two days in a row. You have to picture the boat—it's an open, express-style fishing craft with a flying bridge. No cabin. There's a settee on each side of the boat toward the back, one covered with camera gear, the other with fishing gear. We're out about forty miles and the seas are around eight feet. There were times we were rolling so hard you couldn't see the sky. You also have to remember that we're not off the coast of Massachusetts. This was Guatemala. There's no Coast Guard to come out and rescue us. We're on our own. I think we were both asking ourselves, 'Is it really bright to be out here? Is there any intelligence in this?' But at the same time we're thinking, 'There are fish out here!' When that sailfish shows up, your mentality changes.

"Then the call comes from Kiwi: 'Fish in the spread!' One mate brought in the teaser bait, the other mate got ready to cast the second bait to bring the fish close. Mark was in position to make his cast with the fly rod as soon as the fish got close enough. Then Kiwi screamed, 'Hold on!' As we slid out of one of the waves we'd bottomed out of the trough and tilted, and the next wave slammed into us broadside. I was able to grab the bridge and hold myself up but Mark was blindsided. All he could do was turn his back, and the wave busted him into the fighting chair and then into water in the boat, which was knee deep. Mark was doubled over in pain. I was a navy SEAL and have medic training, and I got him over to the settee. He couldn't straighten out but there was no blood. I looked around and noticed that the mate who was going to cast the second teaser was standing exactly where he'd been standing when the wave hit. It was like he had Velcro on his feet. He said matter-of-factly, 'The fish is still here.' I guess my fishing instincts are pretty strong because I don't think I hesitated a second before grabbing Mark's fly rod and making a cast. The fish didn't take.

"There was camera gear floating everywhere in the boat, but fortunately it was under-

TALE 28

water gear and not damaged. The boat drained amazingly quickly; it must have shed four hundred gallons of water in a minute and a half. Mark finally straightened up and said, 'I can be in pain here or in pain on the dock. Let's fish.' So that day, we ended up catching two sailfish and a dolphin, which Mark caught. At two A.M. that night, Mark knocked on my door and said, 'I need aspirin.' I asked if we should try to get him to a hospital. He said, 'No, I'm just sore.'

"Day three, we motored out again. The seas were still terrible. Mark was in great pain but he was hanging in there. Despite the conditions, we brought four or five sailfish to the boat. There were no more injuries. On the fourth day conditions were just as bad, but other guests must have been getting cabin fever, as there were a few more boats out there. Over the radio, we heard that a few boats had spotted blue marlin and that one gear fisherman had brought one in. As the day went on, conditions began to worsen. We were really beginning to feel worse for wear, between Mark's ribs and the exertion of trying to keep our sea legs in such heavy seas. We decided to head back in. We'd picked up a few fish and decided it might be more relaxing to fish close to shore for jacks. As we motored in, a fish showed up behind the boat. 'That's the biggest sailfish I've ever seen!' I said to Kiwi. Then we looked at each other and said, 'Blue marlin!'

"It was Mark's turn to cast, and I began yelling for him to pick up the fourteen-weight rod, which was on the settee. The twelve-weight wouldn't be enough. Mark looked stunned, like he wasn't paying attention. He still had the twelve-weight rod in hand. All of a sudden, he put down the twelve-weight, picked up the fourteen-weight, and made a cast. The fish rolled on the fly, missed it, and then grabbed it. Marlin on! The seas flattened out a bit and we were able to follow the fish. It never jumped and we kept a good angle on it. It was two hundred fifty pounds, and we got it to the boat in about forty-five minutes! Afterward, I said to Mark, 'It took you long enough to grab the right rod. I was yelling at you.' He said, 'I never heard you. I didn't know it was a marlin. All I could think was that I hurt so bad, I couldn't fight a fish on light gear.'

"That night, I went into the Tiki Bar and ran into Tim Choate, the lodge's owner. I said, 'Tim, we have one more day. You've got to give us some good weather.' At that point, someone in the bar dubbed us Hurricane Hatter and Typhoon Leon.

"On the last day the seas had leveled off a tiny bit—only four to six feet—and we ran out about forty miles. Pretty soon, a fish showed up and I made the cast. As the fish was about to take the fly, I noticed that the waves were picking up. I hooked up, and Kiwi said, 'We can't chase it.' The seas were not only choppy but rolling in all directions. I looked up and the fish was at the top of a wave, tail-walking along the surface. He was ten feet over my head, eye to eye with Kiwi. I was thinking, 'This is not right.' We got that fish in and I said to Kiwi, 'We're getting our butts kicked, Mark's in pain, and we can't get in the water to get our photos. Let's call it.'

"On the way in we got one more chance. A small fish showed up behind the boat and Mark hooked him. The water was calmer as we were closer to shore, and Mark handed me the rod and went in with his camera. The light was good and he took a bunch of shots.

"We learned later that the camera had not advanced and that we got zero photos.

"When I recount the story of that trip, some people say, 'What bad luck!' I look at them and respond, 'You mean, what good luck!' We caught fish—including a blue marlin on a fly, which is no small feat—we didn't break any rods, and we had only one injury. Once we got home, an X-ray confirmed that Mark had two cracked ribs. It was brutal. It was scary.

"And I don't know anyone who would say that it wasn't a productive trip."

Scott Leon grew up fishing the waters of the Mississippi and Louisiana coasts and began fly fishing as a teenager in the Bahamas. He has fly fished all over the world, almost exclusively in the salt, and maintains a particular affinity for pursuing big yellowfin tuna with a fly rod. Scott was an editor for *Fly Fishing in Salt Waters* for six years and holds a master's degree and five bachelor's degrees. He is a former U.S. Navy SEAL.

TALE 28

SAILFISH OFF GUATEMALA

The San José/Iztapa region on Guatemala's Pacific coast is recognized as one of the most reliable sailfish destinations in Central America—perhaps, in the world. Fish average around ninety pounds, with sailfish up to 150 pounds taken with regularity. Pacific blue marlin are also present, and reach four hundred pounds and more. The season for Pacific sailfish extends from late October through May, with peak seasons occurring in late December and again in late April. The "bait and switch" technique for attracting and hooking billfish on a fly demands some exceptional teamwork between the captain, his crew, and the angler. A teaser bait (without hooks) is trolled behind the boat. When the fish rises to the bait, one crew member reels in the teaser to draw the fish closer to the boat. At this point, the fly angler steps into position, prepared to make what might be the cast of a lifetime.

MAN ONE, BEAVER ZERO

Those who have waded saltwater flats to cast to bonefish or redfish understand how animals that seem relatively harmless when you're in the boat can take on a more menacing aura when you're on their turf. That three- or four-foot sand shark is no maneater, to be sure, but that boat is a few hundred yards away and he's circling kind of close, and didn't you have a cut on your knee that was bleeding a bit when you put on your flats boots this morning? While river anglers might occasionally encounter other land animals (moose, bear, etc.) around the water, there aren't many river creatures that are likely to cause distress as you enter *their* world. Unless you happen to be Macauley Lord.

"It was July of 1991, and I was helping conduct a fly-fishing school for LL Bean up at Grand Lake Stream, near the northeastern corner of the state," Macauley began. "It's a wonderful landlocked salmon river, with a rich history. If Maine has a tweed-and-single-malt river, it would be Grand Lake Stream. I was there with four or five other instructors and we had a terrific heat wave. It pushed the river temperatures up to an unbearable level—in one pool, the water reached eighty-one degrees. The salmon are generally distributed throughout the river at this time, but with the heat the fish that hadn't returned to the lakes were all stacked up at the base of the dam at West Grand Lake. The bottom line under such conditions: no salmon fishing. The upside—if you're an instructor, at least—was that we were free to go snorkeling after hours.

"If I had my choice between casting to fish above water or watching fish underwater while snorkeling, I'd have no hesitation in choosing the latter. Seeing the fish's world from underwater is a religious experience for me, much more powerful than fishing. You feel as if you're in a different universe. There are a few places that we liked to snorkel. Up at the dam pool, above the no-fishing line, there would be lots of salmon, as there the water's much more oxygenated. Sometimes we'd also snorkel the Hatchery Pool. My favorite spot was a place called the Meadows.

"This one day in July, I opted for the Meadows. I hiked in near the bottom of the stretch, through a tunnel in the trees and a clearing that opens up on the river. It was about five-thirty in the afternoon. It was quite warm and there was plenty of light to make for good visibility. I like the architecture of this stretch of water, as there are plenty of logs—good fish habitat. I had my swim fins, mask, and snorkel and I was off. I saw some suckers right off the bat, and then what looked like a few salmon, though it was a sandy bottom, not really good salmon water. I began swimming upstream and saw some smallmouth bass, a species I really enjoy fishing for. Up at the top of the stretch, there's a bend where the river curves right. There are some deep holes up there, and a big beaver lodge. I thought, 'Great, I've never seen a beaver lodge from underwater!' I began to swim toward the lodge. I got to about thirty feet away and, out of nowhere, this beaver appears between me and the lodge. I was a little uneasy, but not exactly frightened. I stuck my head out of the water and the beaver was still there. I figured that whatever was going to happen was going to happen, and I was going to stick it out. I stuck my head back under the surface, thinking that it would be interesting to see what a beaver looks like underwater.

"The beaver continued to swim very purposefully away from its house, to my right, then behind me, then to my left, then in front of me again. He was swimming around me in a perfect three-hundred-sixty-degree circle. There was no variation in his speed. He swam one circle, then began another. I'm not a beaver biologist but I figured that this behavior meant something, and it wasn't particularly good. Three-quarters of the way through the second circle, the beaver did a ninety-degree turn, directly toward me. At this point I was getting nervous. I was thinking of those big teeth—teeth that take down big trees—and those claws. I was thinking, 'This thing is really going to hurt.'

"I don't normally think of myself as a quick-thinking person, but at this moment I felt under attack. When beavers feel threatened, they will often respond by slapping the surface with their tail. Anyone who's encountered this sound while quietly stalking a trout on a pond or stream knows it's a jarring experience. All I could think of as the beaver bore down on me was to respond like a beaver and splash. Lacking a tail, I put my hands on the surface and made as much percussion as I could. When the turbulence cleared, the beaver was gone. It had completely vanished and I never saw it again that afternoon—not that I spent a lot more time in that particular pool. I like to think that my relatively fast thinking that afternoon saved my life, though I can't recall any accounts of beavers taking a human life.

"While I've never sorted out why that beaver chose me as potential prey, there may be some explanation of what occurred on a higher, more spiritual level. Some of my friends think I'm going to burn in the hot place because I like to fish for bass. If God is a salmonid lover, this may have been His way of saying, 'Hey Mac, stop messing with smallmouth!'"

TALE 29

Macauley Lord is the author of the *LL Bean Fly-Casting Handbook*. He has taught at the LL Bean Fly Fishing School since 1986 and was its head instructor from 1996 until 2005. The fly-casting columnist for *American Angler* magazine, his articles have also appeared in *Fly Fisherman* and *Saltwater Fly Fishing* magazines. As an emeritus member of the casting board of governors at the Federation of Fly Fishers, he trains and certifies fly-casting instructors around the country. He is the former editor of *The Loop*, the quarterly journal for certified fly-casting instructors. Macauley is a Kentucky native, a 1978 graduate of Bowdoin College, and he did graduate work in natural resource policy at the University of Michigan. With his fly rod and backpack, Macauley has trout-fished throughout the American West and has bonefished in Belize, the Bahamas, and the Seychelles islands in the Indian Ocean. Macauley bass-fishes avidly in Maine from a kickboat and has trained guide staffs at fly-fishing resorts in the Bahamas and the Seychelles. Teaching remains his first love: "There is no feeling in this world like teaching someone to fly-cast," Macauley said. "Seeing my students' joy in casting a fly out into the fish's world is something I'll never get enough of."

LANDLOCKED SALMON ON GRAND LAKE STREAM

Landlocked salmon are perhaps Maine's greatest fly-fishing attraction, and Grand Lake Stream is a favorite landlock venue for Downeasters and visitors alike. Just three and a half miles long, Grand Lake Stream connects Big Lake and West Grand Lake; fish will be present in the river in greatest numbers in the spring and fall, as many return to the cool depths of the lakes at the height of summer. Landlocked salmon evolved from spawning Atlantic salmon that were trapped inland due to geologic unrest some ten thousand years ago. Though smaller than their ocean-going brethren, landlocks bear the same genetic make-up as *Salmo salar* and are equally game fighters, especially on a five- or six-weight. In the spring the fish are focusing on smelt, and streamer patterns (such as the famed Gray Ghost) fished down and across are the order of the day. As the water warms, the salmon of Grand Lake Stream focus increasingly on caddis and stonefly imitations. The river is also home to brook trout and smallmouth bass, though bronzeback fans will find excellent angling in the lakes and on the nearby St. Croix River.

TOASTING THE GLENFIDDICH

Whether it's in the classroom, on the playing field, or in the workplace, we often find that our most trying experiences prove to be our most gratifying. This explains why anglers are willing to travel thousands of miles and spend thousands of dollars for the very real chance of not catching a fish. The rivers of New Zealand are renowned for being especially stingy with their trophies, even when conditions are ideal. When the rivers get out of shape, the challenges intensify—but so do the rewards, as Tom Montgomery can attest.

"In the winter of 1987, my brother and I found that we both had time on our hands," Tom began. "I suggested that we take an extended fishing excursion in New Zealand. I had been there a number of times previously, and have gone a number of times since in various capacities as trip leader, photographer, and tourist. At the time, my brother, Jock, was living in Asia, leading treks and whitewater expeditions out of Kathmandu. In our family, he's the real adventurer, I'm the fly fisherman. I really wanted to make this trip with him to expose him to the incredible possibilities of fishing—and adventure—in New Zealand. We had six weeks to spend.

"In my earlier travels in New Zealand, I had met a young guide named Tony Entwistle, who at the time was doing a great deal to establish the country as a trout-fishing destination. He's gone on to become one of New Zealand's preeminent anglers. He told me about this wonderful, remote river that went by the code name of the 'Glenfiddich.' The river saw little pressure and held good numbers of double-figure fish—a real angler's El Dorado. One of Tony's guide friends had caught his first double-figure fish there, and the guides had nicknamed the river for the scotch they lifted to toast his catch in the local pub. Few people knew about the quality of the fishing on the Glenfiddich, and understandably the locals wanted to keep it that way. But for whatever reason Tony trusted me, and gave me its location. Most of the few who have fished it helicoptered in. As we had ample time but little money we elected to tramp in.

"It was quite a hike. At one point we left the trailhead, came over a crest, and descended into a dale. Fog soon closed over us, and it wasn't long before we realized we were lost. Knowing that there was no trail into the river, we'd each come equipped with a compass.

The only problem was, our two compasses were pointed thirty-five degrees in different directions! We split the difference and pushed forward and this was a good guess. Before long we could hear the roar of the river, but it was hard to follow as the sound bounced around fifteen hundred feet below us in the deep valley. Eventually we made it to the water in a gorgy section. I peered down into the tea-colored water from a bluff and immediately spotted some feeding fish. Jock made his way downstream from the fish and got into a position to cast. With a little guidance from me on the bluff, he promptly hooked up with a six-pound brown—just like that! I'm sure it was the biggest fish he'd ever hooked, and it was a thrill. Jock was about to land the fish when it made a last run—the tippet held, but somehow the leader twisted around the rod, which snapped just a few inches from the tip. This was a major setback, a bittersweet success that would prove characteristic of the rest of this journey. Now we had one rod between us and four days remaining on the Glenfiddich.

"Then the rains began.

"For the better part of the next three days, we were confined to our tent as the river went from tea-colored to chocolate brown, and rose, and rose, and rose, nearly four feet. We passed the time reading, talking, eating snacks, and occasionally checking the mark we'd left below our tent to chart the rise of the water—it was eventually swept away. Heavy rain can always be part of New Zealand backcountry fishing, and I've even heard stories about anglers moving their tents and camping on the steep-sided banks of the Glenfiddich as the river flooded. It didn't get quite this bad, though we were ready for evacuation and a night of inclined camping. But frankly I wasn't as worried that we'd be swept downriver, or be forced to pitch our tent on a mountainside, as that we'd have to return to the pub and give the guys there, who were cheering us on, a shallow report of our meager success. A six-pound brown is a pretty nice fish by any standards, but given the reputation of the Glenfiddich, this one fish would barely get us a seat at the bar.

"As we idled away our time in the tent, it was my hope that we'd get a falling river for one more day of fishing, and then a clear day to hike out. More than anything else, I wanted to see Jock have a great day on the river. As it turned out, the fishing gods were with us.

"Late on the third day of the deluge the rain let up and by evening the river was falling. By late morning of the fourth day the skies had brightened and the river was coming quickly into shape with good light for spotting fish. I put Jock down at streamside and began spotting from the high banks and bluffs. Almost within sight of our camp I spotted a big brown that was surface feeding in a back eddy. I told Jock where to place his cast and he put it on the

OPPOSITE:
Tom Montgomery's brother, Jock, prepares to release a behemoth brown landed on a fateful trip to the Glenfiddich.

TALE 30

money. Not long after, he had an eight-and-a-half-pound fish in the shallows. In a picture I shot that eventually made it to the cover of a fly-fishing magazine, Jock looks stunned, even mesmerized. Soon after, he repeated the process in another pool, this time landing a nine-and-a-half-pound fish on a small nymph. This was the kind of fishing we'd dreamed about from our rain-soaked tent. After three days of no fishing Jock was having the kind of day any trout fisherman would kill for.

"Late that same day, as shadows were starting to crisscross the deep pools and we were just about ready to head back downstream to camp, I was hiking along another bluff when I spotted a huge fish feeding in the shallows, right at the head of a very large pool. I thought that it must have been twelve or thirteen pounds. I pointed out the fish's location to Jock. Jock pointed out to me that it was my turn to fish. I didn't argue. While I admit that I wanted this fish, and while I was sure that Jock would easily spot it from the bluff, I wasn't sure he'd be able to tell me when to strike. Watching, I had noticed that my fish had an annoying habit of dropping back fifteen feet or more to take a nymph, then sinking invisibly into the tea-color depths, and finally reappearing in the shallows at the head of the pool. Once I even though I'd lost him for good when he disappeared from sight for almost a minute.

"I climbed down from the bluff, crossed the river well downstream from the fish, and rigged up an eighteen-foot leader, a Pheasant Tail nymph, and a tiny yarn indicator. Jock traded positions with me and got on the bluff. Ready to go, I waded into the river and made two false casts followed by a delivery that I still remember as a precise mixture of length, angle, and anxiety. My trimmed indicator was nearly invisible, but for a moment I could see it as it drifted in the mix of foam and surface detritus. Then I lost sight of it and had to make a fast decision: if I lifted the rod, I could be tight to the fish of a lifetime, but if I wasn't I'd likely spook it by ripping the line across the pool. However, if I let the nymph continue its drift I might miss the take and perhaps my only chance at the fish. I chose to lift the rod. Luckily it came up solid. Instantly the fish was all over the pool, pushing my five-weight and my nerves to their limits. Of course it seemed like forever, but in time Jock was able to net and weigh the fish for me. The light was pretty much gone by this point so we never did get a good photo.

"This was our last fish on the Glenfiddich, a male, and it weighed ten and a half pounds on our scale. Later my brother confided that he couldn't tell what happened after the nymph landed and began its drift, that the fish seemed to just drop back into the pool and disappear. Then he noticed my bent rod.

"When dawn came the next morning it was a beautiful, clear day with the river in still better condition than the day before. But we had committed ourselves to hiking out as it was time to try another river and, besides, we were out of food. The hike out was completely uneventful. In fact, we exited the beech forest right at our minivan.

"We had other adventures as we made our way south on that New Zealand trip, and ran into other American anglers along the way, some of whom were having a tough time as that was generally a difficult season on the South Island. We commiserated with them. But we had this secret story of success, this secret history that we shared that buoyed us through our own difficult days.

"I've thought about this trip often over the years, and though Jock and I both have had a fair share of interesting adventures since then, nothing has quite lived up to our time in the valley of the Glenfiddich."

Tom Montgomery is a photographer and fly-fishing guide living in Jackson Hole, Wyoming. In the early eighties he ran the saltwater fly-fishing program at the Southern Cross Club on Little Cayman, as well as guiding summers in Montana, Idaho, and Wyoming. Currently, he leads winter fly-fishing trips to New Zealand, Argentina, and Chile, and in the late summer he guides on the Snake River near his Wyoming home. As a freelance photographer Tom has been published by most of the specialty outdoor magazines, including *Fly Fisherman, Fly Rod and Reel, Gray's Sporting Journal, Field & Stream, Outdoor Life*, and *Sports Afield*. In addition, he has worked on assignment for *Men's Journal, Esquire Sportsman, Forbes*, and *Forbes/FYI*. Tom's clients in the fly-fishing industry include Trout Unlimited, Sage, Orvis, Winston, Patagonia, and Simms. He also works as a life-style specialist photographer for a variety of commercial clients. Tom has a B.A. in English literature and was educated at Middlebury College, Vermont, and St. Peter's College, Oxford University.

TALE 30

CODE NAMES

It's not uncommon for anglers to mask the identity of a special pool—or a special river—with a code name, like the Glenfiddich. Perhaps the best-known "coded" river in literature is the Two-Hearted River, which Hemingway used in the famous short story of the same name. In this tale, protagonist Nick Adams encounters a giant brook trout that quickly breaks off, leaving Adams dry-mouthed and shaken. Although there is a Two-Hearted River in Michigan's Upper Peninsula, fishing historians and literary critics alike agree that Nick was actually fishing on the East Branch of the Fox River, near the defunct lumber town of Seney, some twenty-five miles south of the Two-Hearted. Hemingway visited the area in 1919 and recounted to a friend that he and an accomplice had caught two hundred brook trout of up to two pounds in a week's angling; the author also alluded to a much larger fish that he lost. The East Branch of the Fox and the Fox River continue to support healthy populations of brookies.

AN ISLAND ESCAPE

The quest for exotic game fish often brings surprises. And sometimes those surprises extend far beyond the end of your tippet, as high-tech visionary and philanthropist Gordon Moore recounted.

"A few years back my wife and I, along with another couple who we've fished with for years, made a trip to Australia," Gordon began. "The focus of our trip was going to be big-game fishing for black marlin, but we ended up adding another week to the excursion so we could fish for barramundi on Bathurst Island. Bathurst is easily the most remote place I've ever visited in my life. To get there we had to fly to Darwin, take a small plane to an aboriginal village, and then take a boat that eventually put us on the island. On Bathurst, we saw no evidence of human beings, aside from our guides and the cook who manned the campsite, which was set up on a sand spit. The Tiwi, an aboriginal tribe, do inhabit portions of the island, which falls under their governance.

"On Bathurst, they fish for barramundi in saltwater cuts, which resemble rivers. There are huge tides in this part of the world, twenty-foot plus, and the barramundi move in on the tides to ambush baitfish. There are also saltwater crocodiles (*Crocodylus porosus*). Some of these creatures can attain lengths of twenty-five feet or more and will eat anything they can catch, including, on occasion, man.

"As we arrived at Bathurst, one of our guides made mention of the crocodiles. On the first night we were there, my friend and one of the guides went out with a flashlight to see if they could spot any of the reptiles. Crocodile eyes glow in the dark, a kind of ruby red. It didn't take long for the fellows to spot two sets of eyes in the cut. The first croc had about a foot of space between its eyes, the second one had about six inches. When my friend decided that it would be interesting to try to land one of the reptiles for further inspection, the guide said, 'Better go for the small one, mate.' We had some spinning gear with us and he set up a rod with a large plug. As you'd expect, crocs are pretty aggressive, and it wasn't many casts before he was playing the beast in. Crocodiles aren't great fighters on the rod and reel and they soon had it to hand. The guide tied the croc's legs and covered it with a skiff, the thought being that the rest of us could have a closer look in the light of day.

"The next morning, we all soon learned of my friend's nocturnal catch. I had a video camera along on the trip and set it up to capture the action. I don't think any of us realized just how fast the action would be. During the night the crocodile had struggled out of the rope. When the guides lifted the boat up, a six-foot crocodile zipped past us, back into the water. Any ideas I had about a crocodile not being able to move quickly on land were quickly erased.

"It turned out that the barramundi fishing that week was not as good as it might have been, but there was no shortage of adventures. Our bathing facilities—the cut in front of our camp—was infested with crocs and sharks, which made washing up quite a stimulating event. During dinner, for fun, we tossed a hook baited with meat into the cut right where we'd been bathing a few minutes earlier and attracted the attention of a few good-sized sharks. One evening toward the end of the week our 'dinner guest' turned out to be a saw-fish, a sharklike creature that's actually a member of the ray family and can reach lengths of twenty-five feet. I spent three hours and forty-five minutes walking up and down the sand with thirty-pound conventional trolling tackle trying to get this prehistoric-looking thing in. When I hooked it, it was slack tide. When the big tides started running, the fish began using the current to its advantage and eventually broke me off.

"Even the insects on this isolated island were a handful. As we sat around the fire each evening, we were accosted by a bug called a greenfly. It was similar to a horsefly but larger and even more persistent. We had to swat them with a gin bottle to kill them. We kept a tally, and our records showed that we killed three hundred and sixty in all.

"After contending with crocodiles, sawfish, and greenflies, we went marlin fishing. It seemed tame in comparison."

Gordon Moore is cofounder of Intel Corporation and chairman emeritus of the corporation's board of directors. Prior to Intel, Gordon cofounded Fairchild Semiconductor in 1957. A California native, Moore earned his B.S. in chemistry from the University of California at Berkeley and his Ph.D. in chemistry and physics from the California Institute of Technology. In 1968 he cofounded Intel, serving initially as executive vice president. He became president and chief executive officer in 1975 and held that post until elected chairman and chief executive officer in 1979. In 1987 he relinquished the CEO title and was named chairman emeritus in 1997. He is most widely known for his 1965 prediction that the number of transistors the semiconductor industry would be able to place on a computer chip would double every year. What was intended as a rule of thumb quickly became known as "Moore's Law" and a guiding principle for the delivery of ever more powerful chips at proportionately lower costs. He updated Moore's Law in 1975 from a doubling of chip capacity every year to once every two years. Moore is less well known for his philanthropic work even though he has been contributing to science, technology, education, and conservation projects for decades. He is currently the chairman of the executive committee for Conservation International and a director of Gilead Sciences, Inc. He is also a member of the National Academy of Engineering and a fellow of the Institute of Electrical and Electronics Engineers. He served as chairman of the board of trustees of the California Institute of Technology from 1995 until the beginning of 2001 and continues as a senior trustee. He received the National Medal of Technology in 1990 and the Medal of Freedom in 2002. In 2000, he and his wife, Betty, formed the Gordon and Betty Moore Foundation, which funds initiatives in three areas of interest to the Moores: global environmental conservation, science, and the San Francisco Bay Area. Their environment program includes the Wild Salmon Ecosystems Initiative dedicated to the preservation of the diversity and function of wild salmon ecosystems throughout the North Pacific.

BARRAMUNDI: AUSTRALIAN FOR "FUN"

Many consider the powerful barramundi to be Australia's foremost indigenous sport fish. A member of the Centropomidae family, barra are found in fresh, brackish, and salt water in the waters of the eastern Persian Gulf and the Indian Ocean from southern China and Japan south to New Guinea and northern Australia. Barramundi can grow to lengths of six feet and can weigh up to 130 pounds. A pale gray-green in color (fish that spend more time in marine environments are more silvery), mature barras feed on crustaceans and small fish. Like their cousins the snook, they prefer to wait in ambush for prey around heavy structure. Barra fishing requires accurate if not delicate casts. The heavy flies used for barramundi make delicacy all but impossible!) Their strike is ferocious, and the barramundi's battle for freedom can be punctuated by tremendous leaps.

TALE 31

UP THE RIVER WITHOUT A DORY

Many officebound anglers fantasize about the life of a fly-fishing guide. Just imagine: many days—perhaps *every* day—out on the river, getting paid to help people catch fish. What could be better?

OPPOSITE:
*A youthful
Brian O'Keefe
lands a beauti-
ful Deschutes
redside around
the time this
tale takes place.*

Like any job, however, guiding has its downsides. There are the hours of prep time before you even meet your sports, hours of cleanup time after you drop them off at the lodge or their watering hole of choice. There's the occasional inhospitable client who has little respect for the fish, the fishery—or you. There's the anxiety that can arise if the fish haven't been cooperating all week and your client has to fly home tomorrow (and your tip hangs in the balance). And there's the monotony that can arrive if one is compelled to float the same stretch of river *day after day after day*, where each day plays back as a repeat of itself with slightly different faces in the front of the boat.

These are some of the occupational hazards that can plague the guiding life. But they pale in comparison with a spring day in 1978 when one of fly fishing's great free spirits, Brian O'Keefe, experienced a Job-like test from the fishing-guide gods on central Oregon's Deschutes River.

"It was early June, the time of the great Deschutes salmonfly hatch, and I got a call from a writer for *National Geographic*. He was doing a story on the Warm Springs Indians and wanted me to take him out for a float. Better yet, he had permission to fish all of the reservation side of the river, which is off limits to most anglers—meaning the fish would have seen few flies and would be especially willing. We met at the Warm Springs boat ramp, rigged up, and launched my boat, a brand-new Lavro eighteen-foot river dory.

"As I'd anticipated, the fishing was quite good. The writer, who was weighed down with about thirty thousand dollars' worth of Nikon camera equipment, was taking lots of photos of me, the fish we were catching, the canyon. Things were going perfectly. I was young and in my glory—that rhymes with 'dory,' which I'll return to soon.

"At around ten-thirty A.M. I was on the bank when a smallish rattlesnake came out of the tall grass and struck my leg without warning. My waders protected me from the actual bite but I jumped a mile high and landed in knee-deep water. The snake swam out to me hissing and striking, which was odd behavior. I pushed it away with my rod. It kept coming back at me and I kept pushing it away. All the while I was wading backward into deeper and deeper water. There comes a point when being 'snake friendly' becomes a sink-or-swim deal—literally! The snake would not take 'no' for an answer, and thanks to its aggressive behavior I decided it might not be long for this world. I turned my Hardy-made, System Six reel over to the flat side and gave the snake one hard smack on its head. It curled up in a ball and sank out of sight. As I gathered my composure, a raft overflowing with ten yahoos, complete with a keg and a pirate flag, came floating by. I yelled, 'Hey, did you see that? I just killed a rattlesnake with my fly reel.' One of the fellows mumbled, 'And I thought we were drunk.'

"A couple of hours went by without incident. As we were floating along, I realized that I was rowing about thirty thousand dollars' worth of camera equipment in my new Lavro. At the time, that seemed pretty cool! Eventually we stopped at a little island about halfway to the Trout Creek campground and got out to fish. About twenty minutes later the writer pointed downstream and said, 'Is that our boat?' Holy s**t!

"It turned out my new drift boat had come with a round anchor instead of a pronged anchor and it had rolled off a ledge and come loose. Our ride off the island—and the thirty thousand dollars' worth of Nikons—were free-floating down the mighty Deschutes. I cinched up my belt and dove into the water and swam—floundered—the hundred and fifty feet to shore. My Seal-Dri waders filled up like a water balloon and it was tough to do a headstand to drain them out. Finally I got inverted and received the cold shower I deserved. Then I was off and running after the boat. The air was about eighty degrees and Seal-Dri waders are like a sweatsuit even on a cool day. Two miles later I found the boat, safe and sound, circling in an eddy as if waiting for me. I *tied* the boat to a tree and hoofed it back to the writer on the island. I yelled out to him that I was going upstream to flag down the next boat and get him a ride to the mainland. Eventually, a boat came by with one person and two huge golden retrievers and the writer was rescued and licked from head to toe. We walked back to the boat. I had forty excuses about the new boat, the round anchor, et cetera. Suddenly things weren't going so well, and my earlier glory was fading before my eyes.

"The rest of the float went okay. We both caught some nice trout, the evening was warm, and I actually started to relax. I pulled the boat up to shore at my camp at Trout Creek and we started unloading everything into my old truck for the ride back to his car at the Warm Springs boat ramp. Normally, I would have had his car shuttled over to Trout Creek so he could go on his way, but he had invited me to accompany him to a dinner at Kah-Nee-Ta Resort on the Warm Springs Reservation, and free dinners were my kind of thing—still are! It's a rough, rutted road out of Trout Creek, and about two miles beyond camp I got a flat tire. You guessed it. My spare was flat too. With heavy hearts, we walked away from the vault of Nikons in my piece-of-junk truck. Back at the boat ramp, the guy with the dogs offered to give us a lift back to my truck to get the tire off and then take us into Warm Springs. My trophy dinner date with the *National Geographic* superstar was looking like a nonevent. When we got back to the truck, I went to get the jack out from behind the seat. Oh, no!— somehow I had left my keys back at camp! Pop goes the wing window—twenty-five dollars in those days—and I'm in the truck. We unloaded the Nikons into the other truck with the dogs, and I sent the writer, the cameras, the dogs, and their driver on their way. I walked back to camp to another dinner of baked beans.

"I'm sure they were all glad to be rid of me and my bad juju."

Brian O'Keefe has fished and photographed the world. His photographs have appeared in the *Los Angeles Times,* the *New York Times, USA Today, Men's Journal*, and just about every fishing magazine you can imagine. In addition to his photography work, Brian is a tackle rep for Scientific Anglers, Cloudveil, and Maui Jim. He is also a master-certified fly-casting instructor from the Federation of Fly Fishers (FFF). Brian and his wife, Judith, live in central Oregon.

THE DESCHUTES

The lower Deschutes river flows one hundred miles through sagebrush-covered high desert and tall basalt canyons from near Warm Springs to its terminus at the Columbia. It is home to the Deschutes redside, a subspecies of rainbow trout called "desert red band trout"or *Onchoryncus mykiss irideus.* Averaging between thirteen and eighteen inches, the fish are not extremely large by western river standards, though they are broad-shouldered and understand how to use the Deschutes's powerful currents to their advantage. Thanks to rich subsurface insect life, the redsides of the Deschutes are less surface-inclined than many anglers would like. However, from mid-May to mid-June, the upper sixty miles of the river see a periodically prolific salmonfly hatch. While surface activity can be sporadic (it doesn't take too many of these big bugs to satiate the fish), action can be fast and furious should you catch it right.

TALE 32

NO FISH FOR A TIGER

It's been said that fly fishing for Atlantic salmon is a great equalizer. The fish don't care how much money you have, what clubs you belong to, how high your IQ is, or how well received your latest movie has been. They only care about how your fly is presented—and if the bite isn't on even that doesn't matter. Just ask Mark O'Meara, who witnessed some Irish salmon's snubbing of one of the greatest golf champions of all time.

"I go over to Ireland to fish for Atlantic salmon twice a year," Mark began, "and one of my favorite rivers to fish is the River Blackwater. One visit is just after the Master's tournament in April. The other is in the summer, just before the British Open. The spring is a great time to be on the Blackwater, as this is when the river gets its run of bigger fish. I was there a few years back at the Careysville House, with a group that included Tiger Woods, who is a dear friend. That particular week, the fishing had been a bit slow, though we'd been fishing pretty hard. Of course, anyone who fishes for salmon or steelhead on a fly understands that there's always the possibility of getting shut out. We weren't shut out but we were doing none too well, especially Tiger.

"One morning, Tiger and I were on a run with two guides—Sean McManmon, who is a member of the Irish Fly Fishing Team and a guide at the K Club in County Kildare, and a local ghillie named Paddy. Paddy was a slightly older gentleman and had one of the thickest Irish brogues that I've ever heard. It was barely comprehensible. Tiger and I had worked our way through most of the run, and breakfast time was coming around. Sean, Paddy, and Tiger decided to take a break and grab a sandwich. I reminded Tiger that the best way to catch a fish is to stay in the river and keep fishing, but they all retired to the bank. They were barely on shore when I hooked into a nice fish, about seven or eight pounds. I played it to hand as they went to the ghillie's hut for their snack. As they were coming back down to the river, I hooked into another fish. I played it for a while as they looked on, and it eventually came off. I went over to the bank, and I could see immediately that Tiger was getting a little worked up about his lack of success. I said to him, 'Don't worry, the fish are in here. Let's put you right in the middle of this run where I've been getting some takes. I'll stay with you and get you all fired up. When your confidence is up, you'll get a fish.'

"I stayed with Tiger in the river for a while to help him get in the swing of things. He was in a nice long run and it was just a matter of getting into a rhythm—cast, swing, step, cast, swing, step. After a time, I left Tiger to his own devices and joined Sean and Paddy up on the bank. It was a pleasure to watch Tiger cast. The mechanics of golf swing and a fly cast are pretty similar, and as you might expect Tiger's golf swing translates into an excellent casting form. Though a fish would roll out in the run every now and again, Tiger was having no luck. As he made his way downstream I could see that Tiger was beginning to rush his casts a bit, and I sensed he was getting frustrated again.

"As we watched Tiger cast through the bottom of the run, Paddy, who had been pretty quiet most of the morning, suddenly spoke. Apropos of nothing, he said, 'Boys, if those salmon only knew who was on the other end of that line, they'd be stackin' up to take that fly.'"

Mark O'Meara took up golf when he was thirteen and turned pro in 1980, shortly after graduating from Long Beach State University. Since turning pro, Mark has won more than a dozen PGA tourneys, including the AT&T Pebble Beach National Pro-Am (five times), the Master's (1998), and the British Open (1998). He is an avid and accomplished fly fisherman and fly tyer and recently teamed with PGA TOUR Design Services to build TPC of Valencia, California. Mark lives in the Orlando, Florida, area with his wife, Alicia, and children, Michelle and Shaun Robert.

BLACKWATER SALMON

Rising in the mountains east of Killarney, the River Blackwater flows through counties Cork and Waterford until it reaches the Irish Sea, seventy-five miles later. It has traditionally been one of Ireland's most prolific Atlantic salmon rivers, yielding between five thousand and six thousand salmon per annum. Like most European salmon rivers, much of the Blackwater is private, though there are ample beats available for lease. (The largest lessee is the Blackwater Lodge [www.ireland-salmon-fishing.net], which holds beats on fifteen miles of the river; the Careysville House [+353-58-54424], where Mark and Tiger fished, offers beats on one and three-quarters miles of prime water.) While Blackwater salmon (and Irish salmon in general) run a bit smaller than the fish that return to neighboring Scotland, the beauty of the rolling countryside of the valley, the welcoming charm of the villages that dot its banks—and the promise of a fresh Guinness at the local pub—more than make up for the absence of trophy specimens.

TALE 33

MOTHER KNOWS BEST

Many a young angler's first streamside adventure is led by a father, eager to school his progeny in the sportsman's traditions. For Leigh Perkins, however, the fly-fishing gene was passed along and nurtured in good part by the fairer sex, in the shape of his mother, Katherine.

OPPOSITE: Another day in Atlantic salmon paradise.

"When I was eleven I was kicked out of the Hawken School in Cleveland—near where my family lived—for playing hooky to go fishing in a nearby creek," Leigh recalled. "I was first sent to a boarding school in Connecticut called Forman. There were a few streams nearby, one of which held brook trout, and I was able to further refine my angling skills. When the teachers at Forman determined that I might make a reasonably productive citizen, I said good-bye to my little Connecticut streams and went on to a more challenging school in North Carolina called Asheville. While there was some good bass, bluegill, and crappie fishing on a lake near the Asheville School, it wasn't exactly a fisherman's paradise. Fortunately, my mother was there to help fill in the fishing voids.

"The best part of my continuing education in the outdoors during the Asheville years took place in the summers when I went on fishing trips up into Canada with my mother. Between my freshman and sophomore years, we went on my first Atlantic salmon trip to the Madeleine River on the north shore of the Gaspé Peninsula. We reached the camp by a long hike on a woods trails and slept in tents right on the river, which we could hear flowing past us in the dark. There was no refrigeration, so we dammed a little feeder stream to make a pool where we could keep whatever salmon we caught alive until it was time to go back. We had two pools on the river where we fished, one right in front of the camp and the other about seventy-five yards upstream. It was a wild, remote river and there were plenty of salmon in it, making their way upstream to spawn. I would climb trees and look down into the pools and watch them holding there so I could tell my mother where to place her fly.

"We were using the finest tackle that was available in those days: bamboo rods, silk lines, and gut leaders. It would all be considered hopelessly obsolete and primitive today. You had to be good to make it work, and even then it was tough. Mother was still learning, and I was an absolute novice. The first few salmon we managed to hook all broke off. But there was something so magnificent and powerful in the way those strong, silver fish ran and jumped that we didn't mind at first. Then we got a little desperate, since we wanted fish to eat. We finally managed to catch some, and I think it was then that I graduated from bass and bluegill to the great game fish that I have spent so much of the rest of my life fishing for all over the world.

"My mother and I made other trips for salmon while I was at the Asheville School, and we both got better and came to love the fishing more and more. We went to the legendary rivers in New Brunswick, the Restigouche and the Upsalquitch, and while salmon fishing was pretty much a man's sport back then, Mother's reputation as a sports lady—especially as a wing shot—had preceded her, so she got on to some of the best water at the best times of the season. Since I was her fishing buddy, I got to go with her.

"She was not much for the fixed routine of the camps, which called for a leisurely breakfast followed by a morning of fishing, then lunch and a little rest period, followed by some more fishing and then dinner. This schedule was considered sacrosanct, but Mother didn't care. She would get a guide to take her out early, and often she would catch a fish before breakfast. Soon everybody else in camp started following her example. The guides didn't much appreciate it, but it was a lesson to me. You take advantage of opportunities, especially when they are as rare and special as being on one of the world's great salmon rivers.

"When I was sixteen, on one of those trips to the Restigouche, I was using a sixteen-foot, two-handed rod made by Leonard—one of the Orvis company's strongest competitors in those days—and casting a big fly—a number two Green Highlander. I got a take from a very large salmon, and to this day I can see that fish coming out of the water with its hooked jaw wide open and its thick silver body hanging over the river. I managed to hold on and land the fish, which turned out to weigh thirty pounds. It was the thrill of my young life, and I think my mother took more pride in that fish than I did. I have never caught a larger salmon.

"Many years later, I was able to return my mother the favor. In July 1969 I took her to the most famous Atlantic salmon river in the world, the Alta, in Norway. It was a chance for me to pay her back, just a little, for all the memorable fishing trips she had taken me on. Not just anybody gets to fish the Alta, and those who do are willing to pay dearly for the privilege. But I was able to get on at a bargain price because of the Orvis travel business.

"The Alta is a big river, too big to wade, so you fish from a large canoe. At that time, the guides fished using a trawling method, with the guide rowing for control and slowly losing ground to the current, swinging the stern of the boat from one side to the other to position the angler, who doesn't even cast, really, just holds his rod and leaves some line in the water and lets the boat position the fly. Not my idea of a particularly interesting way to fish, and I got into trouble with the guides right away. They wanted us to use the fifteen- and sixteen-foot Norwegian two-handed rods, which were traditional. I said I would stick with my nine-and-a-half-foot Orvis impregnated-bamboo rods, which you cast with one hand. Since I was paying, that seemed my prerogative.

"Well, I missed three fish, two of which struck short of the fly, so it didn't have anything to do with the rod. But the autocratic ghillie took my rod away from me, gave me one of the long two-handed jobs, and said, 'Now you will fish with this rod.' I was furious and I said, 'No, I won't.' I wasn't too terribly surprised when my own mother went along with the guide. Soon after, I found myself being put ashore, almost as though by a mutinous crew. I knew exactly what was in Mother's mind. She had come a long way to catch a big Alta River salmon, and she knew how much that depended on the guide. If your guide doesn't like you, he can make damn sure you don't catch a fish. Mother figured that with me out of the boat, she'd go along with the guide and have a lot better chance at a fish. The injury to her own son's pride was a small price to pay.

"As it turned out, Mother did catch a fish that day, and I got very, very cold trying to fish that huge river without waders. I managed to catch three grilse, but the real accomplishment was that I managed not to drown myself.

"My regard for the ghillies was not exactly high, and I wasn't shy about letting it show. So Mother took me aside, just like I was ten years old, and told me to adjust my attitude or we wouldn't catch any fish. So much for being the big shot and the host.

"I never used the long Norwegian rods, but otherwise I did what I was told and it worked. We caught fish. None of ours was over twenty-two pounds, but one member of our party caught one that weighed forty-six pounds. When he flew back to Michigan, he carried the fish on his lap."

Leigh Perkins was CEO of the Orvis Company, Inc. from 1965 to 1992. He now devotes his efforts to a variety of conservation causes and divides his time among homes in Vermont, Florida, and Wyoming.

THE FUTURE OF ATLANTIC SALMON

Atlantic salmon have been swimming treacherous waters the past few decades. When Leigh and his mother, Katherine, first fished the rivers of New Brunswick and the Gaspé, fish were quite plentiful. Over the past twenty-five years, the number of returning fish has plummeted to a fraction of historic runs. While biologists and fisheries managers have been unable to pinpoint the reasons for these declines, likely factors include commercial fishing, reduced food availability at sea, degraded river habitats, and ecological problems linked to salmon farming. In recent years, some rays of hope are beginning to shine through the doom and gloom prognosis of the North American salmon's imminent extinction. In 2004 and 2005, some of the healthiest runs of fish in years have returned to the Miramichi and Restigouche. These returns would seem to indicate that some of the conservation efforts that have been undertaken to save Atlantic salmon—primarily, measures to curtail or reduce commercial fishing through various compensation and alternative employment opportunities—are starting to have a positive impact. Though just as it's a mystery as to why a salmon will one day pounce on a fly and the next day disdain it, no one knows for sure what most affects the well-being of a run of fish.

THE GREAT TROUT ROUND-UP

Generally speaking, fly anglers use that little point at the end of their fly called a hook to connect to their prey. These hooks come in myriad shapes and sizes—sweeping bends, sproat bends, round bends, long shanks, short shanks, steel, nickel, bronze, barbed, and barbless—just glance at a catalog of fly-tying materials to see what I mean! Most of us are more concerned with the nuances of the fly pattern we've affixed to our tippet than with the specifics of the hook that protrudes from the conglomeration of feathers, fur, or hair that we've selected for the moment. The bottom line is: we're able to feel that delirious pull of a sport fish, and, with a bit of luck, bring it to hand, thanks to that hook.

That is, unless you're able to work a little cowboy magic, like Perk Perkins did on not one occasion but two.

"I was fishing at dusk on the Lamoille River in northern Vermont," Perk began. "I was fishing to a pod of rising fish, but I could hear by the way the leader was going through the air over my head that it was badly fouled. There was not enough light left to change flies and I didn't have a penlight with me. I figured it was dark enough that the trout wouldn't notice, so I continued to cast. I landed my fly—and its accompanying bird's nest—in the midst of the fish and heard a rise about where my fly had landed. I struck and could feel the weight of the fish. He was on.

"Nothing felt at all out of the ordinary as I played the fish in. As I got him closer, I could make out this horrible snarl near the end of my line. The fish was there too, but I could clearly see the fly hanging six inches below the whole mess. When I brought the fish to hand, I realized what had happened. The fish had risen through the snarl to take the fly. In setting the hook, I'd closed the snarl like a noose and had lassoed the fish. I felt this was quite odd. It was even stranger when it happened a second time, some ten years later.

"I enjoy fishing still water and was out on a reservoir north of San Francisco with my good friends Christine and Michael Fong. It was a good time to be fishing the reservoir, as the water was turning over, sending lots of threadfin shad to the surface. The reservoir's rainbows were keying on them there. It was almost like fishing for bluefish or stripers in the salt, where you seek out balls of baitfish with the assumption that the bigger fish are working underneath and around them. We were cruising around the lake looking for rainbows crashing on bait, and then we'd cast into them.

"It didn't take long for us to come upon a ball of feeding fish. We were taking turns working the bait ball. Michael took a fish, and then Christine. When my turn came, I threw a streamer into the melee, made a few strips, and soon had a fish on. I was impressed with how aggressively the fish fought. When I got it to the boat, I was surprised to find a modest-size rainbow—though I could quickly see why it had fought so well. It was lassoed around the tail! The hook was nowhere close to the fish's mouth! Christine and Michael got quite a kick out of this. I thought at the time that it gave credence to the adage that goes, it's better to be lucky than to be good.

"It turned out that I wouldn't be fishing that reservoir much more in the future, as we soon left San Francisco for the East Coast. Before we departed, our friends threw us a fantastic going-away party. Everyone who attended was asked to bring a picket sign to the party. The sign that Mike brought read, 'Don't Go! Start the Fish-Lassoing Society with Me.'"

Perk Perkins has led Orvis as president and CEO since November 1992. He came to work for Orvis in 1977 and has held many positions in the company. Perk is an avid and accomplished fly fisherman, wing shooter, canoeist, cross-country skier, and bird-watcher. He dedicates considerable energy to conservation issues, and serves as vice chairman of the Nature Conservancy. He has led Orvis's support of conservation (5 percent of pretax profits) with the mantra, "If we are going to benefit from our natural resources, we must be willing to take action to protect them."

A SHORT HISTORY OF LEADERS

Leaders have been part of fly fishing from the very earliest days of the sport, and it can be assumed that anglers since the time of Izaak Walton have been occasionally finding their terminal gear in a bird's nest of profanity-laden disarray. The earliest leaders are believed to have been constructed from the strands of hair from a horse's tail (fly lines were made of greater concentrations of the same material). In the early 1700s, strands of silkworm gut were braided together to create leaders that were almost transparent. These were often referred to as "catgut" leaders; though no cats suffered in their construction, these gut leaders were extremely finicky and required moistening before each use, and great care in general. The first nylon leaders didn't appear until the early 1940s and were a decided advance over worm guts, providing greater strength, flexibility, and resistance to abrasion. Today, tapered leaders are the norm, where the leader begins with a heavier/wider diameter of nylon and diminishes as it reaches the end. In the past few years, fluorocarbon leaders (made of polyvinyliden fluoride) have gained some prominence, for they are believed to provide a higher strength-to-diameter ratio than traditional nylon leaders and are less visible in subsurface fishing situations.

TUNA FROM HELL

"Be careful what you ask for," the old saw runs, "because you just might get it." This was precisely Ross Purnell's experience as he satisfied a dream of catching a yellowfin tuna on a fly rod—an experience he never wishes to repeat again.

"My first and last adventure for yellowfin began in Venice, Louisiana. Venice is about as far out on the Mississippi Delta as you can go, and it exists to service the fourteen-hundred-odd oil rigs that rest out in the Gulf of Mexico. Helicopters and boats are taking off day and night, bringing out supplies. In addition to the folks who supply the oil rigs, there are a few fishing charters that operate out of Venice. One of the captains—Peace Marvel—specializes in targeting yellowfin on a fly. Some of the guys who fish yellowfin bring the tuna up through chumming. This fellow does it by motoring out to the rigs—way out—where the tuna are busting on baitfish. You see, flying fish are attracted to the light of the flares that burn on the oil rigs more or less all the time. The flying fish can soar along for a hundred yards or so at a time. When they set down, a bad fate awaits them—namely, the yellowfin, who are ready for dinner. The tuna really slam into them.

"Captain Marvel took us out a hundred and twenty miles off the coast of Venice, to a rig called Mars. Considering that we were in a twenty-foot boat, the trip out to the rig was an experience in itself. The Mars rig is quite a facility. Almost two hundred people live and work there. The flare itself from the burning oil soars twelve stories high. You could see it miles and miles away. It's surreal, like something out of a Hieronymus Bosch painting of Hades. We left Venice around four in the afternoon and showed up at the rig around seven P.M., with plans to fish all night. Just as the captain promised, flying fish were skittering across the surface, and we could make out the tuna waiting below them. The captain cut the engine a half mile above the rigs and we floated down to them. The fishing involved long casts with poppers and streamers, which we'd strip back to the boat. The first fish I attracted took a 7/0 popper. It came up like a Polaris missile and crashed down on the fly. It wasn't on for long but I got a sense of what lay ahead.

"I switched over to a monster Clouser Minnow with the biggest dumbbell eyes I'd ever seen and cast over near one of the pylons of the rig, where more tuna were busting on flying

OPPOSITE:
A school of yellowfin tuna await the chance to torment an angler like Ross Purnell.

TALE 36

fish. I could feel the heat from the flares as I stripped the fly in, and then boom! a tuna took it, and in the first run took four hundred yards of line, mostly straight down—we were in three thousand feet of water. It was about one-forty-five A.M. I'd looked forward to this moment for six months, but within half an hour I was begging the captain to let me break the fish off. To bring the tuna up, you have to dead lift it from the bottom. Tarpon twice the size are a pushover! Fighting this fish was killing my back. When I hooked it, Captain Marvel said it would take two and a half or three hours to bring it in. When I asked again to break it off, the captain said, 'You break this fish off, I'm going to call you every week to tell you what a wimp you are!' I've never not wanted to catch a fish so badly. When I hooked the fish, some guys on the rig came out to watch. By the time we got it in, we were five or six miles away. It was just an hour later. My back was still aching five days later.

"Yellowfin tuna are interesting creatures. They have huge eyes, and when we had this fish up at the boat I really had the feeling that the fish was looking at me. Their eyes make them seem more like a mammal than any other fish I've caught. In this respect, this quest felt like big-game hunting. My fish was sixty-five pounds—sixty-five pounds of the best sushi I've ever had in my life."

Ross Purnell is editorial director at *Fly Fisherman* magazine in Harrisburg, Pennsylvania. He was born in Calgary, Alberta, and grew up fishing the famed Bow River, eventually becoming a full-time guide and owner of the Bow River Company. A graduate of the University of Calgary and Mount Royal College (journalism), he worked in the newspaper business as a reporter and editor before landing a job with *Fly Fisherman* as the content director of its Web site in Fort Collins, Colorado.

TUNA OFF THE RIGS

Pound for pound, yellowfin tuna (*Thunnus albacares*) are among the strongest fish in the sea. They're easily identified by their body shape and namesake fins. Off the coast of Louisiana, yellowfin average about seventy pounds, with some fish reaching 200 pounds. The myriad oil platforms that rest south of Venice form an artificial reef of sorts that attracts baitfish and, in turn, predators. These deeper rigs attract larger pelagic species, including blackfin, skipjack, and yellowfin tuna. The Mars platform, mentioned in Ross's story, is a mammoth structure, 36,500 tons and the size of a city block. It rests in water of nearly three thousand feet and, incidentally, was featured in the movie *Armageddon*.

METEORS, KAMCHATKA-STYLE

For anglers who've made the trek, the Kamchatka peninsula of far eastern Russia offers an unforgettable experience. According to the Wild Salmon Center, the thousand-mile-long peninsula hosts the greatest diversity of salmonid fish on earth, including five species of Pacific salmon, kunzha (white spotted char), lenok, steelhead, and resident rainbow trout. Since Wild Salmon Center and its sister organization, Wild Salmon River Expeditions, began leading ecotrips to the region to assist scientists through "nonfatal" capture of fish (namely, fly fishing), many anglers have had the thrill of catching the rainbow of their life-time . . . again and again! This, combined with largely unspoiled scenery that includes active volcanoes, very large brown bears, and Steller's sea eagles, makes for a fishing trip that's out of the ordinary, to say the least. The sense that you are in a very special and very Russian place extends beyond the fine fishing and omnipresent vodka. For Tim Purvis, the ambience of Kamchatka manifested itself in a rare sky show one evening.

"I was with a group of anglers fishing the Sedanka, which is essentially a very long spring creek, running somewhere in the vicinity of ninety miles. We were staying at the Middle Camp on the river and the fishing had been quite good. We were taking many fish on dries. Most of the fish were eighteen inches, but more than a few reached twenty-three inches. We took even larger fish when we'd swing a mouse pattern across the surface—very explosive fishing, when it's on. The camps on the Sedanka are quite comfortable. Guests sleep in yurts, with a dining room consisting of two old containers that have been joined together, and with windows and doors cut into the sides.

"After dinner on this one evening, a group of us gathered around the firepit to play Mandavoshka—a Russian dice game that translates roughly into 'crabs' and has its roots in Russian prisons. Four of the guests had turned in to read. The dice players were head guide Mike Van Wormer, another guest named Don Hobbs, the camp's translator, Natasha, and young Alexei, the camp brigadier. The camp's bear dog—named Bear Dog—was also there. A fire was going in the pit and we were passing a bottle of vodka around. Though the sun had set, there was a dusky glow on the horizon. Above the glow was a large orange star, very vibrant, with a certain aura about it. Natasha pointed and said, 'That's Jupiter.' 'Ah, Jupiter!'

a few of us muttered. 'Wonderful!' After a few more rolls of the dice and a few more shots of vodka, Don looked up at the horizon and pointed out that Jupiter had moved. 'Ah,' we surmised. 'Satellite!'

"We got back to our game, checking the sky occasionally to track the progress of the satellite. It had moved quite a way from the horizon and was taking a decidedly upward trajectory. At some point, it had our collective attention. The satellite got brighter and brighter, and then shot over our heads, sprouting new colors as it flew above us. Then little parcels of the satellite started bursting off it in all kinds of colors. It's not a satellite, we decided. It's a meteor shower! The idea of a meteor shower captured our imaginations and we were hooting and hollering. Vapors were drifting off the fragments that had separated from the larger meteors. We were wishing that we had the right sort of camera to capture this great natural phenomenon on film. Someone suggested that we could get a better view from a bluff above camp, and we left our dice and vodka and ran up to the top of the bluff. As we ran up there we heard a series of dull thuds. Then it was gone.

"At the top of the bluff, behind the camp kitchen, our Russian guides were having a smoke. We were excited at what we'd witnessed, and Sasha, one of the guides, sensed our agitation. Sasha's English was better than that of the other guides, and he said, 'Don't worry. Just missile.' Sasha had served as a sniper in the Russian military in the occupation of Chechnya and knew a bit about the way things worked. With Natasha's help, he went on to explain that had we counted, we would've heard sixteen thuds—one for each warhead that was discharged from the missile. The missiles are fired every few years from the Kola Peninsula in far western Russia, which is thirteen time zones away. A few of the other guides confirmed that they'd seen the missiles before. It didn't faze them in the least.

"The next hour or so was spent wedged in the kitchen with everyone jabbering in half-English, half-Russian, toasting friendships with the ubiquitous vodka and agreeing on the folly of governments. There's nothing like a nuclear attack to bring people together!"

Tim Purvis works for John Eustice & Associates, a leading fly-fishing travel company based in Portland, Oregon. His piscatorial travels have taken him to Patagonia, Iceland, British Columbia, the Kola Peninsula, and Kamchatka, as well as through the western United States. A native of northern England, Tim now lives in Troutdale, Oregon, with his wife, Ellen, and daughter, Lucy.

RAINBOWS OF KAMCHATKA

The native rainbows of Kamchatka—*mikizha*, in Russian—are large and willing. On some systems, the fish average 20 to 22 inches; on others, the average size is 24 inches and even greater! To date, outfitters have focused their efforts on the Zhupanova, Sedanka, and Kal-gauch rivers. Though the fish in these systems have become slightly more wary, the good news is that new rivers are being opened up to fishing each year. A few outfitters offer "adventure floats" where you'll have chance to be among the very first—if not *the* first—angler to fish a river! Kamchatka offers such bountiful fishing opportunities in part because it was closed to outside development until the breakup of the Soviet Union in 1990. The Wild Salmon Center, among other conservation organizations, is working diligently to curb the enthusiasm of various extraction industries so that key watersheds in Kamchatka can be set aside in perpetuity. It's a worthwhile effort: after all, it's estimated that a quarter of the world's Pacific salmon return to natal rivers in Kamchatka.

TALE 37

SALMON BY PULLEY

Perhaps a guide's greatest fear is that a client will hinge the relative success of a fishing excursion on the number and/or size of fish that are brought to hand. There are so many other things to appreciate on a fishing trip, be it the beauty of the natural surroundings, chance encounters with other nonfinned fauna, new knowledge one may gain from the guide's experience, and the camaraderie one might enjoy with a fishing partner. All of these elements are essential to a successful trip . . . but at the end of the day, no matter how well these criteria have been met, it's still nice to have caught a few fish, the bigger the better.

When the five species of salmon are running in Alaska, catching fish is generally not a problem. Sometimes the multitudes of fish and the lingering presence of anglers past makes for some interesting catching methods, as Tim Rajeff once discovered.

"Back in 1986 I was doing a lot of guiding, and I decided I wanted to take a break from the Lower Forty-eight," Tim began. "A few good friends of mine—Brian O'Keefe and Jan Krieger—had worked in Alaska at a place called the King Salmon Lodge on the Naknek River, and I accepted a gig there. Jan was my best friend at the time and I was excited for the opportunity to work with him. I was also excited at the prospect of doing lots of fly-outs to some remote waters. Unfortunately Jan bailed out and decided to continue his sixteen-month surf safari. Oh well—Alaska would be an incredible experience even if Jan couldn't make it.

"Since my particular area of fly-fishing expertise has always been casting, I'm a fairly good teacher, and this made me a natural for working with the beginners. It was satisfying to make the connection with newcomers to the sport. After giving them the rudiments of casting, we'd go after grayling with dry flies, Dolly Varden, and char. We weren't hunting the big rainbows that I would've fished for on my own, but after a while I didn't care. By the Fourth of July, I had learned the Naknek and Brooks rivers well enough to put my sports on fish pretty regularly. This was a wonderful time to be in Alaska. Life is exploding in early July. There are a zillion birds, sockeye salmon are thick, and bears are everywhere.

"One day around this time, I had a father and his twelve-year-old whom I took fishing. The dad was hoping to catch rainbows. The son, Jamie, was happy catching sockeyes and watching the bears. To make things a bit easier for Jamie, I'd set him up with a spinning rod

OPPOSITE:
When the sockeyes are thick in the rivers of the Bristol Bay region of Alaska, it's hard not to catch them.

TALE 38

with a fly, split shot, and a bobber. Both father and son had had a number of fish, the weather was fabulous—our day was pretty much complete. We were just about finished when we came to a spot on the river where there was a snag on the far bank. The father was fishing upstream, nymphing for rainbows. I suspected that there might be a bigger sockeye below the snag and asked Jamie to cast about thirty feet out. There was a dark cloud of fish—hundreds of them—in an area of water the size of a modest bedroom, just in front of the snag. I told Jamie I'd be back and went upstream to see if I could help his dad get into some fish. I'd taken about twenty steps when I heard Jamie hollering. I turned around. After many years of guiding, you have an instinctual sense of when something is wrong—when a client has hooked a species you wouldn't expect to find where you're fishing, when a fish is especially big, especially small, or foul-hooked. When I looked back and saw the angle of the line vis-à-vis where the fish was jumping, I knew something was weird. But Jamie was having a ball, and his dad was cheering him on. Everything was good.

"As I ran back downstream the fish kept jumping like crazy. It must have jumped five times in twenty seconds. As I got closer, I saw what was wrong: someone had gotten their line stuck in the snag, about thirty feet of monofilament with a fly dangling off the end. One of the fish from the pod had grabbed the dangling fly just as Jamie's line had floated over. His fly had hooked the monofilament that was attached to the snag on one end and the fish on the other, and it was sliding up and down the line. Jamie started backing up on the bank, and both lines held, so the fish was easing closer and closer to shore. When the salmon's body touched the gravel it went absolutely berserk. We were treated to an acrobatic show that would put Cirque du Soleil to shame! The sockeye flipped over, did three cartwheels, then tail-walked across the water, toward the shore. As the fish tail-walked, the line broke free of the snag. Jamie realized that the fish was no longer on the rod, screamed, and threw the rod down. In the meantime, his dad had worked his way downstream to take in the acrobatic show and the fish was now flopping on the gravel. Jamie tried to scoop the fish up, but each time he missed it and bumped it closer to the river. I grabbed the end of the line from the snag just as the fish hit the water. It was only four inches deep, but that was enough to get its motor going. I had maybe five feet of line between me and the fish. We're all screaming now, splashing around the shallows chasing the fish, which was rooster-tailing, kicking water all over us. The line started burning out of my hand. When the fish reached eighteen inches of water, it began jumping again, and it finally broke the line.

"As the fish disappeared, Jamie and I looked at each other. I was worried that he was going to be bummed out that this fish had gotten away, but instead he began laughing and gave me half a dozen high fives. We were soaking wet and giggling. The smile on Jamie's face as he turned to ask his dad if he saw the little acrobatics show was unforgettable.

"I'm sure that Jamie, who must be grown up now, remembers that fish that got away much more clearly than the dozens of fish he hooked and landed."

Tim Rajeff is the founder of Rajeff Sports (www.rajeffsports.com) in Vancouver, Washington, a distributor of fly-fishing products. Growing up a few blocks from the famous Golden Gate Angling and Casting Club, he began fly-casting at a very young age. Tim and his brother Steve both progressed to become some of the most highly regarded flycasters in the world. Among Tim's achievements are a gold medal from the World Casting Games in single-hand fly distance and a national first place in 1984 for the combined accuracy and distance championship. Most recently Tim and Steve took the top spot for OLN's televised Fly Fishing Masters, a national fly-fishing competition that tested both fishing and casting skills. Aside from competition, Tim has guided in Alaska, built and managed a camp on the Ponoi in Russia with his soul mate, Katherine Hart, and taught countless schools, clinics, and private classes worldwide. He currently presides on the FFF's board of governors and serves as a host on *LL Bean Guide to the Outdoors*, which is featured on the Outdoor Life Network.

SATED ON SOCKEYES

Sockeye salmon (*Oncorhynchus nerka*) are generally not the primary reason that anglers travel to Alaska, though they provide good sport on a 6- or 7-weight rod and can save a guide's day when more prized species are not cooperating. The number of fish that return to the Bristol Bay region each summer is mind-boggling; ten to thirty million fish are harvested each year, providing one of Alaska's most important commercial fisheries. Sockeye, which generally run 4 to 8 pounds, favor river systems with lakes. When fish are moving toward their spawning grounds, they're disinterested in taking a fly. However, when they pause to rest, they can be enticed to strike, especially if the fly is presented directly in front of them. Once hooked, sockeye are more inclined than pink, chum, or chinook salmon to jump and cartwheel. Odds are very good that if you're able to hook one, you'll be able to hook twenty.

LUCK OF THE IRISH

Learning a new river is at once thrilling and frightening for most guides. While understanding the nuances of a fishery is at the heart of the fishing experience, the expectation of putting clients on fish—often, after a very brief apprenticeship—comes with no small amount of pressure. The challenges of learning a new river are significantly heightened when that river is the North Umpqua, and you are from out of state, as Patty Reilly can attest.

"I was invited to guide for steelhead on the North Umpqua River in 1990 when I met the owner of the Steamboat Inn, Jim Van Loan, on the Rio Chimehuin in Argentina," Patty began. "I had guided the northern Patagonia trout rivers for many Southern Hemisphere summers while our home waters in the Rockies were shrouded in snow and below-zero temperatures. In our summers I had been guiding anglers for trout for over a decade in the Rocky Mountain states. Already the steelhead mystique and lure of fishing for anadromous fish had piqued my curiosity. I was intrigued by the idea of fishing for steelhead, and Jim's invitation greatly appealed to me. Plus, there was the attraction of a new river. An invitation to learn the North Umpqua with Steamboat's head guide as my teacher, and the promise of a decent place to rent, with the assurance that a paying job—in a nonguiding capacity—at Steamboat awaited if I couldn't get enough clients to get by—being low guide on the totem pole—was an opportunity I felt I could not let slip by. With all that in mind, that spring I signed off on my Montana summer guiding job for the upcoming season, packed up my 1974 Jeep Cherokee, and headed west.

"Needless to say, in the months between my return to home base in Wyoming from Argentina and my departure for Oregon, I was a bit anxious. I was to reside and guide in a state I had never even visited before, and the North Umpqua had a reputation for being one of the most difficult steelhead rivers to learn. You had to 'pay your dues' to catch fish, let alone to guide other anglers. On the positive side, it was said to be a gorgeous place, and when folks familiar with it spoke of the Umpqua, they seemed to hold it in awe.

"At this point in my life I had guided long enough to not worry about being a female guide, and the sometimes tenuous territory you enter when guiding new rivers. Where I had guided in the Rockies and Argentina my peers were always supportive and I was accepted by them, the outfits I represented, and my anglers. I had reason to believe that any gender biases had already largely been dealt with on the Umpqua, as the inn already employed a female guide named Pat Lee, now acting manager of the inn. What I was to learn later was that out-of-staters were a way larger issue and blatantly frowned upon. Nor did I understand just what a close-knit community the world of steelheaders was, especially on this river. Some might refer to them as an elitist group of fishing snobs, but in the seasons to follow I found a few among this group delightful and still call them friends.

"I arrived in June, well before the start of the summer steelhead run. My first days of exploring the Umpqua were a dichotomy in motion. On the one hand, it was one of the most beautiful rivers I had ever seen anywhere in the world. On the other hand, I was terrified by the logging trucks that zoomed up and down Highway 138, which parallels the river. Either they were loaded to the hilt with mammoth trunks heading west toward Roseburg or roaring upriver en route to the harvesting areas. Knowing the pull-outs that dot the thirty-two miles of Fly Fishing Only water was a major factor in learning to guide this river, as almost every pull-out indicated a fishable run or pool. You took your life in your hands trying to find a pull-out to access the river. The sound of airbrakes squealing, as angry logging-truck drivers showed their contempt for the conservationist stance the Steamboat Inn had taken, was a far cry from the guiding I had done in the parks of Grand Teton and Yellowstone. It was not uncommon to see bumper stickers urging 'Eat More Spotted Owls.'

"After a few days of scouting and dodging logging trucks, I had the privilege to meet my teacher, one of the main reasons I was willing to take a gamble and head west. His name was Tony Wratney, and he had been guiding on the river for some years, though still fairly young in age. Tony had the reputation as being a punk at that time, as I was to later learn. But Tony knew the river as well as anyone. Now, and not by choice, he was given the annoying task of having to train someone else to fish it—and potentially give away his secrets as well. He was not pleased but he did it, and at first he was surprisingly gracious. When I didn't have fishing sessions with Tony, I was tromping about by myself trying to learn this amazing river.

"My first two weeks were unforgettable . . . unforgettably bad. The river is infamous for its slippery basalt ledges, and I fell into the river every single day of those two weeks. I had never been so humbled in my life. Things improved when I took some sound advice to give up cleated sole bottoms and go for corkers—suddenly I could stay upright in the Camp Water! Once I figured out how to stand, I needed to get a handle on reconciling the clarity of the water to the depth. I went in over my waders on mere 'walk ins' as I stumbled on that learning curve. Then came the poison oak on my elbows and—when I went from waders to wet wading—onto the legs. There were also the bruises from navigating the treacherously rough rocks on the sides of the river left from the blasting of the highway. The game was to look for worn trails down to the rocks that held corker marks, as casting from these spots had likely produced fish before. Sometimes they did, but being part contortionist helped in some of the descents to these coveted locations.

"Not long after my apprenticeship had begun, I learned that Tony and Jim Van Loan had some strong disagreements, perhaps on the guiding program at the inn. Consequently, Jim had threatened to designate me, the newcomer, as head guide and first on the roster for guiding clients. I never completely understood the dynamics of the situation or its history. I do know that I expressed my concern to Jim, along the lines of, 'It is insane to make me head guide, especially as I've never even caught a steelhead!' Suffice it to say that shortly after hearing mutterings of these arrangements, Tony no longer took me fishing. Any meaningful communication other than mere pleasantries with the other guides working out of the inn also ended.

"I continued to spend my days learning the river, fishing and not catching. When I wasn't fishing, I was reading every book I could find on steelhead fly-fishing techniques. The Umpqua was a special river and this new species of fish was fascinating, but my anxiety about the guiding season remained . . . and it didn't get better when I learned that to catch one steelhead a day was considered great. I thought that perhaps I'd made a huge mistake relocating myself to Oregon from the trout-laden rivers of the Rockies. I had entered what many call the graduate school of fly fishing. I wasn't sure I could cut it.

"On July eighth I reached my first milestone, hooking and landing my first steelhead while fishing with Stephen Cary. I'd passed some kind of threshold. Now for the task of guiding.

"As July progressed, the run of fish strengthened and Steamboat began receiving anglers. Tony and the fellows were keeping quite busy, but I declined to guide for another few weeks and passed over any offered trips. I still had zero confidence, but with more time on the water my fishing improved. I spent a lot of time learning the lower river and befriended Joe Howell who to this day I admire and consider a mentor. His encouragement and coaching made a great difference to my guiding. Fortunately, there were good returns of fish that summer, which made my odds a bit better. I stayed in the lower section of the fly water, and more often than not avoided the inn and the constant inquiries for a personal daily fishing report.

"Finally the day came when I had to guide as all the other guides were busy. The night before my first trip I was grease-line fishing the Tree Pool with my fly barely subsurface. A good-size steelhead came up and grabbed my fly, showing his whole body. In my excitement, I reverted to my ingrained trout-fishing habits. Instead of letting that fish take the fly and return to its lie, I instinctively lifted the rod to set the hook, stung the fish, and had the fly and line come back, draping my body and then landing in a pile at my feet. I marked the lie in my memory and returned downriver to my rented abode, disillusioned and mildly desperate.

"The next morning I arrived at Steamboat at five-fifteen A.M. to meet my guest for the day. His name was Bob Lindeman and he told me he had never fished for steelhead before on a fly and had not done much fly fishing, period. We headed to the Tree Pool. Because Bob was new to this game, I put on a dry fly so he could see it. We got in the swing of casting and following the fly in the early light of morning as we worked our way down the run. We reached the spot where I'd stung the fish the previous evening and, sure enough, my fish came up and latched on to Bob's dry fly. Bob was so stunned that he was a bit slow to react and that steelhead hooked itself. Then it was off to the races! Bob fought the fish in perfect fashion and we soon landed and admired it. I was thrilled, and I know for a fact more surprised and delighted than Bob! I looked at my watch and it was six-ten A.M. His first steelhead, and caught on a dry fly—my first guided trip! It had to be the luck of the Irish on my side, and on that day my infatuation with the North Umpqua truly began. In a lifetime of fishing, that steelhead will never be forgotten!

"By the end of that summer I was accepted by the guides, though Tony later told me that due to the blowup with Jim, he and his cohorts had made a pact not to show me the river. Rude as it was, I could understand their thinking, but by then it was all water under the bridge and we became friends and fishing buddies, and remained that way.

"I guided on the North Umpqua for several more seasons, and Jim Van Loan and the extended Steamboat family could not have been kinder. Before I left my guiding days on the North Umpqua, my old Cherokee proudly wore those Oregon plates!"

Patty Reilly has been a professional fishing guide, fly-fishing instructor, and manager of fishing operations for the past twenty-six years. She has guided and fished in a multitude of locations around the globe and been featured in a variety of magazines and books on fishing. She now owns and operates GuidedConnections (www.guidedconnections.com) from

TALE 39

Jackson Hole, Wyoming. Patty and her company arrange customized fly-fishing, birding, and riding trips to many great locations, with a special focus on Patagonian Argentina and Chile.

THE NORTH UMPQUA

Since the river came to broad notoriety from the dispatches of western novelist Zane Grey in the twenties and thirties, the North Umpqua has held a powerful attraction for steelheaders around the world. Perhaps it's the beauty of the North Umpqua's Cascades foothill setting. Perhaps it's the tremendous variety of habitat, ranging from long runs to pools, pocket water, and everything in between. And perhaps it's the challenge. Unofficial riverkeeper Frank Moore has called the North Umpqua a "finishing school for steelhead fly fishers. If you think you're good and want to improve, you can do so here on one of the most beautiful rivers around." Indeed, skating a Muddler Minnow over one of the North Umpqua's fabled pools is a rite of passage for fly fishers in search of steelhead. If a fish should rise and bump the fly with its nose—or take the fly in a tremendous boil—so much the better!

ONE FOR THIRTY-THREE

Ed Rice is a fly fisherman's fly fisherman. Over thirty-plus years, he has helped pioneer many fisheries, and through a combination of knowledge, inventiveness, and plain perseverance he has shown himself quite capable of catching fish on a fly when others shake their heads and give up. Yet like many gifted anglers, he's loath to talk up his accomplishments.

It should be heartening for the rest of us to learn that even an angler of Ed's prowess can from time to time encounter a challenge that takes a bit of practice to overcome.

"It was in the 1970s, and I was operating International Sportsmen's Expos," Ed began. "I had the chance to invite a lot of interesting anglers to present at the shows we held. I had heard about a fellow named Billy Pate and his experiences going after billfish with a fly rod. I asked him to come to the show. We had a chance to chat and his stories about billfish were intriguing. My first experience with billfish was in Costa Rica, going after sailfish. It was a little different than I expected. I thought it would take all day to land a hundred-pound sailfish. Instead, it took all of twenty minutes.

"At that point in time, not many people had gone after marlin on the fly. I had fished for them with conventional tackle and knew that they'd account for themselves a bit differently than the sailfish. I wanted to try it. For me, living on the West Coast, striped marlin were the closest marlin species available, and Cabo San Lucas—on Baja California—was the closest venue to pursue them. I booked five days down there with a skipper named Didier Van Der Becken. He had a twenty-one-foot center-console boat and was set up for teasing fish in—the accepted method of fly fishing for billfish. When we got out on the water, there were huge schools of bait everywhere. The marlin were there too. Some of the bait balls were box car–sized to begin with—there were as many as twenty marlin attacking them! You could see the fish right up on the surface; they were glowing, lit up like neon in the excitement of their feeding. By the time the fish had been through the bait balls, they were the size of a refrigerator.

"We tried the teaser technique for a while, but it wasn't working. Then we decided to try casting into the bait ball. I had a fifteen-weight Sage rod and a SeaMaster tarpon reel. We killed the boat and drifted up to the one of the bait balls. I chose a fish and cast to it. As

I stripped in, two marlin were on the fly instantly. The fish on the right engulfed it. In my excitement, it looked like it was a thousand pounds. It was probably more like a hundred. I set the hook and the fish was in the air right away. It greyhounded, skipping across the surface like a stone. It didn't flop when it jumped, it kept on jumping, nothing like the sailfish I had caught.

"Forty-five minutes later, we had the fish next to the boat, on its side—all ready to bring in. I yelled 'Gaff it!' to the mate but soon realized there was no gaff on the boat. Then I yelled, 'Bill it!' The mate didn't seem to understand. I tried to bill it myself but couldn't quite get hold of the fish while keeping a hold on the rod. Didier couldn't help, as he was keeping the boat steady. The mate tried to grab the front of the bill and soon let go. To be landed, marlin need to be grabbed toward the bottom of their bill. The fish went out ten feet from the boat but came back in again. Then the mate grabbed the leader. I cried, 'No toque—Don't touch!' It was too late, and the tippet popped. One striped marlin lost.

"I should've been crestfallen. But when I looked up, there were big flocks of feeding birds as far as I could see. That meant many big balls of baitfish . . . and many more marlin. This certainly wouldn't be my last opportunity to land a striped marlin.

"Our experience with the first fish seemed to set the tone for the week—one fish after another hooked, fought, and lost. Shortly after losing the first fish, I hooked another, got it to the boat, and we couldn't bill it. It was like a replay of the loss of the first fish. As the next five days elapsed, I lost fish in almost every conceivable way. Several times, I had other charter boats run over our line while I was playing the marlin in—either they didn't understand how the fly line operated—it was still very new to fly fish for billfish then—or they just didn't care. It was frustrating, to say the least, to have someone run over the line after battling a fish for forty-five minutes. A few times, Didier accidentally ran over my line when he misinterpreted my hand signal. The first time this happened, we were seconds away from landing a fish in the back of the boat. I signaled to slow down and he thought I meant back up! The second time, we were trying to gaff a fish in front. I put my hand up to signal 'Stop,' and he thought I wanted him to go forward. Another fish gone. I can't really fault him, as we were blocking his view of what was going on. All in all, we lost thirty-two fish over the course of five days. Not a single marlin in the boat.

"You get pretty worn out fighting striped marlin after striped marlin. For nearly five days, I'd played fish after fish, almost nonstop. I had bruises all over from bouncing around the boat and my hands were cut to shreds from maneuvering the line and trying to land the fish.

OPPOSITE:
Taking a billfish will inevitably change the way you think about fly fishing.

TALE 40

By the fifth afternoon I had one leader left. I'd tied five the night before, but the first four were shot. I rigged up the last leader—sixteen-pound test with a hundred-pound shock tippet—and promptly hooked into the biggest fish of the trip. It was one hundred fifty, maybe two hundred pounds. All hell broke loose with that fish. It sounded and I couldn't get it up. We followed it for miles. We'd shut the motor off and let the fish run, hoping to tire it out. It would almost spool me, and we'd have to give chase again. After an hour of this it simply spit the hook. Just like that. As I reeled the line in I felt a good take. It turned out to be a dorado, about thirty pounds. Finally, we got a fish to the boat. A nice consolation prize, but not what we were looking for.

"At this point I was heartbroken. I'd hooked a total of fifty fish, hooked and played thirty-two of them, and had nothing to show for it. My tippet was shot and it was time to go home. As we motored in, another huge pod of fish presented itself. 'I have no more tippet,' I told Didier. He said, 'I have some.' He rummaged around under the gunwale and pulled out a spool of monofilament. I grabbed it and gave a good tug. It wasn't very strong but it was the only game in town. I wrapped it on my leader. I was fresh out of billfish flies. The best I could do was a 3/0 Lefty's Deceiver. I tied it on and threw it out into the melee and started stripping in. One fish was right on it. He followed it to within ten feet of the boat, then turned with the fly. I lifted the rod slowly to snug the fly down the bill for a good hookup, then struck. The fish jumped countless times. It was probably two hundred and fifty yards away before it stopped jumping. It seemed to have traveled the entire distance on the surface. In the course of losing thirty-two fish I'd learned that the best way to get the fish to the boat was to keep them jumping and moving, let them tire out. So that's what I did. I brought it up slowly but surely. About sixty feet from the boat, it half-jumped, but I could tell it was exhausted. When I had it at the boat the mate gaffed it—but he gaffed it right in the belly! The fish fell off but didn't break the tippet. We finally gaffed it properly and hoisted it into the boat. It was ninety-eight pounds. The tippet I'd used from Didier's bag was later tested at six pounds, nine ounces. It would've been a world record except the tippet diameter was too large."

Ed Rice grew up outside of Chico, California, with a passion for fishing and hunting. By the time he was in his twenties, he had spent every dime he could scrape together to explore the world, with fly rod in hand. In the mid-1970s he founded International Sportsmen's Expositions (ISE) in Eugene, Oregon, growing the company to a base of 2,000 exhibitors and seven events in five different states before selling the business and retiring in the late 1990s. Ed has helped pioneer many exotic destinations, new species, and new techniques, including long-range, blue-water fly fishing. His adventures were frequently profiled at various ISE events. Ed has visited forty countries on six continents and has caught 237 species of fish on a fly rod, more than anybody in the world.

STRIPED MARLIN OFF CABO SAN LUCAS

Cabo San Lucas lies at the tip of Baja California, where the Sea of Cortez and the Pacific commingle. A constant source of bait—squid, shrimp, and forage fish—attracts throngs of sport fish to these waters. Roosterfish, dorado, tuna, and wahoo are all present, and blue and blue-and-black marlin make regular appearances. Many consider Cabo the striped marlin capital of the world. Fish range from 50 to 300 pounds, averaging around 125 pounds. Although fish are present year-round in the waters off Cabo, late fall/early winter is considered the very best time; it was December when Ed encountered the large pods of fish working the bait balls. Most outfitters use the "bait and switch" method, teasing the marlin close to the boat with a hookless plug so that the fly angler can have a shot at glory.

A.M. WHITEOUT

A good fishing buddy is an invaluable commodity. It's someone who can amuse and enlighten you on the long drives (or flights!) to the next destination. It's someone who can (you hope) whip up a great camp meal, knows how you like your coffee, and is willing to help you drown your sorrows after a bad day on the water. In best-case scenarios, it's someone who enjoys the same fishing style that you embrace—or at least is willing to occasionally indulge your big-fish-only/dry-fly-even-if-there's-nothing-happening whims.

OPPOSITE: An angler battles a Lahontan cutthroat on Mann Lake, with majestic Steens Mountain due west.

When you find a good fishing buddy, you want to hold on to him or her. But when an unseasonable snowstorm blows in, keeping track of your buddy can become a tricky proposition, as Don Roberts explains.

"I had taken my teaching degree at Washington State University in Walla Walla and was trying to decide where I'd launch my educational career," Don began. "This was in the early seventies, when there were actually jobs available for teachers, and recruiters even came on campus to conduct interviews! One of the schools seeking new blood was Grant Union High School from John Day, Oregon. I decided to speak to them, as I was somewhat familiar with the area and knew there was some decent fishing in the region. My first interview was with the school superintendent for the region, a very conservative-looking fellow. At that time I had a beard and longer hair—I was a bit of a hippie, I suppose. The first question the superintendent asked me was, 'How long have you had your beard?' My somewhat smart-ass response was, 'Up to six inches.' There was a pause and then I said, 'This interview is over, isn't it?' He nodded.

"In the next room down the hall, the principal of Grant Union was waiting for me. He had his feet up on his desk and a markedly different air about him. Our exchange went something like this:

'Are you religious?'
'No.'
'Do you like to fish?'
'Yes.'
'You're hired.'

"I later learned that the principal—Charlie Dannen—was looking for a fishing partner to join him on Sundays. Given my non-churchgoing proclivities, I fit the bill.

"Charlie and I went on to become good friends. He was not much of a fly fisherman. He actually preferred using bait—or, more accurately, he preferred propping up a rod by the lake and taking in the surroundings. But no matter. He was good company in the car and around the campfire and was patient while I hustled up and down the streams we visited in eastern Oregon. As a principal, Charlie was pretty conventional, but he was slightly eccentric in his outlook on life. He liked people who were open to new ideas and able to entertain conflicting viewpoints. He also enjoyed stirring the pot with an occasional outlandish remark. This didn't always play well in John Day, which is a pretty conservative town. I recall one occasion when Charlie was at a football game, which is a big social event in those parts. Apropos of nothing, in the midst of a large group of folks, he said, 'Any town that can't support a whorehouse doesn't deserve a school.' This offhand remark had the makings of a major scandal in John Day, and the school board moved to have Charlie fired. He went before the board and wouldn't back down a bit. It turned out that Charlie's other fishing partner was a local attorney, who of course came to Charlie's defense. He encouraged the school board to fire the principal. 'You go ahead,' he said. 'I know the First Amendment, and this will make a fantastic case that will really put me on the map.' The school board backed down.

"One place we especially enjoyed visiting was Steens Mountain, out in southeastern Oregon. It's a rugged, wild, isolated place—a real bit of the old Wild West. Sheepherders had semisettled the area, though it's still one of the most sparsely populated regions of the state. Charlie had an old International truck that we'd take over there. The roads were torturous. At some points, if you could do three miles an hour you were rolling along. And the weather could change on a dime, from delightful to deadly. It was quite an expedition to get over there, but the scenery was fantastic and there were native redband trout in the little streams and in Fish Lake, on the western flank of the Steens.

"On one occasion, Charlie and I set out in early September for a long weekend. We reached the little campground at Fish Lake and made camp. We never took tents—a few tarps, inflatable mattresses, and sleeping bags were our home. I should mention that Charlie was a World War II vet. He had a bad limp from an injury he'd suffered, and though he didn't talk about it much it was apparent that he'd seen some harried times in the war. He always slept with an AM radio turned on, usually tuned to some right-wing lunatic broadcasting from Salt Lake City or Denver. 'Know thy enemy!' he'd say. He also slept with a loaded .44

revolver, even at home. It was nothing unusual for him to wake up screaming with the gun in his hand. We didn't have the terminology then, but I'd say that Charlie suffered from posttraumatic stress disorder. Anyone who knew him and camped with him was always sure to sleep at least thirty feet away. Even then, sometimes you'd wake up in the morning to find him staring silently at you, holding his gun.

"This night in September, we bedded down with a sky filled with stars, a beautiful late-summer evening. I had my sleeping bag about one hundred feet away from Charlie, underneath a juniper for protection from the elements. As mentioned before, in the Steens the elements can present themselves pretty quickly, and I wanted to be prepared. I dozed off to the murmur of the radio. As the night wore on, I had the odd sensation of being in a deeper and deeper slumber—like being under anesthesia, in a different state of consciousness. I woke up with the sense of being buried. In fact, I had been buried—by two feet of fresh snow. I pushed the snow away from the top of my sleeping bag and looked out on a landscape that was completely white. Two things immediately sprang to mind. One, I didn't know where I'd put my waders and, two, I'd lost Charlie. My first instinct—to roust him out—was tempered by a healthy respect for the .44 that had potential to come into play should Charlie be startled. Still, I was concerned. Then I remembered the radio. I trudged around our rough campsite, listening for the crackle of the AM signal. Soon I located it and, content to know the location of Charlie's resting place, proceeded to start a fire and make coffee.

"Perhaps a half hour later, the snow above the radio stirred and Charlie's head eventually popped up. He looked around for a moment, then asked nonchalantly, 'Got the coffee ready for me yet?'"

Don Roberts has spent (some say misspent) a lifetime scouring the watery recesses of the planet in search of fish and fish tales, but also something far more slippery: insight—those experiences that teeter on the edge. His travels have taken him from north of the Arctic Circle in Russia to the pampas in southern Chile, from fabled rivers in Scotland to billabongs in the Australian bush, and, of course, to an array of waters across North America. Don's credits include founding editor of *Flyfishing the West* magazine; contributions to numerous national periodicals, including *Gray's Sporting Journal, Wild Steelhead and Salmon, Patagonia*, and *Outdoor Life*; authorship of three books, including *River Odyssey*, recently published in Japan; and a work in progress addressing the challenges of fly fishing for winter steelhead. While careening from distant outlands to the merely outlandish, Don maintains that a crooked road and eternally damp skivvies are good for the soul. For Don, writing and travel are just another way of saying "Gone Fishing."

THE WONDERS OF THE STEENS

Steens Mountain is situated sixty miles south of Burns, Oregon, a monolithic fault-block mountain in the midst of Oregon's vast Alvord Desert. From the valley floor of the Alvord to the east rim of the fault block, Steens Mountain rises 5,500 feet in less than three miles! The Steens's unique "sky-island" habitat provides an oasis of sorts in these harsh environs, providing sustenance for bighorn sheep, pronghorn antelope, mule deer, elk, and a three-hundred-head wild-horse herd. It's also home to some surprisingly fertile fishing grounds, especially when one considers the region's aridity. On the west side of the mountain, anglers can pursue native redband trout in the Donner and Blitzen River, which winds through canyons near the tiny town of Frenchglen. Several productive lakes are dotted around the Steens, including Mann Lake on the east side, which is home to Lahontan cutthroat, the largest member of the cutthroat family. Lahontans are indigenous to regions of the Great Basin in Nevada, southern Oregon, and eastern California; they were introduced into Mann Lake.

SURFACE ACTION

Given the choice, ninety-nine out of a hundred fly anglers will show a preference for a fishing experience that involves a surface presentation. Fishing, after all, is such a visual experience and the surface take puts everything on show. Next best to a surface take is sight-fishing a clear flat or creek, where you can pick your prey, make your cast, and watch the fish evaluate your offering—or hit it with reckless abandon. Perhaps it is more than the graphic appeal of surface or sight-fishing that attracts us. Perhaps seeing the fish at or near the surface offers the angler a level of comfort and security. Under these circumstances, the fish seems closer to dwelling in our familiar, air-breathing environment. While coming upon fish feeding on or near the surface is a source of excitement, there are times when an angler can get a little more surface action than he bargained for, as Jim Scott recalls.

"Something that makes Belize special for fly anglers is the presence of adult tarpon year-round," Jim began. "This adds a nice dimension to the fishing here, as in many parts of the Caribbean tarpon may only be present during certain seasons, or as they migrate through. Many of our guests—especially those fairly new to flats fishing—will begin by focusing on bonefish. Our bones are not that big relative to what you'll find in the Keys or the Bahamas, but they're certainly plentiful. After a few days of ten or twenty bonefish, anglers are ready for a little variety. Some will choose permit, which are admittedly a challenge—even here. Anglers will find slightly better odds choosing tarpon.

"On the day in question, we had a few guests fishing out of our property in Ambergris Caye who decided they wanted to go after tarpon. They drew the right guide, Ernesto 'Nesto' Gomez, one of our best and someone with a real feeling for tarpon. They set out early to fish Long Caye, which is just south of Ambergris, due east of Belize City. It's all sight-fishing, of course, and as they cruised around the banks of a small island of the caye, Nesto spotted a very large fish in the shallows. He figured it must be a tarpon, as this was a spot where he'd frequently encountered them before. He directed his guests' attention to the fish, and one of the anglers took his position in the casting station with his tarpon rod. Guests generally carry several rods, so they're ready for whatever game fish they might encounter. The guest loaded up the rod really nicely and dropped the fly right in front of the cruising fish. It was a

perfect cast and the fish made a beeline for the fly. Right as the fish was taking the fly, Nesto realized that he'd been mistaken. 'That's a big 'cuda!' he cried. But it was too late. The angler was already setting the hook. In a flash, the fish took off like a banshee. Since it was in shallow water, its natural instinct was to head for deep water. And sure enough it came dead straight at the boat.

"The angler was stripping in line as fast as he could, as by now he could see the fish screaming at the boat. Barracuda are extremely fast for short distances, and he was fighting a losing battle. As the angler feverishly stripped in line, his buddy was rummaging around in the bow of the boat trying to locate his camera so he could capture the moment for posterity. By the time he stood up, the barracuda was almost at the boat. We can only guess what was going through the 'cuda's mind at this moment—perhaps he thought a large rock had presented itself in its path to freedom. Whatever the case, as the fellow in the bow stood up, the four-foot-long barracuda launched itself into the air, teeth bared, and flew right into the boat, hitting the would-be photographer on the inner thigh! Those razor-sharp teeth instantly cut the poor fellow open. The only good thing to be said at this juncture is that the fish didn't hit a private place, though a few inches over could have made this a very bad situation indeed.

"At this point, Nesto said in a very calm, matter-of-fact voice, 'Guess the fishing is done for today. We're going to the hospital.' This, of course, is a logical plan of action. But in the short term there's one guy gushing blood in the bow and there's still a four-foot 'cuda breakdancing in the middle of the boat. As the two guests applied pressure and ice to the wound, Nesto climbed over the center console to immobilize the fish. We sometimes keep the 'cuda guests catch, as they can be good eating. This was not a catch-and-release scenario, especially after the mayhem the 'cuda had already wreaked on the day. The fish was neutralized. Nesto got the ravaged angler to a hospital, where he was stitched up, and the next day he was out fishing again.

"Though my guess is that he and his buddy were a little less interested in 'tarpon' fishing."

Jim Scott moved to Belize in 1987 to work with the Peace Corps and has stayed ever since. He began working in the hospitality industry in Belize in 1990, both guiding and managing properties, and in 2001 he became general manager of El Pescador's Punta Gorda property (www.elpescadorpg.com). Jim grew up fishing Michigan's Upper Peninsula, and has since fly fished throughout the American West, on the Pacific for bluewater species, and exten-

OPPOSITE: This barracuda's smile says a lot about why you don't want him catapulting toward your mid-section.

sively on the flats of Belize. "Nothing beats the combination of hunting and fishing that you experience when you're sight-fishing on the flats," Jim said. "It doesn't get any better."

TIGER OF THE REEF

There are eighteen species of barracuda swimming the oceans of the world, but the barracuda that comes to mind when we imagine a missilelike fish slashing through mullet is likely the great barracuda (*Sphyraena barracuda*). Great barracuda are indigenous to the Atlantic, Caribbean, and Pacific, can range up to six feet in length, and tend toward a solitary existence. They often feed by locating a school of fish, marauding through the school with their mouths open to immobilize as many fish as possible, and then returning to feed on the remains. Great barracuda can attain speeds of up to twenty-five miles per hour for short bursts; anyone who's ever seen a barracuda attack its prey can attest to its speed! Though barracuda do not tend to be a focus species for fly rodders on a flats vacation, they respond very well to poppers and other surface presentations, and provide a visceral (and, as we learned above, potentially *eviscerating*) experience. Note: Many people enjoy the flesh of barracuda, but in certain regions the fish can ingest an abundance of a naturally occurring poison called *ciguatera*, which forage fish accumulate from feeding on algae that grow on some forms of coral. The flesh of barracuda that reside in an area where *ciguatera* occurs can be toxic.

CUT!

Television programs featuring the sporting life—hunting, fishing, and the like—provide a window into a multitude of exotic outdoors experiences that many of us have never experienced . . . or perhaps even considered. *American Sportsman* introduced generations of anglers to the wonders of Patagonia and the possibilities of Iceland. Today, programs such as *In Search of Fly Water* bring the jungle rivers of Brazil or the Okavango Delta—along with their toothy denizens—to your living room. The folks who are featured on the programs are generally professional anglers, and their great expertise is evident from the tremendous numbers of fish they catch. They *always* have fish on.

Or so it seems.

A few years back, Beaver Shriver had a chance to experience outdoor television from the inside, and the results were quite eye-opening.

"Before I joined Frontiers Travel, I did a good bit of guiding, much of it in the mountains of Virginia," Beaver began. "On one occasion, I was asked to participate in the taping of a popular outdoors program of the day. The show's format featured a celebrity host—a former sports star—and a celebrity guest. My role would be to guide them.

"Like most outdoors programs this particular show had a corporate sponsor, and part of the mission of the program was to showcase the sponsor's products. Among the sponsor's assortment of offerings were outboard motors and all-terrain vehicles. Part of the conceit of the episode I was involved in was that we were going to be using these modes of transport to get into the back country to reach the river we'd be fishing. The only problem was that we were going to be fishing a small mountain stream up in the Allegheny Mountains that was ill-suited to motorboats and closed to four-wheelers. This would prove to be less of an obstacle than I would have imagined.

"The first shot of the day that we'd need to capture would highlight the sponsor's outboard. The host, the guest, the camera crew, and yours truly assembled on a river not at all connected to the mountain stream we'd eventually be fishing. The idea was that we'd get a shot of the boat roaring up the river, away from the confines of civilization to that secret honey hole. Unfortunately, we couldn't get the engine going. We tried to start it, tried to

TALE 43

start it, but the motor wouldn't turn over. All the while, we were drifting farther and farther away from the camera crew. We finally rowed to shore, got the engine fired up, and shot some footage of the boat roaring up the river . . . again and again, to make sure we had something that would work.

"When we were finished with the motor boat sequence, we had to show the sponsor's four-wheelers. While it was true that we'd never be able to get a boat into the stream where we were going to fish, it was equally impossible to get a four-wheeler in. There were no trails that were appropriate for a quad and, as mentioned before, the area where we'd fish was part of a preserve and closed to mechanized vehicles. We retreated to a location where ATVs were permitted and shot some scenes of the intrepid anglers climbing through the hardwoods toward that magical pool.

"With the obligatory product scenes captured, we were ready to fish. We hiked into the stream, camera crew in tow. Soon, we'd face the greatest challenge to successfully taping the show segment: the fact that the celebrity guest didn't know a fish from a fish stick. The stream in question has a good population of native rainbows, but despite my best tutoring efforts I couldn't give him the tools necessary to catch a trout. The celebrity host, who was a decent enough angler, couldn't entice a strike either. A fishing show without any fish—no matter how beautiful the surroundings or how well the sponsor's products are showcased—is not much of a show. After a few hours of nothing, with the host and the guest fishing, the director asked me to give it a whirl. Pretty soon I was able to hook a fish. I passed the rod to the host, the cameras whirred, and he played the fish in. Before the fish was all the way to hand, the director called 'Cut!' and asked the host to pass the rod to the guest. The host let the fish play out a bit of line and dutifully passed the rod along. The celebrity guest understood enough about the game to be able to reel in the fish. The rainbow, which was pretty hot the first time around, came in the second time with far less spunk. I don't think fish understand the concept of 'takes.' As the guest brought the fish to hand, the host looked at the camera, smiled, and said, 'Whaddya know? This one looks exactly like the fish that we just caught!'

"Now, if I'm flipping through the channels on television and come across a fishing show, I feel compelled to watch it. I can't help but wonder how long it took to catch the fish that are shown, who actually caught them, and how."

Beaver Shriver grew up fishing the trout streams of the eastern United States from Virginia through New England. He owned and operated a fly shop, along with his two chocolate Labs, for seventeen years. Presently, Beaver is the director of marketing for Frontiers International Travel, giving him the opportunity to fish the world from Christmas Island to the Seychelles and just about everywhere in between. A graduate of Dartmouth College, where he played ice hockey (a potential professional career was iced by shoulder injuries), Beaver is married to Erin, a spa consultant and accomplished saltwater fly fisher. They have a lovely daughter, Bianca.

THE BIRTH OF *AMERICAN SPORTSMAN*

American Sportsman premiered on ABC in 1965 with Curt Gowdy, the preeminent sportscaster of his time, at the helm. It's hard to imagine a time before cable and a zillion niche-marketed channels, but that was television at the time, and ABC made a bit of a gamble to nationally broadcast a program dedicated solely to fishing and hunting. It wasn't a complete shot in the dark, however, for the show was created thanks to the favorable response generated by a 1964 segment that aired on *Wide World of Sports* featuring Gowdy and angling legend Joe Brooks fishing for brook trout in Argentina. "The audience knew where to find us—Sundays at three P.M. EST on ABC, January through March," Gowdy recently reminisced on ESPN.com. "Millions stopped what they were doing, tuned in, and sat back to watch the granddaddy of all fishing shows." Since the original *American Sportsman* went off the air in the mid-1980s, fishing programs have been relegated to weekend morning slots on cable channels. A revamped version of the show, *The New American Sportsman*, was launched in 2002 on ESPN Outdoors. Curt Gowdy passed away in the winter of 2006.

TALE 43

THE MONEY HOLE

Guides who work a particular fishery with great frequency gain an intimate knowledge of the waters in question. With a sniff of the air or a glance at the water level or clarity, they will often have a pretty good sense of how things will go—though they'll be loath to dampen a client's spirits with their prediction if the prognosis isn't good. Even on the direst days, however, most guides will have a secret spot in mind, a little riffle or sheltered eddy that's consistently produced a fish or two, no matter how trying the conditions. These spots—honey holes, money holes, whatever you'd like to call them—can save an outing, and in some cases a guide's tip.

OPPOSITE:
The Grand Tetons provide a stunning backdrop for anglers floating the Snake near Jackson, Wyoming.

During one week in September, John Simms was amazed to find that a reliable pool had been transformed, quite literally, into a money hole.

"Thirty years ago, when people would come out to fish in the Jackson area, they'd come for a week or two weeks of fishing," John began. "Now it's quite different. Even if people come out for a week, they usually only book a day or two of fishing. Likewise, there are a few more guides on the rivers these days. When I first began guiding in the early seventies, there were three or four of us. Now there must be three hundred or four hundred guides working the Valley.

"When I had clients for longer periods of time, real friendships developed. I got to know them well and we'd spend time together after fishing, having dinner or drinks afterward. Fishing with these clients was like fishing with old friends. It was about twenty-five years ago when I had one of my regular clients, a radio station owner named Chris, come out for a couple of weeks of fishing in mid-September. Around this time—the autumnal equinox—we tend to get a brief period of rough weather, maybe two to four days of snow, sleet, cold, whatever. Once the equinox storm passes, the weather is glorious, with warm, sunny days and cool nights. The fishing really turns on in late September and continues through the end of October.

"This client and I had been fishing for a few days on the Snake River when the equinox storm came in. It was a cold, rainy, miserable day, but we went out anyway. I had been designing some neoprene waders at the time, and I figured that we'd stay warm enough

TALE 44

in those. We put in at Pritchard Creek, down one of the lower sections that we fish. We'd floated about three miles and the fishing had been pretty slow when we came to a long pool and stopped. I said to Chris, 'Why don't you fish the upper part of the pool with a dry fly. I'll fish the bottom with a shooting head and a streamer.' The pool was about a quarter mile long, and there was a large eddy on our side of the river. I had to wade out pretty far—about waist deep—to get my cast beyond the eddy so I could get the fly to swing. As I worked my way down the tail of the pool, I had one of those moments when the wind died down and the light was just so, and I could see the bottom of the river quite clearly. I saw something shiny in front of me, maybe a beer can. I hate to see trash in the river and thought I could get a hold of it between my rod tip and my fly line and move it toward the shore. As I was flicking it around, I realized that it wasn't a beer can, it was a dollar bill. I got it caught between line and rod and eased it toward me. It wasn't a dollar bill. It was a hundred-dollar bill! It had caddis larvae attached to it. I yelled up to Chris, 'Gosh you won't believe this, I just found a hundred-dollar bill!' He waved back at me and I continued fishing, but I was keeping a careful eye on the bottom. Within another four feet, I found a fifty-dollar bill. A little farther down I found another hundred-dollar bill.

"Though Chris was a good friend, he was a client as well and wanted to be catered to. He wasn't catching any fish, so I figured we'd better keep pushing downriver. Before going back to the boat I walked along the edge of the pool to the bottom. By the time I got through the pool, I'd found three more hundred-dollar bills, for a total of five hundred and fifty dollars.

"I've always enjoyed searching for things. When I was involved in the ski business, I would scour the slopes for watches, money, whatever might have gotten dropped and buried in the snow. Had I lived in the gold rush days, I'm sure I would've gone to California or Alaska looking for gold.

"The rest of that day I kept looking for hundreds, but we didn't come upon any more. We didn't come across many fish, either. There are six or eight floatable sections of the Snake, and over the course of the week we fished a different stretch each day. At the end of the week, Chris's son came to Jackson to join us. I figured we'd float back down from Pritchard Creek. We fished our way the three miles down to the long pool. I jokingly said to Chris's son, 'Keep your eyes open, this is the money pool.'

"He looked down and, sure enough, he picked up a hundred-dollar bill.

"I got Chris and his son set up on the pool and began hunting around. Pretty soon, I had found three more hundred-dollar bills. When we were done fishing the pool and were floating down, I spotted another hundred-dollar bill, stuck on a twig. I grabbed it. I was all booked up guiding for the next month and couldn't get back to that pool and scour the area like I wanted to. I mentioned my little secret to a friend who really could use the money. He took an inflatable kayak down there with a little spotting scope I made him and found three more hundreds. A total of thirteen hundred and fifty dollars had been found. I'd found nine hundred fifty, a lot of money for a guide back then.

"I spent my winters at that time doing avalanche forecasting and control for the Forest Service, and I worked alongside a lot of ski patrollers. Some of the patrollers were fishing guides in the summer. One day, a few of us were sitting at the top of the mountain, telling guide tales, good days, terrible days. One fellow named Smiley recounted a day he'd spent with a couple from Chicago who were very disagreeable. They were constantly arguing with each other and, to make matters worse, the fishing had been awful. They'd caught one whitefish between them.

"Though Smiley usually enjoyed his clients, he was glad to get to the end of that day. At the takeout as they were getting into the vehicle, the husband reached for his wallet to settle up and exclaimed, "Oh Jeez, I lost my wallet. I had fifteen hundred fifty dollars! His wife berated him for losing his wallet and paid Smiley for the day. It turned out that the stretch they had floated was ten miles above the pool where I had found the first bill, and they had floated it two weeks before my first lucky trip.

"When I first came across the bills, I thought there had been a drug deal gone bad or a bank robbery. I had all these bizarre conjectures. After hearing about the lost wallet, I had a recurring dream where I could see the wallet drifting along the bottom of the river, with suckers and whitefish occasionally pulling a bill out.

"The guides who know me all call that pool the Money Hole."

John Simms began fly fishing as a kid for bass, panfish, pike, and trout in western New York State. When he moved to Colorado in 1960 to take a job as a professional ski patrolman, he began fishing the West's great waters. John moved to Wyoming in the mid-sixties, working as a ski patroller in the winter and a fishing guide in the summer. "It was a great life that I didn't think could get much better—but it did!" Around that time, John started a back country–oriented ski equipment company called Life-Link International, as well as a fly-fishing equipment company, SIMMS Fishing. "At that point I had to travel the world testing my equipment in both winter and summer, Christmas Island to Alaska via Tierra del

Fuego!" In the mid-seventies, John developed a serious addiction to dry-fly steelhead fishing and has fished British Columbia seriously ever since. In recent years, John has turned his formidable creativity to sculpture, which he creates on a large scale in steel and bronze. His sculptures have won many awards. Some of John's public art can be experienced at the Omniplex in Oklahoma City; the Bellevue City Park in Bellevue, Washington; the Hudson Gardens in Littleton, Colorado; and close to home at the Tetron County Library in Jackson, Wyoming.

IN THE SHADOW OF THE TETONS

Framed by one of the West's most spectacular and recognizable backdrops, the Snake River hosts thousands of visiting anglers each year, drawn as much by the majestic mountain views as by the fishing. The Snake undergoes many changes in its 450-mile course, from its headwaters in Yellowstone National Park to its terminus with the Columbia River in eastern Washington; in the reaches in and around Grand Teton National Park, it's a gently flowing river that is home to an endemic trout species, the Snake River cutthroat. Snake River cutts are distinguished by their very fine spots. Like other cutthroat trout, they are a free-rising and willing fish, eager to take large dry flies that may or may not mimic emerging insects. The Snake River cutts' eagerness to please and the ready availability of knowledgeable guides make this section of the Snake an ideal destination for novice anglers.

BOXING WITH BEARS

Many a good fishing tale involving Alaska also involves bears, namely grizzly bears and brown bears. It's estimated that there are thirty-five thousand to forty-five thousand such creatures in the forty-ninth state. Sighting one of these powerful animals can provide an awe-inspiring exclamation point to an already incredible trip; a closer encounter will count among an individual's most hair-raising experiences. While grizzlies (*Ursus horribilis*) prefer rugged mountain settings and are less likely to be encountered, brown bears (*Ursus arctos*) are as stimulated by the rewards of a good salmon river as any angler. During summer months when the salmon are in, bears and fly fishers—at least those with the good sense to keep a healthy distance—generally can coexist peacefully.

Finding yourself between a bear and a fresh kill is one of the most precarious situations an angler can find himself in. Under such circumstances, there's a real chance that the bear will charge, and short of being a fast and accurate shot with a high-powered sidearm, your odds are not good. One bear on the Alaska peninsula learned the hard way that adventurer/outfitter J. W. Smith can be almost as combative when defending *his* food.

"Back in the early eighties I had a lodge on Painter Creek, on the southern shore of Bristol Bay, at the beginning of the Alaskan peninsula," J.W. began. "It was an undeveloped place, very little in the way of other anglers. But after a while, I guess I got a little restless and began looking for something a little wilder. What I found was a stream called Main Creek, over on the Pacific side of the peninsula, at a place called Amber Bay. I had flown over the creek a few times and had seen large pods of silver salmon there. Upstream, there were also great populations of arctic char.

"There was no easy way to get a plane in there, but we eventually figured out a way to land on the soft sand beaches: we'd partially deflate our tundra tires and touch down wheel-first. With a landing technique under our belts, we set up a tent camp out there and would run small groups to the camp at the height of the silver run, generally August and September. On one occasion, we took a group of Texans out there, bankers and developers, big wheels. This was a fun-loving bunch of guys, very adaptable, too, as we'd learn. The fishing could be pretty amazing—big silvers, cast after cast. At low tide, you could fish in the ocean

where Main Creek entered the salt. One of the fellows hooked a silver that went berserk and dashed back to the ocean. He took everything, fly line and backing both. The following day, the same fish made its way back into the creek, line still in tow. We got a hold of the line but weren't able to land the fish. At least that fellow wasn't out a fly line!

"During these fellows' stay, we had some rough weather come in—not uncommon on that part of the peninsula. It didn't seem to bother the Texans very much. When they couldn't fish, they'd take some golf clubs they'd brought along—seven and nine irons, I recall—and play a version of Alaska golf, which was, hit the ball down near the brown bear on the beach and then back. The fewest strokes won, and there was a two-stroke penalty for peeing out of turn—these boys liked to bend the elbow a bit. To the best of my knowledge, this was the first golf match ever played on that part of the Alaskan peninsula.

"After a few days of such shenanigans, I knew we had to figure out a way to fly these fellows back to Painter Creek Lodge, as they had a plane to catch to take them back home. It was only about an eighteen-minute flight, but the visibility and the wind had been too rough for them to make it out with any degree of safety. When we finally got a blue-sky break, we pulled everyone out of there in a hurry, four flights in small airplanes. In all the hubbub, there had been some confusion among the guides, and everybody had flown out. Generally, we always leave someone at camp to keep the bears at bay. That night, back at the main lodge, I could imagine that the bears were havin' one helluva party in our tent camp. But there was nothing I could do until the weather improved again.

"Two days later a high-pressure system came in and we were able to fly back to the camp. I had an old friend and client named Sam Haddon along with me, who's now a federal district court judge in Great Falls, Montana, and Sam's friend Moose. As we walked through the tall grass at the edge of the beach, we got an inkling of what awaited us: we could see the butt of a bear sticking out of the cook tent. When he turned around, his nose was bright pink from the powdered pink lemonade he'd gotten into. That bear lumbered across Main Creek as we approached and assessed the damage. It looked like half the bears on the Alaskan peninsula had beaten a path down the hillsides to our camp. All the food had been torn into and parts of the tents had been torn down but, miraculously, not completely torn up. The trees surrounding the tent were white with flour that the bears had tossed around, and there were foot-and-a-half-long turds with candy wrappers in the middle.

"Sam, Moose, and I worked the rest of the day and were able to get things into a semblance of order. The bears were still around, mostly juvenile males, five hundred to six hundred

OPPOSITE: If they had their druthers, most anglers would prefer a less—eh, intimate— encounter with a brown bear than photographer Brian O'Keefe had here.

TALE 45

pounds. Not big as brown bears go, but plenty big enough. During the day they kept their distance, but at night they were ready to continue their bear party. Now some folks, when they're in bear country, like to cache their food up in a tree. If I have any kind of structure, I'd rather sleep with my food, as I'd prefer to fight the bears than be hungry. The first night we were back in the camp, that's just what I did. I was in one tent with the food, and Sam and Moose were in another tent forty or fifty feet away. I could hear the bears bumbling around outside, and one was particularly close to the tent. As I'm huddled inside, a paw comes inside the flap of the tent. It had a strong smell, like musty fish. At that moment, I could make out very clearly the imprint of the bear's face on the tent. Instinctively, I punched the bear right in the nose through the tent. With a yelp and a loud whuff!, he jumped back and ran toward the trees. Giving him a right jab probably wasn't the smartest thing to do, and it hurt my hand, but I was too dumb to be scared.

"That was only the beginning. The bears kept coming around the tent all night. I figured I couldn't go out there and box with them and keep my unbeaten record intact, so I moved to plan two. I picked up my shotgun and loaded it with seven-and-a-half birdshot—light enough so it would just sting 'em a bit. Now brown bears have small, beady eyes, and you can't see them very well at night. I could hear them grunting around the tent but couldn't see them too well, so I spotlighted them and yelled until they were fifty or sixty feet away. Then I'd let 'em have it with the birdshot. The ground would shake when they'd run away. I shot the gun seven times that night.

"Somewhere around the third or fourth bear, I called over to Sam and Moose. 'I can't get no damn sleep. Why don't one of you guys come over here and take over with the shotgun?' Sam just laughed and shouted back, 'No, you're doing a fine job.' I stayed awake and listened to them snore."

J. W. Smith grew up in east Tennessee, fishing the Clinch River and trout/smallmouth streams in the Appalachian and Smoky Mountains. After attending the University of Tennessee, he spent four years as a Tennessee game warden, five years as an Alaska game warden, and seven years as a U. S. Fish and Wildlife special agent. After leaving the federal government, J. W. developed Painter Creek Lodge on the Alaskan peninsula. He and his wife, Dawn, have exploratory-fished extensively, and pioneered remote fishing adventures in Alaska, British Columbia, the Bahamas, Mexico, Honduras, Brazil, Argentina, and Bolivia. J. W. is currently co-owner of Rod and Gun Resources, Inc. (www.rodgunresources.com), a hunting and fishing sporting tours agency.

SILVER SAFARI

The Pacific side of the Alaskan peninsula gives anglers access to very large coho (silver) salmon in as remote a location as you can imagine. The silvers here are larger than elsewhere in Alaska, averaging 12 to 14 pounds, with some fish over 20 pounds. They grow heftier because they have to travel around the peninsula from the Bering Sea to reach their natal streams and have an extra four weeks to gorge themselves on smolt and baitfish before entering fresh water. The fish are also plentiful; during the visit described above, Judge Haddon caught seven silvers on seven casts! J. W. Smith eventually went on to establish a camp at Nakalilok Bay, near Amber Bay; the camp now operates as Alaska Wilderness Safari, and serves anglers from July through September. Visitors fish for silvers as close as a few hundred yards from the sea, and the fish are very aggressive, receptive to skated Pollywogs—and just about anything else thrown to them. (At low tide, you can even stalk silvers where the river enters the salt.) Incidentally, the tent camp has a seismic bear perimeter system (formerly used by American troops in Vietnam) that emits an increasingly audible tone when anything large (such as a bear) approaches. The system helps the staff keep the critters away from the food tent and guests.

THREE'S THE CHARM

Fly fishing holds many thrills and pleasures for its adherents, but few are more rewarding for grown-up anglers than watching their children catch their first fish. Many emotions are wrapped up in that moment: fear, that the child will lose the fish and associate disappointment with the fishing experience; hope, that the daughter or son will value the experience and take up the sport, gaining the parent a lifelong fishing pal; and pride, that the child has mastered enough of the rudiments of the cast to hook up in the first place. One can barely imagine the pride that Bill Taylor must have felt watching his youngest daughter hook three fish on Canada's most famous Atlantic salmon river—including her first large salmon—while a gaggle of grown-up sports looked on.

OPPOSITE: Casting to autumn Atlantics on the storied Miramichi.

"I'm a fortunate man in many ways, not the least of which is the fact that everyone in my family likes to fish," Bill began. "My wife, Suzanne, is a very competent fly fisher, as are my two daughters, Jessie and Kelsey. We'll do a number of fishing trips in the course of a season, though the trip we look forward to most happens in October, over the Canadian Thanksgiving holiday. Each year at this time we'll visit the Miramichi, which happens to be the most productive Atlantic salmon river in North America. Fall is a great time to be there. The sun is lower in the sky and the fishing can be good throughout the day.

"A few years ago we were on the Miramichi, staying with our friends Keith and Bonnie Wilson, who are the sixth generation of their family to operate a lodge on the river—Wilson's Sporting Camps. There were a number of anglers at the lodge, and fishing had been slow. Between eight of us—my family and four friends—there had been two to three salmon taken each day. The girls and I were fishing around the fringes of the better water, as the prime spots were reserved for the paying clients. We'd been at it on this particular day for about four hours, and none of us had done anything. At one point in the afternoon, Kelsey and I were fishing on one side of the river, Jessie and Suzanne on the other. Kelsey, who was nine at the time, had a five-weight rod and reel with perhaps fifty yards of backing—not your recommended salmon rig, though certainly enough to handle a grilse [an adult salmon that has spent only one year at sea and weighs about five pounds]. The river was high and I was wading downriver from her so I could catch her in case she took a dunk. We were working our way through the run, enjoying a pleasant fall day, when Kelsey hooked a fish. It was a grilse, but still a nice fish for a small girl. She played it in through a few jumps and a couple of short runs, I tailed it, and we took a few pictures.

"After releasing the fish, I moved back downriver and Kelsey resumed casting. I'd barely had time to strip my line out when I hear a shout—Kelsey had hooked a second fish. This time, she had a large salmon and it's really carrying on. I reeled back in and hustled back upriver to help her. Again, she's only got a five-weight and fifty yards of backing, but she handles it admirably. I gave her a few tips but refused to take the rod when she wanted to surrender it. Pretty soon Kelsey's got the fish in close and I tail it. By this time, four or five

male guests of the lodge have gathered on the other side of the river and they're clapping and cheering. This was Kelsey's first proper Atlantic salmon, nine or ten pounds, and she was as excited as the fellows across the way. We took a few more pictures and then released the fish.

"Any time you land an Atlantic salmon on a fly, you have reason to feel pretty good. Catching a nice grilse and a salmon on almost back-to-back casts—especially when no one else has touched

Kelsey, Bill, and Jessie Taylor pose with a salmon that Jessie landed a few years before Kelsey's big day.

a thing—is almost cause for celebration. But Kelsey wasn't done yet. I returned to my spot below her and we continued working down the run. In less than half an hour she hooked another fish—this one bigger than the last. The fish was thrashing around on the surface and, though she had never hooked such a fish before, she knew that unless she followed the fish downstream, she was going to run out of backing pretty quick. I think she was following the fish—it may have been pulling her. By the time I got to her, she was just about to go over her waders. I grabbed her around the waist and carried her back to shallower water while she continued to play her salmon. By this time, a small crowd had gathered across the river to take in the show. Despite the small rod and a very limited amount of backing, Kelsey played the fish fabulously and soon I tailed it. This salmon was twelve or thirteen pounds.

"On that trip, we were sleeping in a little camp near Wilson's, but taking our meals in the lodge. When we walked into dinner that night, all the old regulars—all fellows I know—were sitting around telling their tales; we later learned that only a couple of other fish had been hooked by the dozen or so other anglers. When they saw Kelsey, all the guys stopped talking, stood up and clapped. Kelsey turned twenty shades of red."

Bill Taylor has worked with the Atlantic Salmon Federation since 1988 and in 1995 became its president and CEO. ASF is an international nonprofit organization dedicated to the conservation and wise management of wild Atlantic salmon and the rivers and oceans where they live. He took up fly fishing when he was thirteen, and began Atlantic salmon fishing as soon as he secured his driver's license. Bill regularly fishes the Miramichi in New Brunswick, and has also fished the salmon rivers of the Gaspé Peninsula as well as northern Quebec, Newfoundland, Nova Scotia, and Labrador. He lives in the province of New Brunswick with his wife and daughters.

THE MIRAMICHI

Canada's most storied Atlantic salmon river, the Miramichi's reputation rests on its prolific runs—on a good year, more than a hundred thousand grilse and large salmon return. With numbers like these, it's no wonder that the Miramichi produces almost half of the rod-caught salmon in North America. The summer run begins arriving in mid-June, with fresh fish entering the river until the close of the season on October 15. The fall run, which shows up in mid-September, comprises the Miramichi's biggest fish, with some eclipsing 30 pounds. In addition to healthy numbers of fish, the Miramichi and its tributaries offer over seven hundred miles of angling water. New Brunswick's regulations and access rites can seem a bit byzantine to the uninitiated. The bottom line is, if you are not a New Brunswick resident you need to retain a local guide to fish, and your guide will be able to lead you to accessible public waters . . . or outline options for securing access to private or Crown-owned water.

A BIRTHDAY TARPON

What makes the ideal birthday gift? A day at the spa? A new set of irons? The proverbial diamond tennis bracelet? If the spouse is a fly fisher, she may have some very specific notions in mind: a weekend at the Joan Wulff Casting School, for example. A new set of waders. Or, perhaps, the latest greatest graphite/boron/titanium magic stick that guarantees tight loops and ninety-foot casts. For Donna Teeny, one birthday gift took a particularly piscine form.

OPPOSITE:
Donna Teeny bows her rod to her very first tarpon.

"My husband, Jim, had taken up tarpon fishing about a dozen years before," Donna began, "and I'd heard lots and lots of stories about what an exciting experience it was. Jim was planning a trip to the Florida Keys in June of 1993, and I said kiddingly—well, only half-kiddingly—that he couldn't go unless he took me along. Hooking up with a tarpon certainly intrigued me, but I was equally interested in drinking in the sunshine. He agreed. We made the trip, and on the day of my forty-sixth birthday—June twenty-second—we booked a day with Jake Jordan, one of the more renowned tarpon guides in the Keys. This would be my very first saltwater trip.

"We launched at eight A.M., a very civilized starting time on one's birthday. It was a short run to the waters that Jake wanted to fish, and Jim was first on deck. We poled around a bit and no fish showed up. Finally, Jim said, 'You take over.' I took the rod and Jake ran us to a spot that he described as his 'favorite.' There was a long stretch of relatively shallow water with white sand and an abrupt drop-off. It was a great spot for a newcomer like me to be able to spot a fish coming out of the deeper water. As he killed the engine, Jake said, 'You know, we can see one at any time.' Sure enough, before Jake had even picked up his pole, he yelled, 'Donna, fish!' He pointed out over the flat and there was a lone tarpon swimming across, as if on cue. I hadn't even pulled any line off the reel. He told me where to cast and how far, and I let it fly. I was scared, to be honest, as this was my first time. Nonetheless, I put it right where he wanted it and began stripping it—away from the fish, as what baitfish in his right mind would swim *toward* a tarpon. 'Donna, he didn't see it,' Jake whispered. 'Pick it up and cast your fly again.' Luckily, the second cast was as accurate as the first. This time, the fish came toward the fly—a Teeny Leech on a 3/0 hook. I made a few long strips and watched the fish open its mouth. To this day, I've never experienced anything like watching that huge fish eat that little fly. Despite my trepidations, I remembered how to set the hook—hard! When the fish exploded out of the water, I also remembered to bow the rod. Jake kept telling me to crank down harder on the reel. I'd caught forty-five-pound king salmon on a fly rod before but tarpon gave new meaning to 'crank down'!

"Nine jumps and fifty-eight minutes later, the fish came to the boat, nearly a mile from where we had hooked it. The fish was one hundred pounds and nearly as tall as me. I think that Jake Jordan was as excited as I was—less than half a day on the water and a first-timer had a fish in the boat in two casts! We cut the day short and headed back to Marathon, where we were staying, at a resort called Faro Blanco. There was a jewelry store at the resort, and Jimmy took me in. There was necklace featuring a tarpon, fashioned in gold. He gave me that necklace for a birthday present . . . though most would agree that I received my present a few hours before on Jake Jordan's boat!"

Donna Teeny has thirty-five years of fly-fishing experience and has traveled from the Pacific Northwest through Canada, Europe, the Kamchatka peninsula, and the Caribbean chasing anything that swims. A writer, photographer, and speaker, she has guest-hosted a variety of television fishing shows. Throughout her career, Donna has taken a special interest in introducing women to fly fishing through fly-fishing schools and designing clothing with a proper female fit. Through the years, Donna has enjoyed giving back to fly fishing as a volunteer and by leading seminars and fishing programs for the Fly Fishers Federation, Oregon Department of Fish and Wildlife, and the Becoming an Outdoors Woman program. For the past nine years, she has managed the Andros Island Bonefish Club in the Bahamas during the high season. This has afforded her an excellent opportunity to chase bonefish, one of her favorite game fish (the other being steelhead). Donna has always had an active role at Jim Teeny, Inc., where she enjoys overseeing the creative end of the business. She's fond of saying that "Fishing is my life and I feel very blessed."

THE LURE OF TARPON

It's believed that tarpon sportfishing with rod and reel began in the mid-1800s in Florida, though reports of a tarpon caught on a handline go back to 1773. In the early days, expensive outfits (costing $70 and up) were rigged with strips of fresh mullet and either dropped to the bottom or trolled. According to J. P. "Gator" Wilson, one Dr. James A. Henschall reported the first fly-caught tarpon in his book *Camping and Cruising Florida*, which was published in 1878. In the next decade the railroad lines expanded through southwestern Florida, opening up what would become some of Florida's most productive tarpon waters to tourists. Dr. Andrew Herd recounts the tarpon fly-fishing exploits of A. W. Dimmock as early as 1908 in *A History of Fly Fishing* and points out that tarpon flies were carried by Abercrombie & Fitch in the 1920s, but the pursuit of tarpon with a fly rod did not gain real momentum until the emergence of Joe Brooks in the 1950's. Whether caught by harpoon, handline, conventional rod and reel, or fly rod, the tarpon's terrific speed and proclivity for tall leaps make it a truly addictive species.

TALE 47

A GAFFE WITH THE GAFF

Losing the fish of a lifetime arouses many feelings. Sorrow. Frustration. Endless second guessing. Perhaps even anger. These emotions are all the more complicated if the fish that's lost is a world record–class tarpon . . . and if the fish is lost not due to any miscue on the angler's part but thanks to a failure on the part of one's skipper. Such is Jim Teeny's tale.

"Back in 1979, I was put in touch with a fellow named Billy Pate who was interested in coming out west to do some steelhead fishing," Jim began. "I told him to come on out. I didn't know much about saltwater fly fishing then, though I understood he was quite involved with it. Billy came out and I took him to the Kalama River and the Washougal River in southwest Washington, and a friend named Steve took him out on the Deschutes. He had a ball. Before Billy left he asked us if we'd like to come to Florida to go tarpon fishing. We didn't think much of it then. A few months later, I got a call from Steve on a Saturday afternoon. He had been watching *American Sportsman* on television and the show featured Billy Pate tarpon fishing. He said, 'I'm calling Billy. We're going!'

"The next June we joined Billy in the Florida Keys for three days. We each jumped four fish and landed three. Steve landed one over 140 pounds. Before we left, Billy said, 'I hope you boys don't think this is what tarpon fishing is all about. I think you're ready for Homosassa Springs.'

"The following year we set up another trip. This time, we'd go to Homosassa to go after the big guys. It's not uncommon for anglers to see fish of over 200 pounds! Getting them to eat and landing them is another matter, however. The first few days out of Homosassa we only jumped a fish or two—we just weren't casting as well as we should have been. I decided to do some experimenting. I took a weight-forward line and measured back twenty-seven feet. I then made a cut and Albrighted a level floating line to the now Intermediate shooting head. The next day we jumped more fish than any of the other forty-seven boats going out of the marina. It was just phenomenal.

"A few days later we were out again and a guide's voice came on the radio. He said, 'There are fish coming your way!' Our guide, Rick, spotted a group of five or six fish cruising fairly deep. It was my turn to cast and I led them quite a ways so that the fly, a Teeny Nymph in antique gold, would have time to sink. As the fish closed in, I began stripping. The biggest tarpon in the group veered suddenly toward the fly, opened its mouth, and took the fly. The fish tried to jump but couldn't make it out of the water. We knew it was over 200 pounds. Several other boats were fishing in the area and could see that we had a big fish on. Every now and again it would come up to the surface, take some air, and roll. [Tarpon possess an air bladder that allows them to breathe in air.] The other guides who saw it estimated the fish's weight at 250 pounds.

"I fought the fish very hard from the outset—at least as hard as fifteen-pound-test tippet would allow. After two and a half hours, I felt like the fish was finally slowing down. When I had the fish near the boat, Rick took out the kill gaff. It was eight feet long. The fish was as long as the gaff and its back looked to be sixteen inches across. I should mention that now I would never kill such a creature, but I didn't know then what I know now. It was by far the biggest fish any of us had ever seen and would certainly be a world record on fly tackle. Before going for the gaff, Rick took off his shoes, watch, and shirt. 'Why are you undressing?' I asked. 'That fish is going to pull me in,' he responded. In retrospect, Rick's uncertainty was a precursor of what was to come. With his first gaffing attempt, Rick put the gaff in the center-top of the tarpon. He hit the fish so hard, the rod vibrated. Steve and I shot a look at each other. We weren't expert at this but we knew this was not the way to do it. This was a wake-up call for the fish, and it exploded. Three hundred yards of line went out in seconds and we were soon chasing him again.

"I brought the tarpon up to the boat two more times. The first time, Rick missed him again. The way he missed it made me think that he really didn't want me to catch the fish. After he missed it, he asked me to break it off. This isn't the kind of request you expect from your guide when you've gone out in search of a trophy tarpon, and you actually get one on the line! I said, 'Rick, this is the greatest fish I've ever hooked in my life. Give me one more chance.' It wasn't too much longer before I had the fish up to the boat again. This time, I had the leader inside the rod. As I stripped the line of my spool to give him slack, Rick grabbed the leader a foot and a half from the fish. There was no more tension on the rod. The head of that tarpon was the size of the lid of a large garbage can. It was floating by the boat on its side. We seemed to be seconds away from landing the fish of a lifetime—for all intents and purposes, it *was* caught. And then Rick froze. Steve and I both said, 'Rick, get him!' But he only stood there. The fish floated on its side for twenty-five or thirty seconds, as if waiting to be hoisted into the boat. When Rick failed to do so, the fish swam to the front of the boat, the leader got caught on some metal trim, and it broke, with the butt section still in Rick's hand. I had fought the fish for four hours and thirty-five minutes clock time.

"Rick's response was, 'Well, he's gone. Let's go.'

"We made the run back to Homosassa in silence, except for the radio. Word of the big fish had made its rounds among the guides and it was all the buzz. If Steve had tried to gaff the fish, I'm certain we would've gotten it. But it was Rick's boat, and it was not our place to try to take control. Had Steve taken the gaff, it would have been the equivalent of mutiny.

"That night, I ran into Billy Pate as he had Steve and me stay at the house he had rented. Billy was wondering if I was okay. He said, 'You know, if you had landed that fish, you would've sent a lot of us home. That's the fish we have all been after.' In retrospect, I suppose the fact that I was from the Pacific Northwest and known more for steelhead and salmon fishing than for jumping tarpon would've made things even worse for the local guys.

"In my heart, I still feel as though I caught that fish. I tried to have a reproduction made so I could have some memento of the battle, but they don't make molds that big."

Jim Teeny originated the Teeny Nymph Fly pattern in May of 1962 at Oregon's East Lake for large cruising rainbow trout. Little did he know, at the age of sixteen, that this fly would help design his future. In 1971 Jim started the Teeny Nymph Co. (now called Jim Teeny, Inc.). The Teeny Nymph has taken dozens of world record fish in both fresh and salt water; Jim has held ten official IGFA world records in the past and has released more than twenty other fish that would have qualified for world records. Jim has always been on the cutting edge of the fly-fishing industry, leading the way in the sinking fly line market with his T-Series lines, as well as numerous subsequent lines. He has appeared on many television shows teaching and sharing his techniques; Jim has also written countless articles for major national fishing publications and created instructional videos, including *Catching More Steelhead*, which won the 1988 Teddy Roosevelt Award for the nation's best "How to" fishing video. His newest book, *Fly Fishing Great Waters*, was published in 2005; production has recently begun on a new television program, *Fly-Fishing Alaska with Jim Teeny*.

THE MONSTER TARPON OF HOMOSASSA

Just as trout aficionados long to one day voyage to the Railroad Ranch section of the Henry's Fork for Opening Day, anyone who has seriously pursued tarpon dreams of fishing the flats of Florida's Homosassa in June for a chance to hook into a mammoth tarpon. The big tarpon begin arriving in April in preparation for spawning later in the year, but the fishing reaches its peak in June. Anglers fishing out of Homosassa can boast five International Game Fish Association (IGFA) world records for tarpon, including a 202.5-pound fish caught by Jim Holland Jr. in 2001, on 20-pound tippet. While old-timers at Homosassa sometimes complain of the crowds and will insist that fishing is not what it used to be, there are still few better places in the world to confront with a fly rod a tarpon approaching or exceeding two hundred pounds.

I CAN'T BELIEVE YOU MISSED
THAT FREAKIN' FISH

Teaching someone you love to fish—like teaching them how to drive—can be a difficult and at times maddeningly frustrating task. There's a very good case to be made for outsourcing this task to a professional, though, as Heather Templeton relates, even a third-party teacher does not guarantee that you'll be spared the frustration.

"Growing up, I had always loved bass fishing," Heather began. "I had the notion that fly fishing was overly precious and ultimately a fake. When I moved to Jackson Hole, I was determined to steer clear of flies and fish only with my spinning rod—that is, until I realized that in Wyoming, only rednecks fished with spinning rods. I reluctantly picked up a fly rod and eventually caught a tiny rainbow on a Royal Wulff. For all the satisfaction I experienced, the fish could've been twenty-four inches. At that point, I crossed over to the fly fisher's side of the river.

"The speed with which I picked up fly fishing was undoubtedly accelerated by the fact that my husband at the time—Carter Andrews—was a renowned guide around Jackson. Unlike some guides who would rather do just about anything but fish on their day off, Carter was crazy about fishing and was out on the river every chance he could get. With Jackson being such a tourist destination, he took a lot of beginners fishing. This was often tough for him, as he would get frustrated watching these tyros miss fish after fish, as their hook-setting instincts were not very polished. He told me once that a client had missed a fish and said 'He didn't take it. He missed it.' Exasperated, Carter replied, 'How often do you miss your mouth when you eat?' He then took the rod from the client and caught the fish.

"Carter was an amazing angler, and I certainly learned from him. However, he was so intense, so focused on the river, that fishing with him was not very much fun. Carter and I eventually went our separate ways. And when I decided to take my new husband, John Templeton, on a fishing excursion, I remembered my early educational experiences on the river with Carter. I'd pass on being the teacher and would retain some good guides.

"John is a very active fellow. He enjoys running, mountain biking, and mountain climbing—not too long ago, he climbed Mount McKinley in Alaska. I mention this because until I came along, he was pretty dismissive about fishing. It seemed too sedate for him. When

OPPOSITE:
The South Fork of the Snake is more intimate than Henry's Fork, and offers prolific hatches.

we had planned a trip from our home in North Carolina to Wyoming, I set up a few days of fishing, including an overnight trip on the South Fork of the Snake. I was pretty excited about our itinerary. John's comment was, 'That doesn't sound like much fun to me.' We'd see about that.

"The first day, I booked us with a fellow named Guy Turk—creator of the great Turk's Tarantula pattern, a true old-school guide. The Snake hadn't been turning on until noon for hatches, so we put on the water at a leisurely ten-thirty. Guy seated John in the front of the boat, a beautifully oiled and maintained South Fork skiff—the angler in front usually does better, as he has the first crack at the fish. John had some notion of the motion of the fly cast from a few brief sessions in the yard, but no fishing knowledge beyond that. Guy did a great job giving him command of the basics. Just as Guy had promised, the fishing really picked up in the early afternoon. John's very athletic and he caught on about casting pretty quickly. His presentations were as adequate as they needed to be, especially considering that the fish were feeding so vigorously there were sometimes two or three fish fighting for his fly. However, his timing for setting the hook was not all it could be. He did catch some fish, and hooked one decent-sized brown, a fish he couldn't get to the boat. Just like Carter, I found myself getting a little frustrated with his inability to set the hook. But remembering how I felt under Carter's scrutiny, I did my best to hold my peace.

"When we got off the river that afternoon, we drove down through Yellowstone, detoured to fish the Firehole and Madison for a little while, and then stopped overnight in West Yellowstone. The next morning we continued into Idaho. I'd booked a guide named Dan Oasis to take us down the South Fork. He's a younger guy, and bald. When he explained that he'd shaved his head to minimize his hair maintenance during the fishing season, I knew we were in good hands. Things only got better out on the river, as we hit the salmon-fly hatch in full force. We were floating the canyon section of the South Fork and there were huge trout—browns, rainbows, and cutts—coming up all along the bank. It's exactly how you want it to be. I gave John the front seat again. Dan did an excellent job of explaining the hatch and how we'd fish during the various phases of the salmonfly emergence. He and John got out of the boat and fished a few riffles and they got into some wonderful fish. John has an addictive personality, and I could see the addiction kicking in. Dan was having a difficult time getting John back in the boat to move to the next spot. It was incredibly gratifying for me to watch John getting hooked, to see it clicking for him.

"John's casting was getting better and better but his setting of the hook continued to be problematic. He missed or lost at least as many fish as he had landed. John was getting all of Dan's attention, and he was getting the first shot at the good water. I felt my competitive urges coming on—he'd had a lot of chances at good fish and he wasn't seizing the opportunity. I wanted to say, 'Either step up to the plate and make the most of this, or get in the back of the boat.' Still, I kept these feelings to myself.

"Toward the end of the afternoon John had this beautiful brown come up and swirl at his fly. I thought he'd miss it, but the fish was hooked. Unfortunately, instead of swimming away from the boat the fish came right at us. This put a bunch of slack in the line so John couldn't strip it in fast enough, and the trout spit the fly. The frustration I had bottled up regarding John's angling technique suddenly burst out. (It might have had something to do with my hormonal state, as I was five months pregnant at the time!) I yelled, 'I can't believe you missed that freakin' fish!' Poor Dan was dumbfounded. 'Normally it's the husband saying that to his wife,' he said. By the end of the day, John caught an eighteen-inch brown. In the picture, he's grinning from ear to ear.

"That night we slept on our cots under the stars on the banks of the South Fork. I think we both knew that we had entered a new world together."

Heather Templeton began fishing for smallmouth bass in Maryland with her brother and a spinning rod. When she moved to Jackson, Wyoming, her love of fly fishing took hold. Heather feels she owes all of her casting knowledge to her self-nominated grandfather Lefty Kreh. She has appeared on several fishing television shows including *Walkers Cay Chronicles* with Flip Pallot. She currently teaches fly-fishing clinics with Lefty Kreh in North Carolina and you will find her hosting a new show on the Fine Living Channel beginning in 2007. Heather is most excited about sharing her passion for fly fishing with her two-year-old son, Jack.

THE "OTHER" SNAKE

For visiting anglers, the South Fork of the Snake River in southeastern Idaho takes a back-seat to the region's other more celebrated rivers—the Henry's Fork of the Snake and the Madison, to name a few. As far as locals are concerned, this is just fine. The South Fork, specifically the forty-nine-mile section between the Palisades Dam and its confluence with the Henry's, is a tremendously prolific river, with populations of almost seven thousand fish per mile, and trout averaging 15 to 17 inches. Rainbow and cutthroat predominate through much of the river, though the presence of browns—some approaching trophy size—increases in the lower stretches before the confluence. The South Fork provides steady dry-fly action throughout the season, with blue-winged olives, pale morning duns, salmonflies, caddis, and terrestrials all making a significant appearance; due to spring runoff, the season here doesn't get into full swing until July. Many anglers opt to float the river, because floating affords access to the most water and the greatest opportunity to take in the scenic splendor of the Swan Valley, where you're likely to encounter moose, elk, and a great variety of bird life.

A HALF–ROD EDUCATION

The romanticized picture many of us carry in our minds of a father and son fly fishing to-gether borders on Rockwellian bliss. We imagine the father patiently passing along the basics of casting, educating his son about the insects that inhabit the river in question …and, of course, sharing whatever wisdom about life that he's gained in his travels on this earth.

If only it always worked out this way. All too often, the long-anticipated fishing trip shared by father and son is a veiled (and desperate) attempt for two people to connect after a life of colliding, or not having had any contact at all. That's a lot to expect from a few days on the river, and such expectations place a great deal of pressure on the guide who finds herself trying to locate a few fish for this twosome—and perhaps trying to salvage a relationship that may be on the rocks.

Jean Williams is the kind of capable, compassionate, and clever guide who is up for the task. And it took only half a fly rod to seal the deal.

"A few years back, a father and son came out to Colorado to fish with me," Jean began. "The father was very intelligent and successful but he was as tightly wound as they get—a triple-A personality. His son, Tommy, was ten, a beautiful little boy, very fragile and still at the cusp of wonderment, still able to build a fort and play in it. It was apparent pretty quickly that they had a broken home, that the dad had a limited relationship with his son, and that this was one of two times a year that they spent time together. I could also see that the boy was terrified of his dad. Generally, the lodge doesn't take kids that young, as there just isn't a lot for them to do. This father was going to have his kid out there fishing all day, dawn to dusk. He expected him to be Lefty Kreh by lunchtime, and probably envisioned himself boasting about his son at dinner. I was thinking that the dad needed to turn off his cell phone and climb into that fort with his kid.

"I was going to have them for four days. At the outset of each of the first two days, we talked about expectations and goals for the fishing. I tried to give the boy some language that would help him relate to the experience. He and I hit it off great—he was exactly my height, which probably helped! But despite this bond things weren't going well. The dad was barking orders at the boy, and the boy was shutting down. I'm sure the dad didn't mean

to do this, but these were the tools he had, the tools that worked well in the business world. I tried to break things up for the boy, tossing him a Frisbee, showing him the flora and fauna. The dad saw this as an interruption in his quest for the big fish.

"I really wanted the father and son to engage, so on day three I decided to take a different tack. At ElkTrout, where I guide, we have an assortment of waters to choose from—some larger rivers, some smaller waters. The idea is that guests can cycle through different beats in the course of the day to have different experiences, without encountering other anglers. There's one little spot that I just love called Upper Troublesome Creek. It's as precious and beautiful as you can imagine, maybe twenty feet across in places, mostly six to twelve feet. The willows close in all around it, creating little cavelike spots. It feels like something from *The Hobbit* or *Peter Pan*. I took the father and son up there on the morning of day three, thinking that this would bring the dimensions down to a ten-year-old size. As we were hiking in, I said to Tommy, 'This is your kind of water. It's a little, fragile place. We might see hawks, eagles, deer, maybe even elk. The fish are very timid, so we'll have to be very quiet.'

"When we reached the creek, I set down the most important rule of the day: 'All the fish you catch, you have to catch together. One guy casts with the top half of the rod, the other guy holds the reel. The guy with the top half chooses the fish and presents the fly. When you hook up, you direct the guy on the reel.' The father reached for the rod and I said, 'Tommy goes first.' I have a few other rules up on Upper Troublesome Creek—you can only dry-fly fish, Mr. Elk Hair Caddis or Mr. Royal Wulff. And you can't take out any more than twenty feet of line, though twelve is closer to right. The dad was dumbfounded at this last pronouncement, as on our first few days out he'd displayed a little launching problem—that is, he felt he had to launch all of his line to *really* be fishing!

"We crept around in the willows for a while, fishing a spot here and there. Each guy gets two casts as rod dude, then you switch. We teased up some small fish, the biggest might have been eleven inches. The dad was having a tough time not correcting Tommy but he was trying. I could see his temperament slowly changing. They were cheering each other on when the other hooked a fish. They had to be a team and strategize. Finally, the dad was being good. He had started listening.

"When we got to the creek, I told them about one particular spot that they had to build themselves up to, one tiny pool where there was a nice rainbow who was difficult to coax up. From past experience, I knew he liked to rest in this little bowl against the bank where he had shade. When we reached the spot, I told Tommy that he had to get a sense of how the

OPPOSITE: An intimate Colorado stream like this provided Jean Williams with an ideal classroom for collaboration.

fly would drift in the current, and to watch carefully. I went forty feet upstream and threw some pieces of grass into the current. 'Don't cast until you see a piece of grass that seems to drift right where it needs to go,' I advised. We stood on the bank and waited for the water to settle. Fifteen minutes later, Tommy pointed out a subtle little suck. The fish had taken something off the surface. 'You've got to count between dimples,' I reminded him, then added, 'We're gonna do one cast and get this fish.'

"Tommy turned and looked at his dad and said, 'We're gonna get this fish.' Suddenly, the two of them were truly connecting. I had chills and was thinking, 'Please God, please let the fish touch the fly.' Tommy said, 'Okay Dad, I'm going to put it right in the seam, just off that branch.' He walked into position as his dad stripped line off. Tommy asked, 'Now?' and I said, 'It's your call. You've got to have your timing just right.' As Tommy counted out 'One thousand one, one thousand two,' his dad was still pulling out line. It's like a big bowl of angel hair pasta in the water in front of him. Finally, Tommy made a little backcast and laid the line out. The Royal Wulff delicately dribbled down the seam, and sure enough the rainbow lethargically sucked it in. Tommy dropped his mouth and cried, 'Oh my God!' and I cried, 'Set!' Now a fifteen-inch rainbow is on. It might as well have been a marlin. The fish just parked. Tommy had the rod tip up, and he was shaking. His dad said, 'He's gonna run, he's gonna run!'

"On cue, the fish went ballistic. He ran between Tommy's legs, then through my legs. The dad had ninety feet of three-weight line in a pile between us. He was trying to reel in the line but wasn't getting anywhere. I was almost free of the fly line, thinking I needed to get the net out. The fish continued to go around us, through us, every which way. I knew that if we didn't do something soon, we were going to lose him. So I said, 'Let's move close and trap him between us.' The fish was still shooting around, but we were closing in. I asked the dad to pick up the pile of fly line and he did so, but then he inexplicably dropped it on the trout. This disoriented the fish and he stuck his head through a gap in the fly line. I slammed my net right through the fly line and got him. There we were, wrapped up in a pile of fly line, with a beautiful rainbow in the middle. Tommy kissed the fish on the cheek.

"We stopped fishing the creek after releasing the fish, just sat on the bank and talked about what had happened. For the rest of that day and day four, Tommy and his dad fished together, with one rod. They realized that fishing was something they could do together."

Jean Williams has worked as a fly-fishing guide for eleven years, ten at ElkTrout Lodge in Colorado, one in Alaska. A native of Denver, Jean also works as manufacturer's representative for Cortland Line Company; in the past she has worked in retail operations for Patagonia. Jean is very active with environmental projects, in particular in association with Trout Unlimited and Patagonia. She continues to work as a retreat leader for Casting for Recovery (www.castingforrecovery.org), a nonprofit organization that provides fly-fishing retreats at locations around the United States for women who have or have had breast cancer. A thespian, classically trained at the National Shakespeare Conservatory, Jean can recite monologues indefinitely to keep clients amused on those days when the fishing is tough.

PRIVATE COLORADO PLEASURES

ElkTrout Lodge (800-722-3343; www.elktrout.com) is situated roughly two hours west of Denver near the town of Kremmling, Colorado, a stone's throw from the Colorado River. The private waters of ElkTrout—which include stretches of the Colorado, the Blue River, and Troublesome Creek—are renowned for their prodigious hatches of pale morning duns, green drakes, blue-winged olives, and more. The Colorado and Blue also offer opportunities for truly big fish; browns and rainbows approaching and even eclipsing thirty inches are landed each year.

Editor: Jennifer Levesque
Designer: Helene Silverman
Production Manager: Jane Searle

The text of this book was composed in DTL Documenta.